Secret Beaches

of the Salish Sea

THE NORTHERN GULF ISLANDS

THEO

HERITAGE

VANCOUVER · VICTORIA · CALGARY

Heritage House Publishing Company Ltd.
heritagehouse.ca

LIBRARY AND ARCHIVES CANADA CATALOGUING IN PUBLICATION

Dombrowski, Theo, 1947–
    Secret beaches of the Salish Sea: the northern Gulf Islands / Theo Dombrowski.

Includes index.
Also issued in electronic format.
ISBN 978-1-927051-33-7

    1. Beaches—British Columbia—Gulf Islands—Guidebooks. 2. Recreation
areas—British Columbia—Gulf Islands—Guidebooks. 3. Gulf Islands (B.C.)—
Guidebooks. I. Title.

FC3845.G8D643 2012   796.5'30971128   C2012-901016-2

editor: Lenore Hietkamp
proofreader: Karla Decker
designer: Jacqui Thomas
maps, artwork and photographs: Theo Dombrowski

 This book was produced using FSC®-certified, acid-free paper,
processed chlorine free and printed with vegetable-based inks.

Heritage House acknowledges the financial support for its publishing program from
the Government of Canada through the Canada Book Fund (CBF), Canada Council
for the Arts and the province of British Columbia through the British Columbia Arts
Council and the Book Publishing Tax Credit.

 Canadian   Patrimoine
Heritage   canadien

 The Canada Council | Le Conseil des Arts
for the Arts | du Canada

 BRITISH COLUMBIA
ARTS COUNCIL

16 15 14 13 12 1 2 3 4 5

Printed in Canada

CONTENTS

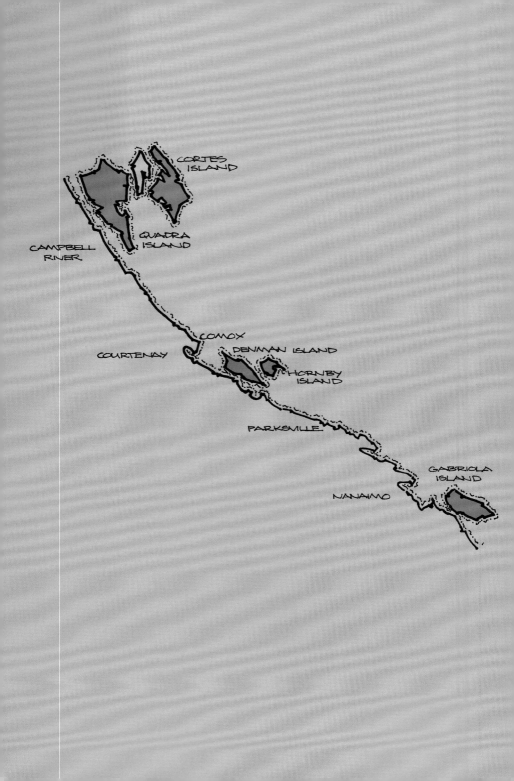

Hornby: Periwinkle Place

INTRODUCTION

For most Canadians the word "north" is both powerful and evocative. At the most basic level, as we are often tunefully reminded, we are the "True north strong and free." Even beyond the anthem, the "north" has powerful associations. The rest of the world, like the anthem, may consider us to live in the "North," but we know better. Most Canadians live within a few kilometres of the US–Canada border, and they will indicate with a broad sweep of the hand that the *real* north is . . . up there. Wherever you are, there is always more north . . . and yet more.

In many places unpeopled and at many times a mite chilly, the north is also associated with the wilderness—and, in turn, with purity, power and large, peckish animals. Might we expect all of these associations to apply to the "secret beaches" of the "northern" Salish Sea? In addition, might we expect that, given the choice between the beaches of the *southern* islands (in volume four of this series) and the *northern* islands, only the hardiest and most adventurous of beachgoers would want to venture far from the much-touted "Mediterranean" warmth of the southern islands? Let's admit it: many are sure that turning from the dry, baking heat of Salt Spring or the Pender Islands, for example, toward Quadra and Cortes Islands is a cue for putting away the bathing suits and digging out the windbreakers.

Yet it is one of the wonders of these northern islands that, in many ways, they may not seem even remotely "northern." In fact, nowhere in the Salish Sea will you find more large, beautiful sandy beaches with warmer swimming water than on some of these northern islands. Indeed, the warmest water north of Baja California is said to be found in remote and unsettled Pendrell Sound in East Redonda Island, a little east of Cortes. Add to that two more surprises that undercut any impressions that these islands are remote, northern wilderness: first, ferry transportation to and from the islands is generally more regular than to many of the southern islands, and second, the populations are generally just as large.

This is not to say, however, that visitors will not discover any sense of the northern islands being more wild, remote and "northern" than the southern islands. This is particularly true of Quadra and Cortes Islands, but to some extent of all of them. In the first place, huge areas of those rugged, large islands such as Quadra and Cortes, and to an extent Denman, are virtually untouched. Second, sections of steep volcanic shore overhung with wet-loving spruce, on some of the islands, can make you feel very far, indeed, from the smooth sandstone world of Garry oak and arbutus you may associate with the southern islands. Add to these contrasts the sense that on these northernmost islands, the Coast Mountains and Vancouver Island mountains, higher and steeper than in the south, seem to crowd close, and you may indeed feel that you have journeyed into the northlands.

Though these islands are much farther apart from each other, and more distinct from each other, than are the southern islands, they have much in common. The most basic unifying factor is that they are all "Gulf" islands and they are all in the "Salish Sea." The "Gulf" in Gulf Islands refers to their location in the "Gulf of Georgia," a term originally given by Captain Vancouver to the area encompassing today's Strait of Georgia and Puget Sound. The term "Salish Sea," first used in 1988 by marine biologist Bert Webber, became official in the United States in 2009 and in Canada in 2010. A generalized term, the Salish Sea includes Juan de Fuca Strait, Puget Sound, the Strait of Georgia and all connecting waters. Among other things, the term "Salish" pays homage to the First Nation people in the area, the Coast Salish.

But the classifications don't stop there. First, the terms "northern" and "southern," used for convenience in these guidebooks, don't correspond exactly to the way they are used elsewhere. Ferry schedules, for example, include Gabriola with the southern islands while grouping Denman, Hornby, Quadra and Cortes Islands with the Northern Gulf Islands. On the other hand, Quadra and Cortes Islands are often considered two of the "Discovery Islands." The term "Discovery Islands," popular with local tourist offices and real estate agencies, derives from Discovery Passage, the main channel for deepwater ships connecting the Strait of Georgia and Johnstone Strait, the body of mostly open water lying between northern Vancouver Island and the mainland. The Discovery Islands are a dense tangle of largely uninhabited islands with only narrow waterways separating them from each other and from the mainland.

Potential visitors who still are not sure that the trek to the "north" is worthwhile might consider some of the ways in which these islands excel in comparison to the southern islands. Among these islands, you can find:

- the largest sandy beaches (Gabriola, Hornby, Cortes)

- the longest shore-hugging nature trails (Quadra, Hornby)

- the best First Nations cultural sites (Quadra)

- the best views of the Coastal Range (Quadra, Cortes)

- the best views of Strathcona Park mountains (Quadra, Denman)

- the highest concentration of public beach accesses (Gabriola)

- some of the longest stretches of shore walking (Cortes, Quadra, Denman)

- some of the most secluded beaches (Quadra, Cortes, Denman)

Along with these distinctive features of the northern islands are many that they share with their more Mediterranean cousins. Foremost of these common features is the distinct "island culture" that so many islands in the Salish Sea seem to encourage. Settled thousands of years ago by the Coast Salish, all the islands since European "contact" have seen successive waves of newcomers attracted to the kind of life best lived on islands. Along with those hoping most to exploit the resources of the islands are those looking for an "alternative" way of life. Thus, in the northern islands as much as in the southern islands, a distinctive island culture has developed.

You will, of course, find the giant summer houses of the wealthy, many jetting in for a few weeks in the summer. Year-round, though, and more fundamental to the islands, are the small organic farms, the fanciful drift-wood dwellings and the arts and crafts studios.

A further feature that all islands have in common, of course, is that somehow you need to get to them. If you have a boat, you can visit many Gulf Islands, some of them heavily settled and some of them virtually untouched. Savary, Hernando, Mitlenatch, East Redonda and West Redonda Islands are just a few of the fascinating islands in the north Salish Sea accessible to boat owners—but not, alas, to the rest of us. The good news, however, is that ships run by BC Ferries allow everyone to get to the five islands treated in this book. Though the service to all of the northern islands is regular, don't expect just to turn up at one of the terminals and wait for a ferry to pop by. Study your ferry schedules carefully at www.bcferries.com/schedules/. Avoid frustration by taking note of some particular details. First, watch for "dangerous cargo" sailings. Unless you're driving a commercial propane truck, you won't be allowed on. Second, though sailings to the three islands approached directly from Vancouver Island (Gabriola, Denman and Quadra) are frequent, those that require island hopping (Hornby and Cortes) are considerably less frequent. Cortes requires particularly careful planning. Even when you think you have mastered the schedules, note that some schedules change over the weekend and over the seasons. If you plan to make several trips, you can save considerably by buying a BC Ferries "Experience Card," a magnetic card that you preload with as much cash value as you like. A final piece of advice: in summer months, be prepared for the possibility of a ferry wait. Fortunately, many of the ferry terminals have attractive shorefronts, even parks, to explore immediately beside them—especially to and from Denman, Hornby and Cortes Islands. You can make your ferry wait just another opportunity for a little intertidal fun.

Once on the ferries, you will find that, compared to many of the routes in the Southern Gulf Islands, those in the north are short and sweet. You will have to be quick with your camera if you are going to take advantage of the opportunity to capture some wonderful slices of scenery. The only long trip is that between Quadra and Cortes Islands. Rather than being an inconvenience to be tolerated, however, this part of your trip may well become the best 40 minutes of your day. Indeed, of all the Gulf Island seascapes mustering their resources to enchant you, north or south, nothing rivals those splashed around you during this crossing. Come in the springtime when the peaks and crags of the Coast Mountains are thick with snow, and you will have a hard time restraining the exclamations. As if the geography weren't enough, this boat ride happens to give you some of the best chances on the coast for spotting orcas, Dall's porpoises, and even whole schools of Pacific white-sided dolphins.

Once ashore, though, your real adventures begin. Unfortunately, finding small, out-of-the-way beaches is not easy on any of these islands, unlike on some of the southern islands. If you simply drive curiously along the roadways, hoping to chance upon a path to the shoreline, you are unlikely to see any shore outside of the signposted parks. Only Gabriola Island, among this group, has many indications of public trails to the shore, and even these are scattered and hidden behind vegetation. All of the islands have a few signs, some evidently put up by enthusiastic and welcoming locals, but often they are faded or visible only once you have threaded your way to the end of a narrow byway. For the most part, you will have to keep this book close by you if you are going to find some of the most charming—and secluded—shorefront spots in the Salish Sea.

THE GULF ISLAND BEACH

And what will you find at these shorefront spots? As most locals insist, you will find a "beach." Be prepared, though. The word "beach" is used here in the way that most people who live on coastal British Columbia would use the word—loosely. For us, a "beach" is simply a shorefront. It can be covered with sand, pebbles, boulders or even slabs of rock. We all know that some people, usually from southern climes, become (politely) superior when they consider our use of the word "beach." To them, unless it is an unbroken expanse of golden sand bashed by surf, it is not a beach at all. Let such people take themselves elsewhere. The rest of us know what a beach is, and we love our beaches!

MAPS AND DIRECTIONS

Quite apart from the difficulties with trail signs, finding your way around the islands is not always easy, though you may consider that to be part of their charm. Maps can be a real problem, and even more in the Gulf Islands than on north-central Vancouver Island (as noted in the *Campbell River to Qualicum* and *Southern Gulf Islands* volumes). Those planning to use a GPS or Google Maps will often come a cropper, either because those associated databases contain many mistakes or because they simply don't contain information about many of the tiny roads on the islands. Official maps issued by the regional districts or the Islands Trust often pose the opposite kind of problem. They show literally dozens of little roads leading to the coast where, as yet, no such roads exist. At some such places, you will find a track or a path through woods. At most, however, you will encounter nothing but a wall of dense vegetation— that is, if you can even find where the access strip is supposed to be when in front of you stretches a long, forested road with no landmarks.

Other maps are available for these islands, though. Bless realtors and tourist groups! Some maps, complete with symbols for beach accesses (and businesses), are available both on the ferries and online. For the latter, you will probably find it easiest to go to Google Images and search for "X island map." The fly in the ointment, unfortunately, is that among all of these maps you will find glorious disarray. Not only are many smaller roads unlabelled, but also the names themselves vary. In addition, one map showing beach accesses cheerfully dotting the coastline bears scant resemblance to another for the same coast. You are probably best off

Gabriola: Decourcy Drive

buying commercially printed maps in tourist shops and/or grocery shops on the islands and using them in conjunction with this book.

The maps and directions in this book are intended to simplify your getting to your dream beach, not to provide the logistical precision of a moon landing. Nearly all of the directions begin at the ferry terminal, because most people using the book will be visitors to the islands. In the cases of Denman and Quadra Islands, where there are two ferry terminals, the directions begin at the terminal for arrival from Vancouver Island. Second, most beach descriptions are self-contained. Almost all beach entries are accompanied by all of the directions you need, even though the result is that some nearly adjacent beaches duplicate most of the directions. The advantage for visitors, of course, is that you don't need to flip from page to page trying to piece together a complete set of directions.

As you follow the directions, however, be aware that distances between turning points are intended to give drivers only a rough idea whether they should be scanning road signs for an immediate turn or, instead, sitting back and enjoying several kilometres of scenery before eagle-eyeing road signs. Thus, distances under a kilometre are usually rounded off to the nearest 100 m and those over a kilometre usually to the closest kilometre. Even then, however, they are intended as little more than a loose guide. Ultimately, it is road signs and only signs that will get you close to your destination.

Additionally, the maps in this book, like the distances, are simplified. They include all the essential roads you need to get to your destination, but no side roads. To help you further, areas of congested roads are enlarged and those long sections of road with few features are compressed. Use these maps to complement proper road maps, not to replace them.

PUBLIC ACCESS—AND PUBLIC RESPONSIBILITY

Two key principles underlie the writing of the guidebooks in this series:

- The kind of person who will make a point of seeking out a little-known beach will be the kind of person who values quiet beauty and undamaged natural settings.

- In keeping with the ideals of the community of which we are all a part, we should all be able to enjoy waterfront that is, after all, public property.

Even though public property is available for everyone to find, it is important to keep in mind the status of this public property. Most of the Public Access routes leading to beaches are on land zoned for public use lying between private waterfront lots. These routes lead to publicly owned "foreshore," the area between high and low tides. Even when the land above the foreshore is private, the public generally has the privilege of using the foreshore and the water below it, though not the right to do so. When this area is used for a special purpose such as an oyster farm, the public may not be permitted, depending on the nature of the tenure. Usually signs are posted if visitors are restricted from using the foreshore. More detailed information can be found by searching on the web for the pdf document "Coastal Shore Jurisdiction in British Columbia."

BEACH ACCESS WARNING

Quite understandably, many waterfront property owners and other locals want to keep their secret beaches—secret. Who, after all, doesn't enjoy seclusion by the waterfront (other than, perhaps, those who have been working hard at the gym to build the perfect beach body)? More important, what property owners welcome cars blocking driveways and high-decibel midnight parties, not to mention rotting litter, malodorous dog excrement, gutted berry patches, depleted clam and oyster beds or ugly firepits? No one finds such abuse acceptable, neither waterfront owner nor visitor. On the other hand, we need not despair that with increased use will come increased abuse. We can all hope that the more people who visit the shorefront, the more beachgoers there will be to encourage its preservation. Everyone who loves our shores finds in the pleasures and peace of the "secret beach" the inspiration to act on behalf of it and all other areas of natural beauty. In addition, we can hope that with more people using the developed access routes, those access routes currently overgrown and impossible to find will be likewise developed.

BEACHES IN THIS BOOK

Fewer than a quarter of the zoned access spots around the Northern Gulf Islands appear in this book. Why? Many access routes, as already mentioned, fail to live up to their name: they don't provide access. Many, many are tangles of bush or lead down plunging banks. Others are excluded because they are simply too unappealing, or are near similar but more appealing spots. The preferable spots may offer better parking, for example, or an easier path. A few, like the small beaches in the north part of Helliwell Park on Hornby Island, are left out because, for most visitors, they are minor features in a park most remarkable for its cliffside paths. In fact, you will find supplementary routes to the shore summarized at the end of many full entries, beginning with the words "While you are here." Do consider investigating some of these spots. Some will give you a picturesque view, others the beginning of a good shore walk, yet others an alternative access to a beach with a more popular route.

In contrast, a few places have been included whose choice may seem surprising. Prominent among these are those roadside spots (on Gabriola, Denman and Quadra) included simply because it would be criminal not to draw attention to their features. Others appear here, even though they are parks, because visitors from off the islands may know little or nothing about them. Some beaches included are those that, by many people's standards, are not very attractive or, at least, not "proper" beaches. A path may provide the only access to an entire section of coast, or it may be more remarkable for its view, or its function as a launching spot, than the beach at its end. Still, because interests among shore explorers can be as diverse as the shores themselves, a view spot or a kayak-launching spot might be just enough to transform an otherwise ordinary visit.

THE RIGHT BEACH FOR YOU

Let us imagine you suddenly decide that what you need most in the world is an afternoon at the beach. Let us also imagine that what you want most out of your afternoon is complete solitude as you bask in soft sand behind beach logs while finishing off your novel. Or the weather may have turned genuinely nasty before you've had a chance to enjoy your carefully prepared feast. Or you may have a yen to photograph an overwrought sunset. Where should you go?

A quick look at the last section of this book, called "Best Bets," will help you on your way to exactly the best bit of the water's edge for what you want. The categories in this section cover many interests—including playing in the sand, walking along the shore, spotting wildlife or picnicking with those who have walking difficulties. You might be looking for a convenient picnic spot for a birthday party's worth of tiny children with tiny legs. You might want a place where you and your soulmates can find lots of space for parking and spread-eagling in the afternoon sun. You might want to hone your Frisbee skills or watch waves batter complicated headlands. Find the category and narrow in on just the right beach for you.

THE GREAT BEACH EXPERIENCE

Armed with this book, then, and sensitive to the possible impact of your beach-going on local residents and the beaches themselves, you can head out with ferry schedule, camera, sunscreen and picnic basket—or kayak, easel and Frisbee. To be sure that you have a wonderful beach experience, however, consider the following.

Weather The first question that anyone with an iota of West Coast experience will ask before going to the beach is, "What will the weather be like?" Even a sunny day does not guarantee a pleasant experience. As any real West Coaster will tell you, your beach experience is affected by the wind. First, use this book to identify which beaches are partially or fully exposed to which winds. Then turn to the forecast. Unfortunately, most radio or newspaper weather forecasters will tell you little or nothing about the wind, except where, occasionally, they toss in the phrase "windy near the water."

Enter the marine forecast. This kind of forecast is readily available on the web at www.weatheroffice.gc.ca/. Alternatively, you can find the online forecast simply by typing "marine forecast environment Canada" into your search window and follow links to "marine info," then "Georgia basin," then "north of Nanaimo." Soon you will be looking at a prediction something like "winds light this morning, rising to northwest 15 to 20 knots late morning and dropping to 5 knots, variable this evening." In fact, a version of this particular forecast is the one you are most likely to find during the summer (when, let's face it, most of us head to the beach). Many a warm, sunny day with settled conditions begins with barely a breeze. Before long, however, the first ripples spread across the mirror-like surface, and soon the first whitecaps appear. For the next several hours, the straits are alive with the brisk, deep-blue charge of waves.

These conditions, however, can make for some chilly sunbathing or even beach walking. This is where your use of this book can save the day. Unless the day is especially warm, and unless you enjoy the exhilaration of beachcombing with wind in your hair, you will have to make some decisions: wait until late morning, when northwest winds may have subsided; bring a sweater; or look for beaches that are not exposed to northwest winds.

But don't get cocky. This particular daily pattern is common, but in some conditions, and especially during very warm weather, not inevitable. A northwest wind can blow all day long and all night. If, for example, you head off in the late afternoon to Whaling Station Bay on Hornby, expecting a sun-flooded dinner picnic and a sunset paddle over silken seas, you might take one look at the foaming whitecaps and flip through this book to find somewhere nearby that is well protected from these winds. Voila—Little Tribune Bay! Check the forecast, or be prepared to be flexible with your plans.

Although sunny weather is nearly always accompanied by northwest winds, it isn't always. Look to the southeast. The kind of southeast wind that comes with a sunny day seems most often to arise in the afternoon and fade in the evening. Even when this wind is more refreshing than you want, by scanning this book you can find delightful beaches, either fully or partially protected, where you can enjoy a blissful bask. Take note, too,

Hornby: Maude Road—Whaling Station Bay

that during bad weather, any winds are likely to blow from the southeast. Before fully trusting a wind forecast, though, remember that winds can be fluky, curving around headlands just where they aren't wanted.

But don't avoid all blustery days. You might, in fact, particularly enjoy a strong wind. In a storm from the southeast, for example, it can be thrilling to drive to the end of Berry Point Road on Gabriola Island and watch the foamy histrionics. Likewise, kite flying can be a great diversion on a windy day—if you choose a long flat beach such as Smelt Bay Provincial Park on Cortes Island and arrive at low tide. Then, too, there are those (few) stiflingly hot days we have each summer when a windy section of shore feels comfortable, while sheltered beaches bake. Hinton Road on Denman Island, for example, can get blisteringly hot.

And don't avoid foul, rainy weather. In even the worst weather, you can, by consulting this book, find many spots to park your car in full view of the shore and enjoy a cozy car picnic while simultaneously feeding your soul on the splendours of the sea and gulls. In fact, winter, when we are treated to most of the foul weather, is also the best time for spotting sea lions and many species of waterfowl that spend their summers in the far north. Be careful, though, if you venture onto the shore, since both logs and rocks are usually more slippery in winter than in summer.

Sun direction Do you want to sunbathe on a baking bit of shore, or picnic in a patch of cool shade? We tend to think of beaches as being permanently in sun on a sunny day. Because all of the northeast-facing coastlines on these islands are comparatively long, however, a particular piece of shore can be deeply in shadow for much of the afternoon. For the many south- or southwest-facing beaches, however, the reverse pattern holds. The steepness of the bank and the presence or absence of overhanging trees are also factors to consider. You will find in this book many spots that get sun throughout the day but also many that are in full, direct sun during only the morning or the afternoon. Make sure you know what you're in for before you select one beach over another. Even then, consider the seasons. Both the length of shadows and their timing will vary significantly between even June and September, let alone December.

Tides Beaches can, of course, change character completely between high and low tide. This is particularly the case where tides go out a long way. The same beach that is a tempting swimming spot with turquoise waters over sun-dappled pebbles can, at low tide, be a broad swath of oysters, barnacle-covered boulders and tidal pools. Conversely, and especially in winter, you might arrive shod and snack-laden for a favourite shore tromp—only to find the shore under water. You cannot use this book to predict tides, except in a very general way. You can, however, use it in combination with your tide tables to decide when to go to your chosen spot.

Learn about tidal patterns. As most coast dwellers know, we have two high tides each day and, it follows, two low tides. Most coast dwellers also know that the sequence moves forward about an hour each day, so that if, for example, the tide is high at 4:30 p.m. on Tuesday, it will be high at approximately 5:30 p.m. on Wednesday. Not all coast dwellers, however, are familiar with other patterns. In the summer the tides tend to follow one pattern, and in the winter the reverse.

Knowledge of this seasonal shift should help you in your planning: tides are generally high during the day in winter and generally low during the day in summer. That general effect is created because in midsummer, any high tide during the middle of the day will not be very high; in fact, it will often seem like a half tide. Similarly, any low tide in late afternoon or evening will not be very low; it, too, will seem like a half tide. Needless to say, kayakers, who prefer to put their energy into paddling rather than lugging their craft, love these tides. In contrast, if the low tide occurs mid-morning, it is likely to be very low and its companion high tide in mid- to late afternoon is likely to be very high. On wide expanses of beach, this water comes rushing in over the warmed pebbles or sand. These tides often produce the warmest swimming, though the warmth can be a little patchy as the newly warmed surface water is still "floating" over the comparatively colder water.

This, though, is the pattern of midsummer. In early and late summer, the pattern is a little different. If you're looking for days with extreme tides in early summer, expect an afternoon low tide to be extremely low; in late summer expect a morning low tide to be equally low. Confused? Simply search out one of the dozens of websites that provide tide tables. The most official one is that of Fisheries and Oceans Canada (www.waterlevels.gc.ca/).

Children We all associate the seaside with children and sandcastles. Most of the large, sandy beaches on these islands are within parks, but not all. Public access routes can certainly lead you to many wonderful spots with sand and warm tidal pools. In addition, consider that even a small area of sand can provide scads of fun. Beaches with no intertidal sand often have a huge natural sandbox of loose, dry sand among beach logs. Remember how much fun it was, as a child, burying your father's legs or plowing trucks through collapsing landscapes?

Many of the most beautiful and memorable beaches on these islands, though, don't have a single grain of sand. Should families with children never enjoy these beaches? Do consider bringing your children to these beaches simply to challene the stereotypes. Children can play for hours in rocky tidal pools trying to catch "bullheads" (actually sculpins), or building little kingdoms of seaweed, rocks and seashells for their shore crab citizens. Likewise, and particularly with adults leading the way, children can discover wonderful creatures under boulders at low tide that most beachgoers don't even know exist—the frantically wiggling eel-like "blennies," for example, or the bulbous-headed clingfish, or the deliciously slimy leather star.

Some beaches, too, are magical with polished pebbles. Even adults can enjoy sifting through the multicoloured little gems. Other beaches have great skipping stones, or stones perfect for making not sandcastles but rock castles. And don't forget the hours of play that can be had on the tangles of beach logs just begging to be climbed over, conquered or converted into rocket ships. (Do be wary, though: rolling beach logs can be dangerous.)

Because there is nothing much on our beaches that will hurt children, life is made comparatively easy for protective parents. Perhaps the greatest threat is the oyster or barnacle, lurking to inflict the wounds that constitute the rite of passage for all children visiting our beaches. Despite the relative safety of our beaches, remember to toss antibiotic cream and a colourful Band-Aid—or a whole pack—into the beach bag beside the granola bars.

Not all of the beaches in this book are suitable for children, though. Adults will enjoy a steep path down a wooded bank to a secluded nest on a ledge with a dream-like view of overlapping reefs, islets and islands. They will not, however, enjoy watching their children wail as they struggle through a maze of weed-slimy boulders, slithering and crashing to a bloody-handed halt.

So read the descriptions and advice in this book carefully. If you have a high panic threshold and nimble, adventurous children, you can have a wonderful time at some of the lumpier beaches. Do, however, consider what you will be facing and what decisions you will have to make once you get there. And, of course, be prepared to move on if a beach isn't suitable for your children. One of the delights of the islands is that beaches even a hundred metres apart can be radically different.

Signs Glorious confusion and amazing inconsistency reign in the world of beach signs. Some beach access spots are heavily burdened with signs. Many have none. Some have one kind, some another. In some places you will find two access spots 100 m apart, one of them carefully signposted, the other devoid of so much as a stick. In general, the beaches in the Northern Gulf Islands have fewer signs than those anywhere else in the Salish Sea. Often, therefore, you will have to rely on garden-variety common sense and consideration. After all, you shouldn't really need to be told not to litter and to clean up after your dog. Still, the descriptions of beach accesses in the book come accompanied with notes on the signs you can expect to see for some important reasons. First, signs will help you know you're not lost. At several locations, in fact, the only indication that you have come to a public access trail is a single sign warning against collecting shellfish or telling you not to park overnight. More important, signs will help you plan. If you know that you must leave a shore at 10 p.m., there's no point selecting that spot for viewing the annual mid-August meteor shower. Likewise, if you're planning a wiener roast, you will want to know where fires are not allowed. Dog walkers will want to know where Duckhunter must stay on a leash or is not allowed at all. Similarly, if you're mooching for ingredients for your paella, don't come to a beach where the shellfish are contaminated. Signs can change quickly, though, so don't treat everything you read in this book as gospel. Below are the signs you are most likely to encounter.

    Park These islands are unusually well blessed with provincial parks. Visitors will quickly learn to identify the rustic-looking wooden signs with the carved letters, often positioned well before the entrance to a park. More commercial-looking signs in blue and white are often positioned to direct visitors at each major intersection along the entire route from a ferry terminal to the park entrance. Be aware, though, that not all provincial parks are well developed or are suitable for large crowds. Boyle Point Provincial Park on Denman Island, for example, offers vastly different facilities from Fillongley Provincial Park, a short drive away. Regional and community parks vary enormously in their size and facilities but are usually signposted only at their entrances. Among these islands, Gabriola Island is unusually prolific with community parks. In many cases, though, expect the signs for community parks to be badly weathered and, often, nearly illegible.

Dead-end road/No turnaround These are the yellow and black road signs at the beginning of a cul-de-sac that make you feel really, really hesitant about going a metre farther. Because the placement of these signs sometimes seems random, one wonders about the enthusiasm locals feel for having outsiders in their neighbourhood. Not surprisingly, the NO TURNAROUND signs are misleading. Unless you are driving a semi-trailer, you will find yourself perfectly capable of turning around at the end of these roads.

No camping or overnight parking Signs prohibiting camping and overnight parking are probably the most common type at beach access spots on Vancouver Island. Although one might wonder where the harm lies in a camper dozing away for a few hours on a secluded spot, these signs should be heeded. They are comparatively rare on the Northern Gulf Islands, however.

Tsunami warning Dotting the coastline of Vancouver Island, these signs are completely absent from the Gulf Islands. Keep in mind, though, that if you are on a beach when an earthquake should happen to strike, you should immediately move to higher ground.

No fires, fire ban or no open fires Sometimes conveyed through words, sometimes through symbols, these are, perhaps of all the signs, the most important to heed. Because the Gulf Islands, both north and south, are especially vulnerable to the devastating effects of wildfires, many locals have understandably taken it upon themselves to improvise signs. In fact, at some spots, the only signs you will see are several versions of the same warning against fires. You won't have a hard time sensing the depth of the concerns about fire danger.

Dog or pet signs Common at beach access spots on Vancouver Island, prohibitions against pets are rare in the Gulf Islands. All the more reason, therefore, that you should heed them when they are posted. Even

Denman: Chrome Island Lighthouse from Boyle Point Park

when the signs are not posted, you should obviously clean up after your dog and prevent her from wiping out the entire shorebird population of the beaches you visit.

Parking Whether or not your access spot is along a through road or at the end of a cul-de-sac, you might find parking is not great. At a few spots you will see the NO PARKING symbol, indicating you will have to park some distance along a road from the access trailhead. Almost invariably, you will find parking for at least a few cars, usually on the shoulder of the road. You should, of course, be sensitive about blocking driveways.

Public washrooms Other than the provincial parks, few spots have public toilets. The last thing locals or other beachgoers want to face is the unpleasant sight of toilet paper festooned from wild rose bushes. One word of advice: plan! This is particularly the case if you are taking a group or tiny folk with tiny bladders.

Boat launching Only a few of the spots in this book are suitable for launching boats of any weight, such as a dinghy with a small outboard. Many more spots are suitable for launching kayaks and canoes. Information about launching is particularly valuable on the islands, because high-current areas can block easy circumnavigation of some islands—especially Quadra and Gabriola. Launch sites on Cortes may also be of major interest to those wishing to paddle to Desolation Sound. Do check your tide tables, though, and read this book to learn how much shore is exposed at low tide, as well as how easy it is to walk on.

Beach fires Don't even think about having a beach fire during fire season, even when you crave s'mores. Enjoy the tranquility and freedom from eyes full of smoke. And if you see no signs forbidding beach fires, be considerate of others and build your fire well below the high-tide line or in established firepits. Nothing ruins the pristine pleasures of a shiny pebble beach more than an ugly firepit or logs scarred with ashes. In addition, remember that rocks close to a fire turn an ugly orange-brown, permanently blemishing the beach. In any case, be ridiculously careful: a fire out of control on one of these islands would be devastating.

Beachcombing Do you most like to use a public access spot as the beginning of an exploration of a piece of shoreline? Whether you enjoy poking through tidal pools or striding along with the wind in your hair, many

Gabriola: Dragon's Lane

of these access points will allow you considerable opportunity for uplifting waterfront walks. But don't forget the tides. Some carefree rambles can turn at high tide into awkward scrambles beneath overhanging tree branches. At the same time, though some sections of coast are too steep to walk, you needn't worry much about being dangerously trapped by an incoming tide. In addition, consider the season. Many rocky beaches, easy to stroll along in summer, can be dangerously slippery in winter.

Seclusion You may feel motivated to hunt down a small, remote beach to get away from the madding crowds that throng the big public beaches. If so, you should be pleased with the array of fine options among these islands. At many of these places, you can expect to sit for hours at a time, virtually alone, contemplating, undisturbed, the play of light on the waves and the cry of the gulls—or how to initiate That Conversation.

Beaches can be secluded in four different ways, as you will find in the seclusion sections of this book. First, at some spots you can walk almost a hundred metres out to the low-tide line, far away from everyone. Second, some access points are rarely, if ever, used—even by local residents. Third, neighbouring houses are sometimes built well back from the bank or behind a screen of trees. Last, and most spectacularly, these islands are filled with long, wooded trails leading you to shores where you can feel as alone with nature as you could possibly want.

Views One of the remarkable qualities of the view from many of the beach access spots on Vancouver Island is that they combine expansive sea views with a backdrop of the Coast Mountains. Visitors to the Southern Gulf Islands, in contrast, will find that the views, though exquisite, are primarily those created by an overlapping maze of reefs, islets, promontories, bays, and high, forested ridges. Lovers of mountains will nowhere be better pleased than among the Northern Gulf Islands. Gabriola Island is perfectly positioned to look back onto the Vancouver Island mountains above Nanaimo and, from the northeast coast, across the strait to the higher and more jagged peaks of the Coast Range, especially between Jervis Inlet and Howe Sound. From Denman Island and, to a lesser extent, Hornby Island, the Beaufort Range on Vancouver Island seems to loom high above the island as a virtually unbroken wall. It is Quadra and Cortes Islands, though, that surpass all others in the Salish Sea for their mountain views. The highest and most jagged peaks of Strathcona Park seem to rise directly behind Campbell River when seen from Quadra's southwest coast. From Quadra's north-east coast and from Cortes, the most spectacular crags around the Salish Sea cluster high against the skyline. Photographers take note: largely a line of misty-blue silhouettes during hazy summer afternoons, these same mountains during a morning in spring can leap from the distant shore with spectacular detail.

CHECKLIST

With this book, you can set out for a perfect day of beach exploration. You may be alone or with a carful of excited family members. You may be unencumbered or overloaded with paraphernalia. Before you set out, glance down the following checklists of things you may regret not having with you.

For your trip planning
- ✓ tide tables (www.pac.dfo-mpo.gc.ca/)
- ✓ marine weather forecast (www.weatheroffice.gc.ca/)
- ✓ Fisheries notices before gathering shellfish (www.pac.dfo-mpo.gc.ca/)
- ✓ need for fire permits

For the whole family
- ✓ sunscreen, sunglasses, sunhat, other protective sunwear
- ✓ bathing suit and towel
- ✓ beach umbrella, folding chairs, beach mats
- ✓ binoculars, camera, tripod, easel, painting and sketching supplies
- ✓ reading material
- ✓ water bottles, picnic supplies
- ✓ garbage bags to carry away your trash

For your children
- ✓ first-aid supplies and personal flotation devices (PFDs)
- ✓ crocs or water shoes—even in cold weather
- ✓ sunhat, sunscreen
- ✓ dry, warm change of clothes
- ✓ the world's best oatmeal cookies
- ✓ Frisbees, kites, skimboards, inflatable water toys, buckets

For your dog
- ✓ leash and, if needed, muzzle
- ✓ treats, toys, fetch balls
- ✓ water dish, water bottle
- ✓ plastic bags for cleanup
- ✓ old towel

Quadra: Rebecca Spit

PART 1

Gabriola Island

THE SOUTHERNMOST ISLAND INCLUDED in this book, Gabriola Island, like Quadra Island, is only a short ferry ride away from a city. As with Quadra Island, too, part of the workforce of a city—Nanaimo, in this case—has decided they would really enjoy living on a beautiful island and commute to work. Visitors to the island, and especially those looking for "secret beaches," may quickly come to understand why Gabriola Island is so appealing. Like the beaches of Hornby Island, Gabriola's expanses of smooth, firm sand are perfect for families. Also like the beaches of Hornby Island, Gabriola's shores are primarily composed of sandstone. Large areas of shore are composed of smoothly sculpted undulations mixed with strange, lunar protuberances. Another feature of the beaches on this island is the large number well suited to car picnicking and launching kayaks. This relatively small island actually has more publicly accessible beach routes than any other Gulf Island, north or south—and not just more: *many* more. The less encouraging news is that a high number require some detective work to find. Early in the days of the island's development, some enlightened folk not only zoned these many routes but also put in place yellow concrete blocks stamped with the words "Public Access." These blocks aren't everywhere, however, and many are hidden among weeds and bushes. Armed with this book, therefore, and pumped with enthusiasm, you will be able to satisfy your craving for wonderful discoveries.

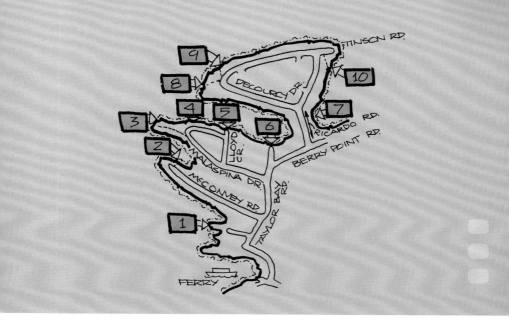

1 DESCANSO BAY REGIONAL PARK
Extensive camping and picnicking facilities near a small, forested promontory separating two narrow bays

Location, signs and parking Within easy walking distance of the ferry, the park can be reached by heading uphill from the ferry and taking the first road on the left, Taylor Bay Road. About 600 m along, you will see a park sign on the left, prominently posted at the beginning of an otherwise unsignposted paved road. About 400 m down this road brings you to the park. A large gravel parking area for day use is located near a grassy field with about a dozen picnic tables. At various points throughout the park, you will see two chief reminder signs, one to clean up after your pooch, the other not even to think about lighting a fire. You are also asked not to disturb the intertidal life, tempting though it is to molest crabs and collect clamshells.

Path Several paths in this park lead to different parts of the shoreline. The most convenient and most attractive leads from the edge of the grassy shorefront area down 11 wooden steps. While the steps are wide and solid, visitors with walking difficulties may wish they also had a handrail. Others, wishing to get their favourite kayak floating, can either use these steps or a gravel slope immediately to the left. Amateur anthropologists might be interested in the ancient First Nation midden.

Beach This odd little beach is a combination of fine pebbles and long, smooth ridges of sandstone. The uppermost part of the beach, a small area of fine loose pebbles and beach logs, is appealing for sitting, but only in the latter part of the day. Though a narrow section of pebbles and gravel leads more or less smoothly toward the low-tide line, the entire left side of the bay is composed of undulating areas of sandstone and small tidal pools. You can also visit a second bay a few dozen metres away, on the opposite side of a wooded peninsula. This long, narrow bay is rather slimy and dank nearest the upper shore, but at low tide it is remarkably diverse, with a long narrow strip of intertidal rock extending more than 200 m from the head of the bay into deeper water.

Suitability for children Like any well-developed park, this one has all the facilities you need to cope with the needs of childhood. Only older children will have a romping good time here, however. Accompany them out along the rocks and tidal pools, particularly in the more northern of the two bays, and you will all find lots to discover in the tidal pools.

Suitability for groups This is probably the best place on the island for a mega-picnic. The large grassy field with picnic tables should make life easy for setting out mountains of potato chips and oodles of Kool-Aid, and the nearby outhouses are handy as well. For most such groups, however, the beach area is small and not very welcoming.

View Your view from these narrow, heavily forested bays is dominated by the nearby features—rock, water and forest. If your eyes stray much beyond the foreground, you will discover that you are looking at the distant northwest end of Newcastle Island and the residential development around Stephenson Point.

Winds, sun and shade You won't find many spots on the island where you are as likely to be oblivious of the elements. Tucked into these deep, forested bays, you won't notice if there is a full-scale gale from the southeast, though a northwest wind can funnel into these narrow channels. Except for the grassy field, which can be sunny for most of the day, this spot can be shady. Wait until late in the afternoon if you want to experience the shore bathed in sunshine.

Beachcombing For the most part, beachcombing is restricted to a little wandering around the tidal pools and rocky sides of the bays. One remarkable exception is available to you, if you time your visit to arrive at a significant low tide. Don a pair of water shoes and head out along the remarkable sequence of sandstone ridges and tidal pools that stretch far offshore into the northern bay.

Seclusion This is a public park. You shouldn't even think about coming to a public park if you want seclusion. Still, because the park is so heavily treed and the shoreline so convoluted, you are never going to be in the midst of a milling crowd—to say the least.

2
McCONVEY ROAD
A slightly challenging access down a rope-assisted rock slope to the side of a small bay with sections of smooth sandstone, pebbles and crushed shell

Location, signs and parking With your scenic ferry ride behind you, plow up the hill and, after about 200 m, take Taylor Road, the first on your left. About 1 km later, turn left onto McConvey Road and follow it to its end in a tree-dotted residential area. Park along the shoulder, being careful to avoid driveways.

Path Used only by a few locals, the path is little more than a barely-tramped route through a grassy area under some firs. More distinct toward the shoreline, the route to the shore becomes unmistakable when you see a section of blue rope put in place by a public-spirited local. The rope is there to help you negotiate the short slope down smooth sandstone, which is quite steep and can become slippery. You can practise a little entry-level abseiling (rappelling) along the way. Clearly, this is not the place to bring the very young, the very old or the very unwieldy.

Beach You will find yourself at the side of a deeply inset bay about 100 m wide. At low tide the intertidal zone is about 100 m long, but since the access route brings you about 50 m from the head of the bay, the waterline is much closer. In fact, you really only want to come to this spot when the tide is out—unless you are happy to find water at your feet as you come down the little slope. The beach is an interesting mixture of shore types. Mostly large, nearly flat surfaces of smooth sandstone, it is intersected with sections of pebbles and dotted with tidal pools.

Suitability for children The scramble down onto the beach is to be reckoned with. Once on the shore, though, most children should find lots to investigate. Because the sandstone blocks extend in long lines from the base of the bay toward its mouth, the resulting cracks and pebbly sections are great places for the relentless pursuit of crabs, starfish and frilled dog whelks. The generally smooth, level surfaces of sandstone encourage galumphing, except near the low-tide line, where seaweed can make the going slippery.

Suitability for groups This is not a good spot for a group, though a few friends in exploration mode may well be impressed that you have guided them to an obscure but intriguing piece of shore.

View From the spot at which you descend onto the shore, your view will be almost entirely of the bay itself. Across the bay, a cliff, some 15 m high at its highest point, is sprinkled with a series of houses. This cliff tapers toward the tip of the bay and appears to be a park, with no houses anywhere. If you have one of those "Aha!" moments, you have just realized that you are getting a rarely enjoyed perspective on the much-touted rock formations known as the "Malaspina Galleries," designated a park. The wildly sculpted hollows in the cliffside are best viewed from the park itself, of course, but from this side of the bay you can appreciate how they fit into the striking geological formations surrounding them.

Winds, sun and shade You won't find many other spots on the island that so successfully funnel every scrap of northwest wind into them. On the other hand, when southeast winds are kicking up foam elsewhere, this bay is like a proverbial millpond—and, presumably, a real one. The part of the beach where you are likely to spend your time is in sun throughout the day.

Beachcombing Come at low tide to wander across and around the pools and low shelves of this bay. Make your way down the comparatively narrow left side of the bay to an equally interesting expanse of sandstone slabs extending almost 100 m from the point at that end of the bay.

Seclusion At few places on the island will you feel so much under the inspection of picture windows directed at your every move. At few places on the island, however, are you less likely to find day visitors. Less-used access routes are hard to find.

While you're here . . . Beside a house numbered 143 on the way to this access path, walk through the lightly scattered trees for an astounding clifftop view both across Descanso Bay and onto the huge low-tide reef below, approachable from Descanso Bay Regional Park.

Gabriola: McConvey Road roadside viewpoint

3 MALASPINA GALLERIES COMMUNITY PARK
A treed promontory sloping down to sandstone-slab shoreline next to the famous Malaspina Galleries

Location, signs and parking Head uphill from the ferry and take the first turn, Taylor Road, on your left. A little over 1.5 km later, turn left onto Malaspina Drive and follow it to its end, about 1 km later. Here you will find a huge paved turnaround, with far more parking space than is ever likely to be filled. Do, however, notice the signs restricting parking in some places. At the end of the parking area you will see a slightly weathered sign giving a little history behind the Malaspina Galleries. Closer to the shore, another sign lists a whole slew of "do nots." Most of these are predictable, concerning unleashed dogs, littering, lighting fires and camping. Others are not: you are not to ride horses, cut trees or—most important, perhaps—use spray paint on these culturally significant rock formations.

Path The path, about 150 m long, is generally level and broad, but a few roots could create problems for anyone with real walking difficulties. As it approaches the tip of the lightly forested ridge, the path drops gradually onto a sloping sandstone shore.

Beach Immediately in front of the trailhead, a sandstone promontory extends about 100 m toward the low-tide line. While this area of tidal pools and ridges is interesting enough, most visitors will find most fascinating the so-called "galleries." Turn left and head a few metres into the bay on the left of the promontory to view the smoothly hollowed-out sandstone formations. Not unlike a giant breaking wave, this formation extends dozens of metres along the steep shoreline on this side of the bay. Unfortunately, an assertive sign warns you against the dangers of entering the galleries themselves.

Suitability for children The biggest problem in bringing children to visit the galleries is convincing them of the dangers of heading directly into the semi-caves. Otherwise, this spot is clearly an intriguing and unusual spot to visit for almost any child who is old enough to distinguish between the ordinary and the extraordinary.

Suitability for groups The large turnaround area suggests that many visitors can be expected. The fact is, however, except for viewing the rock formations themselves, neither the natural features of the park nor what has been added for visitors make it a good place for more than a dozen at a time. If you do wish to lead a larger group here, the sandstone shoreline along the north side of the promontory slopes gradually and smoothly enough that many visitors could explore this large area.

View Not just the close-up view of the rocks but also the more distant views in all directions make this a wonderful place to visit. You can look back toward Duke Point and the southern end of Nanaimo Harbour, but also see past Protection and Newcastle Islands and far up the northern Strait of Georgia. Especially attractive are the small islands offshore from Nanaimo, Snake Island closest to you and, farther away, Five Fingers Island and the Hudson Rocks. This is also a perfect spot for viewing the ferries gliding to and from the mainland, both those from Departure Bay and those from Duke Point. If you happen to be here in the evening, you just might find yourself with a stunning sunset spread out in front of you.

Winds, sun and shade Because this is on a promontory, it can be a very windy spot. Hold onto your hat if the wind is kicking up a storm, though you can duck out of a southeast wind by walking around the peninsula to the right. If you are planning to stay for a while, you'll be able to find about as much shade or sun as you want by choosing your spot wisely.

Beachcombing The wide intertidal zone of crevices and pools at the tip of the promontory is exactly the kind of place that amateur naturalists will love. The array of limpets, chitons, frilled dog whelks and so on is huge. For those whose interest in shore walking is in covering distance, turning right into Taylor Bay will allow them to walk the broad sandstone shelf about 1 km into the head of the bay and the tidal flats adjoining the Taylor Bay side of Gabriola Sands Provincial Park.

Seclusion The park is large enough and wooded enough that you can perch on the shore and feel well away from both the hurly and the burly.

Except for the park, though, this is a densely populated, if well-forested, part of the island. Let your eyes stray too far from the foreground, and you will be aware of many shorefront houses across Taylor Bay.

4
MALASPINA DRIVE
A wooded trail to the south shore of Taylor Bay with its smoothly undulating sandstone shore

Location, signs and parking As you drive away from the ferry terminal, look for the first turn on your left, Taylor Bay Road, and follow it for a little under 2 km. Turn left onto Malaspina Drive for a little over half a kilometre, then right onto Lloyd Crescent. About 100 m later, take your first left, again onto Malaspina Drive, this time the northern end of the loop-shaped drive. Your search at this point requires eagle eyes. Roughly 200 m along, if you look sharply, you will see on the right a faded yellow concrete block and the words PUBLIC ACCESS. Congratulate yourself on your detecting skills, and park along the grassy shoulder of the road.

Path About 75 m long, the path starts off as a clear, largely level track through second-growth firs. As you get closer to the shore, the path tends to become overgrown with salal, but clear enough to bring you to the edge of a smooth sandstone slope down to the shore. Getting down this slope can be a little tricky if the rock is wet and slippery. Be careful!

Beach Welcome to the Gabriola sandstone shoreline at its most quintessential. Backed by an overhanging lip of strata, the shore is largely level and smoothly undulating, except toward the low-tide line, where it becomes slippery with rockweed and intersected with little crevices. The entire intertidal surface, though, is dotted with almost eerily sculpted protuberances. Because no logs collect along the shore, a bench of smooth rock will have to suffice if you are looking for a spot to sit awhile, with or without the comfort of a picnic.

Suitability for children While getting down the steep slope onto the shore might be a bit of a feat for some children, once on the flat rock strata, most children can have a comfortable, even exciting, shore experience. Paddling can be great fun when the tide is almost in, since the shore will appear to be a maze of mini-reefs and islets. Low tide, in contrast, exposes tidal pools and creature-crammed crevices laid out for thorough investigation.

Suitability for groups This is not a good place for a group. Take them to nearby Gabriola Sands Provincial Park.

View Your eyes will be most drawn to the view across Taylor Bay, about 300 m wide at this point. The low landform across the bay is dotted with houses but is prettily treed. Allow your eyes to swing out of the bay and you will see the clusters of houses and treed bumps surrounding Pipers Lagoon, north of Nanaimo, as well as the waters of the straits leading toward Lasqueti and Texada Islands.

Winds, sun and shade Reasonably well protected from southeasterly winds, the bay scoops up every bit of a northwesterly. The morning is the sunniest part of the day, since the upper shore becomes increasingly shady during the afternoon.

Beachcombing Wandering this fascinating, convoluted moonscape is the real attraction of this shore. About 75 m wide at low tide, the rock shelf allows you to walk all the way to the Malaspina Galleries, about 500 m to your left, or to the sand flats of Gabriola Sands Provincial Park, about the same distance to your right.

Seclusion The chances of your finding fellow visitors at this spot are approximately zero. On the other hand, the chances of your feeling secluded are also small. Many houses line this shoreline, even though most of them have preserved groves of sheltering trees.

While you're here . . . Look for a similar PUBLIC ACCESS concrete block between this spot and Malaspina Galleries Park. A wooded trail leads to a pretty view over the sandstone shore on the south side of Taylor Bay and provides another access to this attractive shore.

5

LLOYD CRESCENT
Overlooking Taylor Bay, a
good spot for launching a
kayak or devouring a car
picnic in foul weather

Location, signs and parking Trundling uphill from the ferry, look for Taylor Bay Road, the first turn on your left, and follow it for a little under 2 km. Turn left onto Malaspina Drive for a little over half a kilometre, then right onto Lloyd Crescent. Simply drive straight ahead until you find yourself at the end of the gravel road at shore's edge. Although you won't find masses of room to park or turn around, you are unlikely to have any difficulties doing either at this quiet and little-visited spot.

Path It is the very absence of a path that makes this such a good place to drown your bad-weather woes in the pleasures of brie-and-prosciutto croissants. It is also the absence of a path that makes this a good launch spot for a kayak or two—though you may want to avoid low tides that require you to haul your craft over almost 100 m of shore.

Beach Like the entire southern shore of Taylor Bay, this portion immediately in front of the access route is a wonderfully rolling sequence of sandstone swells punctuated with nearly circular hollows and protuberances. Although this is not the most conventional kind of beach for an afternoon's indolence, you can sprawl either on some of the more welcoming rock mounds or on the small area of grass sloping toward the shore.

Suitability for children The ease both of getting onto the shore and navigating it once there are practical features of this spot. Other features seal the deal in making this a welcoming place for the miniature folk in your entourage. Children probably exist who would feel no temptation to dash around this natural playground of castles and crevices, but they must be few. An incoming tide, as the water heats over the sun-baked rocks, can make splashing around the formations an unusual experience.

Do remember water shoes, though, because the tiny periwinkles clinging to the otherwise smooth stone surfaces can feel sharp.

Suitability for groups If your group would like to experience this kind of sandstone shoreline rather than a more conventional sandy beach, this is one of the better spots on Gabriola Island to do that. Still, be aware that parking is constricted, neighbour houses are close and facilities simply don't exist.

View The curve of the shoreline on this side of Taylor Bay allows you to see the entire end of the bay and the sandy intertidal area in front of the provincial park. Across the bay, the low, treed shoreline is sprinkled with houses. The view outside the bay includes the hills near Pipers Lagoon, covered with suburban development, and the pretty islands a little offshore: Five Finger Island, Hudson Rocks and Snake Island. A lover of sunsets? Time your visit carefully, and you just might be treated to the full whammy.

Winds, sun and shade While a northwest wind whistles straight into this bay, it is well protected from cool winds from the southeast. Though the firs and shore pines that line the low bank don't cast long shadows, the uppermost shore is mostly shady during the afternoon.

Beachcombing For an interesting approach to the Malaspina Galleries, tucked around the tip of the peninsula, head to the left for about 500 m. Walking along the broad table-like surfaces of sandstone constitutes part of the pleasure of your minor expedition to reach the Galleries.

Seclusion While you're likely to be the only visitor at this quiet spot, don't expect to experience an overwhelming sense of isolation. With houses surrounding the entire bay, you should just be grateful that so many locals value the trees around their houses.

6

TAYLOR BAY ROAD

A broad, gravel path sloping
gradually to a flat expanse of
sandstone next to the gravel
and sand tidal flats of Gabriola
Sands Provincial Park

Location, signs and parking In some ways, the driving directions could hardly be simpler. All you need to do is take the first left turn as you leave the ferry terminal. Now that you are on Taylor Bay Road, simply follow it to its end between 2 and 3 km later. Unfortunately, driving is not quite so obvious, because just about 2 km along, at a fork in the road, the main traffic flow will seduce you onto Berry Point Road, unless you are very careful to notice that the narrow left fork is actually a continuation of Taylor Bay Road. About 200 m after this fork, the road comes to an end in a large gravel turnaround in full view of Taylor Bay. It doesn't take much surmising to realize that, in wretched weather, you can easily enjoy a minor feast in your car while savouring a pretty view of Taylor Bay.

Path A broad, crushed gravel path, about 20 m long, angles across and down the face of a treeless grassy bank. Those toting squirming children, tripods or kayaks will appreciate the ease of getting onto the shore, but kayakers will be happiest if they don't arrive when the tide is at its lowest.

Beach Immediately below the path, the shore is composed almost entirely of a large swath of nearly level sandstone. A small area of crushed shell and sand could be a comfortable place for picnicking or settling down with a self-help guide to relaxation. Be a little careful if the rock is wet, since it can be slippery. Immediately adjoining this gently rolling sandstone area are the tidal flats otherwise reached from the provincial park on Ricardo Road.

Suitability for children One of the advantages of using this as an access point for the beach on this side of the provincial park is that you can spread out your base camp on a smooth, sand-free surface. From it, you can make forays onto the sand-and-pebble part of the beach. Water shoes or crocs will make life easier for everyone.

Suitability for groups Although you will find more parking here than you could ever need, this spot is too close to neighbouring houses to make a good place for a group. In any case, nearby Gabriola Sands Provincial Park, with many of the facilities a group requires, leads to the same section of shoreline.

View One of the more restricted views on Gabriola Island, this view, from the end of Taylor Bay Road, is nevertheless both interesting and picturesque. While much of it consists of the shoreline of the nearby park and the steep, low bank across Taylor Bay, outside the bay it extends across the mouth of Nanaimo Harbour to the complex landforms around Hammond Bay. Some will thrill to see ferries both to Duke Point and to Departure Bay gliding past. Others won't.

Winds, sun and shade You may find this spot only a little protected from northwest winds, but from southeast winds you should be well sheltered. If you also need shelter from the sun, you are out of luck unless you provide your own. This bit of shore is in sun as long as there is sun to be in.

Beachcombing When the tide is partly out, you will find lots of walking options. If you are feeling even a little ambitious, head left along the easily wandered sandstone shelves extending all the way along this south side of Taylor Bay as far as the Malaspina Galleries, the weathered sandstone cliffs tucked around the point a little over a kilometre away.

Seclusion Don't choose this spot if you are hoping to find a corner of untouched nature. You won't see many visitors at this spot, but you will see lots of reminders that many lucky folk have shorefront houses around much of the bay.

7 GABRIOLA SANDS
PROVINCIAL PARK
Located on a narrow isthmus,
a day-use park with large,
back-to-back, sandy
beaches

Location, signs and parking Head uphill from the ferry, swinging left onto Taylor Bay Road. After about 2 km, when you see a fork in the road, keep right with the main traffic flow. At this point you are on Berry Point Road. After about 200 m, turn left onto Ricardo Road. Roughly 200 m along, this road will deliver you to the middle of the unusual and beautiful Gabriola Sands Provincial Park. A parking area on the right side of the road has space for more than a dozen cars. Here you will see signs telling you to keep your rambunctious hound leashed and to beware of the dangers of contaminated shellfish. Here you will also see a picnic table and an outhouse. An additional picnic table and outhouse are located across the road near the beach on the other side of the park.

Path From the parking area you need take only a few, largely level steps through a stand of shorefront firs to reach the closer of the two beaches. To reach the other beach, not visible from here, cross the road and the grassy field.

Beach The east-facing beach next to the parking lot is both the more attractive and the more popular of the two beaches. Backed by an array of weathered logs and blessed with a broad expanse of sugary white sand, this beach, about 200 m long, dries at low tide to about 200 m of tidal flats. The second, a west-facing beach, is the same size but doesn't have quite the same feel—in part because it has few logs and is backed by a slope of tall beach grass, and in part because the sand at low tide isn't as fine and firm. Both beaches can become pleasantly warm for swimming, especially near high tide.

Suitability for children If you've brought a carload of little folk frantic to run wild amidst a flurry of decibels, this is probably the best spot on the island to bring them. Whatever bits and pieces you've toted to enhance a day at the beach, you'll have plenty of opportunity to use them on the sandy stretches here. Buckets, spades, skimboards, Frisbees, kites—bring them all. Do, however, be aware that neither beach has flawless sand. A band of barnacly boulders on the east-facing beach can create some grief if they are hidden at mid tide from a happily flailing swimmer.

Suitability for groups Probably the best spot on Gabriola Island for a cavalcade of beach-lovers, this park has not only lots of beach space to spread out but also a large field in case your beach-lovers are also Frisbee and football lovers. You will find only two picnic tables and no picnic shelters, but plenty of comfortable and attractive picnic spots amid the logs. Be aware that the water from the hand pump is not potable.

View Just as you have two beaches, back to back, you have two completely different views, though both of them framed by forested promontories. From the west-facing beach, you look primarily across Newcastle and Protection Islands to Mount Benson and the other high hills behind Nanaimo. On a summer evening, this can be an excellent spot to view an unabashed sunset. The east-facing beach, in contrast, looks out across Pilot Bay and the wide, open spaces of the southern Strait of Georgia to the mainland mountains.

Winds, sun and shade You can't do much better than come to this park if you and the weather can't make up your minds about how much sun and what sort of wind you want. Simply wander around until you find the combination you want.

Beachcombing This is the kind of place where the greatest temptations to walk barefooted are close by. If, however, you are overwhelmed with guilt after eating that third helping of potato salad, your best option for a long-distance tromp is to head down the south shore of Taylor Bay on the west-facing beach. Just over a kilometre will bring you to a satisfying and scenic destination, the Malaspina Galleries. Alternatively, starting at this same beach, you can circumnavigate the entire headland, which is separated from the rest of Gabriola by a narrow isthmus, on the back-to-back beaches. If you choose this walk, you will be most comfortable on the sandstone-slab shore when the tide is at least partly out.

Seclusion You could hardly find a less secluded place on Gabriola Island. Strangely, though, even on a warm summer's afternoon, these beaches can be almost empty.

8

DECOURCY DRIVE
A wooden staircase to an undulating sandstone shore with views of Taylor Bay and Nanaimo

Location, signs and parking Head uphill from the ferry, swinging left onto Taylor Bay Road. After about 2 km, keep right at a fork in the road. At this point you are on Berry Point Road. After about 200 m, turn left onto Ricardo Road and follow it for approximately 400 m. When you come to a fork, you will see that both left and right are Decourcy Drive, a triangular road running around the perimeter of the peninsula. Turn left and go about 300 m, almost to the end of this side of the triangle. At this point, study the left shoulder of the road until you spot a yellow PUBLIC ACCESS concrete block at the base of a telephone pole. The broad shoulder here easily fits two cars, but you could find plenty of additional space nearby. The only other sign, warning you that the area is closed to collecting shellfish, is visible once you are close to the shore.

Path A broad dirt path leads about 100 m, parallel to a fence, through second-growth firs. Even for those with aching or unsteady limbs, this part of the path could hardly be easier. However, this path ends at the top of a flight of about 16 wooden steps. A handrail can help both going up and down, but the stairs are quite steep.

Beach If you arrive at high tide, you will find little beach except for a fairly steep chunk of angular rock. At low tide, though, a stretch of fine sand runs parallel to the shore, and a series of weirdly lunar swellings and bulges rises from the surface of smooth sandstone. One of the larger ones remains beyond reach of all but the highest tides. While this table-top section of the shore is easily explored, the lowest part of the shore is precipitous, more irregular and covered with slippery rockweed.

Suitability for children If your children are a little jaded by the predictable pleasures of the sandy beaches at the nearby provincial park, bring them here at a mid to high tide for a truly strange and wonderful bit of adventuring. As an incoming tide flows over the irregular, sun-warmed rock surfaces, children can splash happily through all kinds of channels, pools and inlets and climb onto rapidly disappearing islets and reefs. Innocent-looking little periwinkles can be devilishly sharp, though, so bring water shoes or crocs.

Suitability for groups The only kind of group that you should even think about bringing here is a small clutch of fellow explorers, driven by curiosity and the desire to see unusual bits of shoreline and unusual viewpoints.

View While your view varies considerably as you meander around the shore, it generally extends from the inner reaches of Taylor Bay directly in front of you across about 4 km of open water between Gabriola Island and the two islands, Newcastle and Protection, largely obscuring Nanaimo. Sunset lovers anticipating a photo-fabulous show can seek this spot out, knowing they will have a perfect viewpoint.

Winds, sun and shade This is the kind of shore where, to some extent, you can vary your exposure to winds. The farther you move away from the bank, in general, the more wind you feel blowing across the shore, roughly parallel to it. Although the middle part of the day is the most sunbaked, the beach is sunny throughout much of the day.

Beachcombing The crevices, pools and rock forms will attract most visitors to wander and peer. If, however, you are looking for a good spot for a fairly easy but geologically fascinating shore walk, this is a good place to start. Turn to your right, and you can saunter around the most exposed part of this dramatically positioned shoreline all the way to a set of stairs just around Tinson Point, about 1 km distant. Thereafter you may want to return by road, but, if you are really determined, you could make your way along the shore to the isthmus, cross over Ricardo Road to Taylor Bay and follow the comparatively narrow shore back to your starting point.

Seclusion This whole area is well settled. Most houses, however, are tucked into trees at the top of the fairly steep bank, so you won't feel even slightly that you have wedged your way into someone's front yard.

9 DECOURCY DRIVE—
NORTHWEST
Concrete stairs down a bank
to a large intertidal area of
crushed shell and sandstone
strata

Location, signs and parking Drive uphill from the ferry terminal and turn left onto Taylor Bay Road. When you come to a fork in the road about 2 km later, keep right with the main traffic flow onto Berry Point Road. After about 200 m, turn left onto Ricardo Road. When you come to a fork you will see that both left and right are Decourcy Drive. Turn left and drive for roughly 300 m. Immediately after the sharp bend in the road, look for a barred gate and a sign saying 285 Decourcy Drive. At present, no other signs are posted. Pull over anywhere on the broad shoulder of this quiet road.

Path Between the fence belonging to this house and the next house along, you will see a broad dirt trail leading under a few firs and arbutus. After about 75 m, the trail comes to an end at the top of a small bank. Here a new set of seven concrete steps and a metal handrail make getting onto the shore easy, even for those with a bum knee or a squirming child. The steps end on smooth stone but require an additional step down, slippery if wet. Take care.

Beach While the uppermost shore provides stone formations more or less suitable for sitting and scoffing muffins or movie mags, this is not the kind of beach most suited to indolence. It is, however, a fascinating bit of shore. Located immediately beside the western tip of a triangular peninsula, this route to the shore gives you good access to a large intertidal area. Composed of swaths of nearly flat sandstone interspersed with significant patches of crushed white shell, the beach extends more than 100 m into Fairway Channel.

Suitability for children Although the smallest children will need a little help getting onto the beach, once there, you can let them loose to leap and prod their way along the level and varied shore. The many low sandstone ridges and tidal pools are rich with periwinkles, hermit crabs, starfish and all the other bio-treasures of this kind of shore. If you and your children put a priority on getting even partially wet, you are best off arriving at mid to high tide.

Suitability for groups This is an attractive and interesting spot only for a small group wishing to explore a shoreline. It is not suitable for a picnicking group, since the neighbouring houses are far too close.

View Because the point of access to the shore is tucked behind a small treed promontory, the view toward Nanaimo is partially obscured. Past Newcastle Island and Stephenson Point, though, the view extends up the northern straits past the distinctive mound of Texada Island and toward the Coast Mountains. The mountains above Jervis Inlet, diminished by distance, make an especially attractive backdrop to the scene.

Winds, sun and shade Fully exposed to winds from the northwest and shady for the early part of the day, this spot can be quite cool until well into the afternoon. Southeast winds don't blow directly onto the shore, but they do skim past it.

Beachcombing Beach walking is the major attraction of this intriguing spot. Come at low tide to enjoy the interesting features of this varied beach. Even at a mid tide, however, walking several hundred metres in either direction allows you to pass around tips of land and find your view suddenly and dramatically changing.

Seclusion Though you won't encounter even minor hordes of beachgoers here, you will be hard-pressed to feel much seclusion. Many, many lucky folk have houses and cottages along the edge of the bank behind this bit of shore.

While you're here . . . About 100 m along this section of Decourcy Drive, en route to Tinson Road, look for a yellow concrete PUBLIC ACCESS block. A pleasant path leads through a broad swath of public land to a continuation of the shore more easily approached by the previous access. The beach is, in some ways, especially interesting because of the areas of fine white crushed shell on the upper shore and the dramatically overhanging chunks of rock along the bank.

10

TINSON ROAD

A broad, level beach with areas of smooth sandstone and sand on the west shore of Pilot Bay

Location, signs and parking Head uphill from the ferry and turn left onto Taylor Bay Road. After about 2 km, at a fork in the road, keep on the main through road by swinging right. At this point you are on Berry Point Road. After about 200 m, turn left onto Ricardo Road and follow it for approximately 400 m. At a fork in the road, both sides of which are Decourcy Drive, turn right. About half a kilometre along, where Decourcy Drive angles back sharply to your left, keep ahead onto tiny Tinson Road. Partway along the right side of the large, teardrop-shaped turnaround at the end of the road, look for a yellow concrete block saying PUBLIC ACCESS. You will find no shortage of parking along the broad shoulder.

Path The smooth, level path runs alongside a fence to the top of a set of 15 wooden stairs. A handrail will help unsteady explorers get up and down the stairs, but be aware that they will have to manage a small natural drop onto the shore.

Beach While the uppermost part of the beach has some sandstone-smooth lumps and bumps that could be used as roosting spots, the most attractive feature of this beach is not its picnicking or sunning area. More than 50 m wide at low tide, the shore is composed of large, level areas of sandstone alternating with equally large areas of sand and crushed white shell.

Suitability for children Almost all children should find lots of diversions on this varied and easily explored beach. The rocks can be a little slippery with weed near the low-tide line, but otherwise expect your children to romp freely through the tidal pools, over the low crests of rock and across the swaths of sand and pebbles. For swimming or even paddling, mid to high tide is by far the best. And, of course, don't forget those water shoes or crocs.

Gabriola: Tinson Road

Suitability for groups You will find plenty of parking, plenty of spacious shore, and, because of the drop down the bank, at least a little separation between you and the locals. Don't guide more than a few shore lovers here, but, if you warn your coven that they will find no facilities, you can bring them here for an attractive and interesting bit of exploration.

View Framed by a photogenic cluster of overhanging firs on the left, your view is otherwise almost entirely of the shoreline of the bay. Roughly 300 m wide and, at high tide, 400 m long, Pilot Bay is mostly surrounded by low, wooded banks and dotted with cottages and houses. The broad sandy beach at the end of Pilot Bay is part of Gabriola Sands Provincial Park, through which you would have driven to reach this spot.

Winds, sun and shade Slather on the sunblock. From morning to mid afternoon, this beach bakes in the full blast of the sun. It is also well protected from the northwest winds that accompany most good weather, so consider the merits of making sure you have a bathing suit for a cooling dip. Don't forget, however, that sunny weather is some-times accompanied by southeast winds—and these can be more than a little brisk here.

Beachcombing One of the main reasons for coming here is to enjoy the gentle but varied terrain of the intertidal zone. Head left for a dramatically sudden change of view as you round Tinson Point. Head right for a stroll to the low-tide sand flats at the head of the bay.

Seclusion You are essentially in an amphitheatre of surrounding houses and cottages so can hardly expect to feel unobserved. Still, you are unlikely to meet more than the odd local on this bit of little-visited shore.

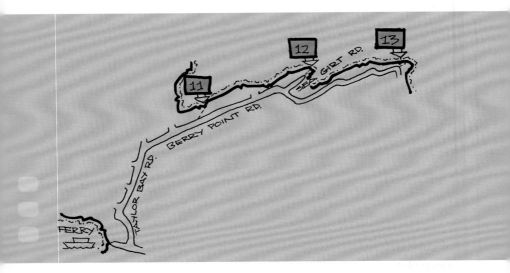

11

BERRY POINT ROAD

A well-hidden but easy route to a shore of strange sandstone bumps adjoining the low-tide line of the large sandy beach of Pilot Bay

Location, signs and parking Head uphill from the ferry and turn left onto Taylor Bay Road. After about 2 km, at a fork in the road, keep on the main through road by swinging right. At this point you are on Berry Point Road. About 300 m along, and about 100 m after the junction with Ricardo Road, look for a house numbered 401 on the right side of the road. Opposite, beside a large hemlock, you should see a dirt track. Berry Point Road is fairly busy, but the shoulder is wide enough to park safely.

Path The broad level path, almost 100 m long, angles through a thick forest of fir and hemlock. It narrows near the shore when it crosses a grassy area beside an overhanging arbutus. Although quite long by Gabriola standards, the path poses no difficulties even for those with gimpy legs.

Beach In a sense you get two beaches in one by coming to this unusual spot. Immediately in front of the point of access, the shore is composed of patches of crushed white shell fragments and lunar bulges rising from the sandstone surface. Cross this area at low tide, though, and you find yourself at the low-tide line of the large sandy beach that fills the end of Pilot Bay and is the chief attraction of Gabriola Sands Provincial Park.

Suitability for children In some ways this can be a more enjoyable and diversified beach for children than that at the nearby park. Only children with the most impoverished imaginations (or tiny legs) won't feel captivated by the galleons, castles and mountain peaks that, to adults, might look just like extraordinary blobs of sandstone. The attractions of this beach are doubled by the fact that children need cross only 20 or so metres of this sandstone if they want to dash at great speed across acres of sand. Be aware, though, that it is only at very low tides that the full range of play areas are high and dry.

Suitability for groups You could bring a small group here to enjoy the unusual features of this unusual spot. You might even enjoy a (shady) picnic on the grassy area. Most groups, however, would be much better off at the adjacent provincial park.

View It is unlikely that your view-seeking eyes will stray much beyond the shoreline of Pilot Bay. The large sandy beach at the head of the bay and the rock-shelf shore across the bay, approximately 300 m away, are the most striking features. Beyond Tinson Point, at the tip of the bay opposite, your view will be of the open waters of the Strait of Georgia and, most probably, a ferry running to or from Tsawwassen.

Winds, sun and shade Shade and wind exposure could be one of the key factors in either attracting you to this spot—or the opposite. The upper shore is dense with shade during the first part of the day and somewhat exposed to winds from the northwest, though not from the southeast. You can find patches of sun, however, by moving along the shore to your right, or, of course, by walking onto the tidal flats.

Beachcombing For adults, one of the main attractions of this beach is likely to be the diverse opportunities for orchestrating some wonderful shore walking. While a barefooted stroll along the low-tide line of the sandy beach is almost *de rigueur*, the most ambitious and imaginative visitors can plan long walks either beyond the beach or along the sandstone shelves to the right, possibly arranging shuttle pickups at the end of Sea Girt Road, almost 3 km distant.

Seclusion Because the trail is so well forested and because the houses on either side are well tucked away into the trees, you are likely to experience the sensation of having found a secret entrance into a well-known space. Enjoy the sensation!

While you're here . . . As you carry along Berry Point Road, roughly 1 km along, turn down clearly signposted Barnacle Road to its end about 100 m along. Here you will find a scrambly approach to a level shoreline of sandstone with outlandish protuberances. Farther along Berry Point Road in the direction of Sea Girt Road, pull over when the road first comes next to the shore. A small trail cuts down the bank to a lovely mixed shore with areas of loose pebbles, sandstone outcroppings and tidal pools.

Gabriola: Sea Girt Road

12
SEA GIRT ROAD

A strange shore consisting of a large, raised shelf of sculpted sandstone and a metal ladder down a cliff face to a sandy bay

Location, signs and parking Head uphill from the ferry and turn left onto Taylor Bay Road. After about 2 km, at a fork in the road, keep on the main through road by swinging right. Now that you are on Berry Point Road, possibly without quite realizing it, keep ahead for about 2 km. Where Berry Point Road swings right, fork a little left onto Sea Girt Road and follow it to its end, in full sight of the shore. You may have to park before the end of this narrow gravel road, possibly tucking into one of the nooks created by a zigzagging cedar fence. In miserable weather, you can easily park at the end of the road with a good view over the shore for as long as it takes to drown your sorrows in your cold chicken and salad picnic. Posted where it is difficult to see is a sign warning against collecting shellfish.

Path Only a few metres separate the end of the road from the shore. Even so, the route, first over a patch of grass and then a kind of natural sandstone ramp onto the level part of the shore, can be a little slippery when wet.

Beach This truly extraordinary bit of shoreline will appeal to those interested in geology and the picturesque. Immediately below the slight but steep drop onto the upper shore, you will find yourself on a kind of raised shelf of undulating sandstone criss-crossed with narrow crevices and tidal pools. At low tide this part of the shore drops off dramatically down a virtual cliff, especially sheer to the right of the access spot. The cliff ends there in a tumble of giant boulders. Just beyond it is a lovely stretch of silver sand, the mouth of Clark Bay. A local has installed a vertical metal ladder down this little cliff, though it is now covered with considerable growth.

Suitability for children This spot is probably most enjoyed by adults, unless they can trust dashing children not to disappear over the edge of the little cliff. The tabletop part of the beach, though, is an attractive and comfortable place to explore. For older children who are good swimmers and aware of possible dangers, this can be a fascinating place for unusual water play at high tide.

Suitability for groups This is not a place for a large group sniffing out a good picnic beach. A small group of fellow beach explorers, though, won't want to miss seeing this spot. Houses are nearby, but, at low tide, enough shore is exposed that your group won't be forced into neighbours' front yards.

View Your view-seeking eyes will likely be preoccupied with the strangely configured shoreline. If you have been wise enough to bring a camera, however, you will no doubt want to focus on a particularly photogenic shore pine on a rugged little bluff to your left. Align your time of year and time of day perfectly, and you just might be able to zoom in on the Entrance Island lighthouse as a large ferry glides past, both of them against a backdrop of the most spectacular snow-clad peaks around Howe Sound.

Winds, sun and shade Although you can duck out of winds by huddling up against the shore, you are otherwise likely to feel as much wind as the straits are dishing up. You are likewise exposed to the rays of the sun, though patches of shade are on offer during the afternoon.

Beachcombing You have little business in coming here unless you want to wander at least a little. To go very far, however, you should turn left and stride appreciatively along the generally level strata of sandstone.

Seclusion Lots of lucky folk have built along this section of coast, so don't expect to have a tête-à-tête with mother nature—or your companion. On the other hand, you are unlikely to see more than the occasional wanderer on this quiet piece of shore.

13

ORLEBAR POINT

A dramatically exposed roadside area with picnic table, park bench and a close-up view of the Entrance Island lighthouse

Location, signs and parking As you head away from the ferry, look for Taylor Bay Road and turn left. After about 2 km, at a fork in the road, swing right, keeping to the larger road. At this point you are on Berry Point Road. Berry Point Road twists and forks, but if you can keep on it for about 3 km, you will find yourself driving next to the shore and coming upon a clearly visible picnic table and park bench. A small parking area has room for a few cars and is rarely full.

Path This is one of the very best spots imaginable for meditatively devouring a gigantic car-feast while a Pacific storm rages and howls around you. In friendlier weather, a kind of ramp allows you immediate access to the shore. Kayakers could easily get their craft onto the shore here, and if the tide isn't too low, into the water. Be aware, though, that the rocks can be a little slippery and the shore a little wave-washed.

Beach This beach is the Gabriola Island shoreline at its most characteristic and extravagant. The sandstone of which it is composed does almost everything you would expect a sandstone headland to do. Knobbly protuberances, criss-crossing crevices, sweeping undulations—all the best features are here in abundance and extend to a low-tide line about 60 m away.

Suitability for children If you want to experience a memorable dollop of scenery, you can come here fairly confident that most children will find lots of prompts for improvised fantasies and unlikely adventures around and over the pools and bumps. The mid to upper part of the beach is the safest, since the low-tide area can be a little slippery and steep. Don't, however, choose this spot over others if pleasing your children is your top priority.

Suitability for groups Any clutch of explorers, photographers, painters or birders worthy of their credentials should be thrilled with the beauty of this spot. They will have lots of room to spread out and wander without running roughshod over the delicate sensibilities of locals. If, however, your group is most interested in comfort and conventional pleasures, they might raise a collective eyebrow if you bring them here.

View It is probably the view, even more than the shoreline, that distinguishes this spot. And it is probably the Entrance Island lighthouse, less than a kilometre away, that most distinguishes the view. Because this is a promontory, too, the whole sweep of the central Strait of Georgia and Coast Mountains lies before you.

Winds, sun and shade If you notice the drastically windswept bushes by the picnic table, you can quickly reach some conclusions about the degree to which this spot is exposed to wind—but that, if you think about it, is one of its charms. The lack of shade trees adds to the sense that this is probably the most "wuthering" spot on the island.

Beachcombing It should go without saying that you will wander over the scoops and waves of sandstone all around Orlebar Point (formerly Berry Point). If you want to venture farther, you can have a wonderful walk on a very similar kind of shoreline by heading left, though you will be walking parallel to the road for some of the way and in front of houses the whole way. Heading to your right brings you to some steep and narrow shoreline where the going can be rough.

Seclusion Though this is one of the most wild and "natural" spots on the island, it is also one of the most densely settled. It seems that many kindred spirits like to share the wild.

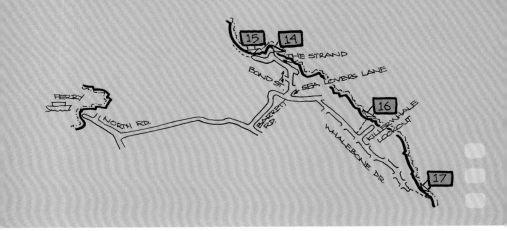

14

BELLS LANDING

A huge parking area and car-width dirt track down a slope to a broad, mixed beach with areas of loose rock and sandstone outcroppings

Location, signs and parking As you drive uphill from the ferry terminal, carry on straight ahead onto the beginning of North Road. Stay on North Road for approximately 4 km, turning left onto Barrett Road. Roughly a kilometre later, swing left onto Bluewater Road and almost immediately left again, this time onto Bond Street. This street comes to an end about 200 m later at a T-junction. Head left along The Strand for about half a kilometre, until you see a broad paved bit of road on your right, ending about 50 m along in a large parking area. Here you will see a carved wooden sign giving the name of the spot, BELLS LANDING, and two other standard signs. One of these asks you not to block access to the driveway on your right. The other warns of the grisly consequences of collecting contaminated shellfish.

Path The path is really a short dirt drive, some 20 m long, sloping toward the shore. Before heading to the beach, however, note the little path beside the waste bin. A few metres down this path you will find a beautifully positioned park bench looking out at the open water through a lacework of tree branches.

Beach The bit of beach at the end of the dirt track is by far the least appealing part of the beach. The compacted dirt is cut through by a dribbling bit of ditch, creating a slightly slimy upper shore. Beyond this entrance to the shore, things perk up considerably. About 50 m wide at low tide, an expanse of small rounded boulders leads to an interesting configuration of sandstone extending an additional 50 m into deeper water.

Suitability for children Older children are likely to enjoy this beach more than those prone to stumbling. With strong shoes and an equally strong interest in finding the world's most purple starfish or tiniest shore crab, most sure-footed children can have lots of fun on this broad and diversified beach. Still, it is not likely to figure high in most children's list of favourite Gabriola beaches.

Suitability for groups If space for parking and space for wandering on a large shoreline, away from a congested residential area, are what you're after for a group, this is the spot for you. Still, this beach is attractive only for walking, not lolling and lunching.

View Because Bells Landing is located on the tip of a promontory, it has one of the most expansive views on this whole side of the island. If you walk just a little out onto the level shore, you can see the whole sweep of Lock Bay and the coastline to Orlebar Point. Off the point, Entrance Island lighthouse looks picturesque against the backdrop of Jervis Inlet and its mountains. If you've brought binoculars, you should be able to pick out both Vance Island and the outermost bit of the Flat Top Islands some 10 km distant, at Gabriola's east end.

Winds, sun and shade The landforms that give you a lot of view also give you a lot of weather. Expect winds from all directions to treat you to as much refreshing or icy blasting as they can. The upper beach is in heavy shade through most of the day, so this part of the shore can be comparatively cool.

Beachcombing You can walk many glorious kilometres southeast along Gabriola's nearly straight and generally hospitable coastline. However, if you arrive when the tide is more or less out, you will probably find most enticing the walk to your left around Lock Bay and across the sand flats of Sandwell Provincial Park.

Seclusion Most visitors to this part of the island go to the nearby provincial park. You are unlikely to bump into others with whom to share the time of day or cheery observations on the marvellous weather we've been having lately.

15
SANDWELL PROVINCIAL PARK
A long, broad path down a bank to a large, isolated beach of pebbles and fine silver sand

Location, signs and parking From the ferry, drive straight ahead onto the beginning of North Road. Stay on North Road for approximately 4 km, turning left onto Barrett Road. About 1 km later, turn left onto Bluewater Road and almost immediately left again onto Bond Street. About 200 m later, at a T-junction, head left along The Strand to its end, about a kilometre later. At the entrance to a large paved parking area on the left, you will pass one of the standard wooden, carved signs used at most provincial parks: WELCOME TO SANDWELL PROVINCIAL PARK. Oddly, you will see a private drive leading off this parking area, but if you head to the farthest corner, you will also see the trailhead and several other signs. After you've registered that you shouldn't start fires or park overnight, you'll discover that a picnic table and restrooms are to be found ahead—after 650 m of path.

Path The "path" is actually a dirt-and-gravel roadbed—hence the sign telling you not to drive down it. Partway down this forested walk is posted a warning, STEEP SLIPPERY SLOPE. Given the length of the path and its slope, you might mull over the possibility that this may not be the best place to come with cumbersome picnic hampers or cumbersome family members.

Beach The beach is one of those minor miracles created by the geographical forces of the open coast of the Strait of Georgia. More than a kilometre long, this beach curves gracefully along a virtually deserted bay. The northern end is backed by a grassy area and a large pond, which opened to the sea in the distant past. The southern end, in contrast, is situated below the sloping treed bank. Throughout its length, the beach is mostly composed of a band of beach logs and fine pebbles leading, at low tide, to a wide stretch of fine, firm sand and tidal pools. Allow yourself a gasp of pleasure when you first see this beautiful shore.

Suitability for children Although the beach is nearly perfect for children, the length of the path to reach it can be an issue for some families. Toting treats and towels, let alone more unwieldy beach supplies, might be daunting for some beach-bound families. Once on the beach, though, any child can run amok over the swaths of enticing sand, shedding clothes and decibels in happy abandon. You really do have to arrive at low tide, however, to enjoy the beach at its best.

Suitability for groups While this beach has washrooms as well as comfortable and capacious picnic space on the beach itself, it does require a hefty bit of hoofing and provides no large area of picnic tables. Thus, though both the park and the beach are huge, this spot may not be quite right for a company picnic.

View At the base of a broad but not deeply inset bay, this beach looks out on a view bookended by two attractively treed promontories. The cluster of reefs and islets to the left, including Entrance Island and its lighthouse buildings, is probably most eye-catching. The whole sweep of the central part of the Strait of Georgia, however, is beautiful.

Winds, sun and shade To some extent, you can adjust your exposure to winds and sun by simply choosing one end of the beach or the other for your base camp. Heading left will minimize a northwest wind and maximize sun. Heading right will minimize both a southeast wind and exposure to the sun.

Beachcombing Even the most indolent will find it hard to resist a barefooted saunter or romp over the silken sand by the low-tide line. If you want to test your mettle, though, head to your right in a pair of strong shoes and you can conquer many kilometres of level, shelving sandstone with patches of sand.

Seclusion On a hot summer's afternoon, you will see others here, of course. Amazingly, though, even if you arrive in hot weather, you may see only a very few others on the shore. In addition, because the only signs of civilization are on the distant ends of the bay, you can enjoy something close to seclusion.

16
KILLERWHALE LOOKOUT
One of four similar spots, a long approach through an open area of grass and trees and down a steep bank to a shore of gravel and rocky outcroppings

Location, signs and parking From the ferry, drive straight ahead onto the beginning of North Road. Stay on North Road for approximately 4 km before turning left onto Barrett Road. Roughly 2 km later, turn right onto Whalebone Drive for about 400 m. Pull over when you see the road sign for Killerwhale Lookout, rather than driving down it. A few metres back from this intersection along Whalebone Drive, you will see two slightly battered signs, one saying PUBLIC PARK ACCESS, and the other announcing this to be a Gabriola Community Park, maintained by volunteers. The list of "do nots" is quite long and, for the most part, much what you would expect, especially concerning dogs, camping, fires and motorized vehicles. Unusually, though, this sign tells you that a $2,000 fine awaits you if you contravene any of these regulations or if you bring your horse, "firearms, bow and arrow, crossbow, or slingshot." Gunslingers and Robin Hood wannabes, be warned.

Path You are unlikely to find any path like this one anywhere except in this neighbourhood of Gabriola Island. Beginning as a broad, level track under trees, it passes first one house and then another as it opens into an area of lawn. While a venerable yellow PUBLIC ACCESS concrete block encourages you along, you will otherwise just have to plow straight ahead across open grassy fields dotted with groves of firs and cedars. This communal land, shared by all the houses surrounding it, ends near the shore with a beautifully situated picnic table behind a clifftop fence. To reach the shore, about 150 m from your starting point, head down the sloping track to the right of the picnic table. A set of 16 aluminum steps brings you down to the beach.

Beach An upper beach of fine, rounded gravel lined with logs leads to a mid-shore area of larger, rounded rocks and a few patches of slightly sticky sand. About 60 m wide at low tide, the gradually sloping shore directly in front of the access spot is bordered by more irregular areas of sandstone slabs.

Suitability for children If you've spun your outing as an exploration and your sure-footed children are happy to accompany you, they will find both the route to the shore and the shore itself a bit of a lark. Once on the beach, they can dart around making friends with the hermit crabs and frilled dog whelks, climbing over rocky outcroppings and so on. Don't be surprised, though, if they soon want to move on to the next beach.

Suitability for groups This is an enclosed area shared by several residential families. It is not a place to bring even a minor entourage.

View At this point on Gabriola Island's northeast coast, the shore curves in such a way that you can see farthest by looking southeast toward the Flat Top Islands at the tip of the island. For the most part, though, your view is of the wide, open stretches of the Strait of Georgia and the Coast Mountains.

Winds, sun and shade Prevailing winds scoot along the shore in both directions but don't blow directly onto it. While mornings are sunny, even baking, up against the bank, by late morning, shade has started to creep down the bank. The rest of the day is mostly shady.

Beachcombing Because the shore slopes only gradually toward the low-tide line along this whole stretch of Gabriola, you can walk for a considerable distance by turning left and, if you like, going as far as Sandwell Provincial Park. Be prepared, though, for walking that is wet at some points and ankle-twistingly uneven at others.

Seclusion This is a well-developed section of Gabriola Island—but it is also developed in such a way that the houses are clustered among trees and set well back into them. Prepare yourself to pass the time of day with the occasional local, but otherwise don't anticipate having more than the rare intrusion into your gently undulating thoughts.

While you're here . . . You may wish to visit several other similar access points along this stretch of road. Perhaps most interesting is that off Sea Lovers Lane, opposite a house numbered 1375, where a steep wood-and-dirt set of stairs put in place by locals leads to a strange shore with areas of soft sand and a raised ridge of rock near the low-tide area. Other access points, next to community parks and very similar to the shore near Killerwhale Lookout, can be found off Whalebone Drive. Hummingbird Community Park, with a set of metal stairs down a steep bank, can be approached via two trails, one across from the intersection with Starbuck Lane, the other opposite the northwest end of Pequod Crescent. A third trail from the southeast end of Pequod Crescent (opposite the northwest end of Tashtego Crescent) leads to a very similar arrangement of staircase and shore. Blue Heron Community Park, next along, can be visited by two trails, the better of these probably being the one at the southeast end of Tashtego Crescent. This may be the most attractive of the four similar spots because the beach has a pleasant area of fine pebbles and several ridges of rock slightly offshore. Oddly, though, while the other access routes have sturdy metal staircases in place, Blue Heron Park requires a bit of a scramble down rough chunks of sandstone.

17 JOYCE LOCKWOOD COMMUNITY PARK

A forested path and wooden staircase to a north-facing wilderness beach of pebbles, logs and large stretches of fine, compact low-tide sand

Location, signs and parking From the ferry, drive straight ahead onto the beginning of North Road. Stay on North Road for approximately 4 km, turning left onto Barrett Road. Roughly 2 km later, turn right onto Whalebone Drive and follow it to its end, a little over 2 km along. Parking is a little tight in this small turnaround, since ditches border either side of the road, but the shoulder is wide enough for comfortable parking. You will have to start down the broad crushed-gravel drive at the end of the road and across a little wooden bridge before you see two signs, one telling you not to light fires, the other giving the name of the park.

Path The generally flat and even path angles gradually toward the shore along the top of a high wooded bank past salmonberries and grand firs. Although you can cut down toward the shore at two or three places, you are best off carrying on to the end of the path. Here you will find a new, well-designed sequence of wooden stairs and platforms bringing you to the beach.

Beach Tucked under a bushy bank, the upper shore is largely a mixture of sand and pebbles lined with a few of those obliging logs so essential to a proper beach. It slopes over a broad band of smooth gravel and small rocks to a gorgeous lower beach of fine grey sand. Stretching perhaps 150 m along the shore, this sandy beach is bounded at both ends by areas of solid-rock outcropping.

Suitability for children Pack your swimming togs, hoist a little backpack of beaching essentials and prepare to give your children a delicious beach experience. You will want to bring water shoes or crocs to manage the area of rocks, but you can otherwise assume your tender-footed children can squeal and run with as much abandon as they can muster.

Sandcastle building and kite flying might well be on the agenda of activities. Swimming, too, can be good, though be aware that when the tide is partially in, some toe-stubbing boulders at the lower edge of the sandy area can be hidden from view.

Suitability for groups This beach isn't set up for allowing a swarm of sun-loving beach-folk easy access to a spacious picnic area with facilities. However, it is far enough from any neighbours and large enough to accommodate as many as will want to find their way here.

View Your eyes will be drawn curiously to the right, down the tapering sweep of shore to the distant tip of Gabriola Island and the small islands tucked in next to it. If you've been visiting the northern end of Gabriola, you may be amazed that, in contrast, the high, forested shore here is so wild and little developed.

Winds, sun and shade If a northwest wind is being a little obstreperous, you can get some protection by moving up against the bank. A southeast wind can be even more of an issue if the day is cool. Add to that the fact that the upper shore is deep in shadow throughout the afternoon, and you will want to come either during the first part of the day or when the weather is baking.

Beachcombing Strike your various romantic poses while sauntering or singing your way along the sand, bare feet kicking up little splashes as you go. If you want to plan a major walk, though, strap on those old approach shoes, acknowledging that your feet will both get wet and need good support, and head out for several kilometres of interesting shore walking. Head left, since the foreshore virtually disappears beneath cliffs if you walk very far right.

Seclusion If you do strike romantic poses as you saunter along the beach, you probably won't have much of an audience. Although this spot is deservedly much loved by locals, it is mostly just locals who even know of its existence or bother to find their way here. In addition, you will find virtually no housing development along this stretch of forested coast, so brace yourself for the possibility of being completely alone.

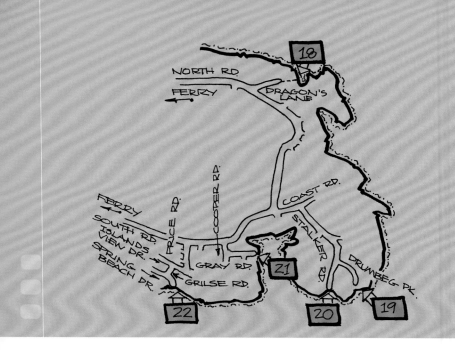

18
DRAGON'S LANE
A narrow, sometimes rough path, some 120 m long, to a mossy bluff on the edge of an unusual little bay of rounded sandstone boulders

Location, signs and parking From the ferry, drive up the hill and turn onto North Road, the first road on your right. Though the distance is great, the route could hardly be easier. Simply stay on North Road for a little more than 10 km until you see Dragon's Lane on your left. Dragon's Lane ends about 200 m later in a large turnaround directly in front of a prominent private driveway. Although you may register some confusion at the apparent lack of a sign, let alone a path, search along the right side of the turnaround as you face the private drive and you will see, nestled in the grass, a yellow concrete block bearing the welcoming words, PUBLIC ACCESS.

Path Though generally level and easy, the path is narrow, a little uneven, and, at one point, can be boggy—as the nearby skunk cabbages testify.

Small bits of wood have been inset into this squelchy section to make the going easier, but they are often not necessary. As the path meanders prettily past cedar, fir and swordferns, the woods open up and you will become aware of walking along the edge of private property with a house. The path proper ends on a lovely, rounded bluff covered with moss, lichen and stonecrop. Come in spring and you'll be treated to the sight of fawn lilies (dogtooth violets). From here, getting down onto the shore can be a little tricky if the bank is wet, so take care and choose the most gradual descent.

Beach If the tide is high when you arrive, you won't have much shore to worry about, since you will be standing on the steep side of a bay, about 30 m across and 100 m from open water. Plan to come at low tide, however, when you can make your way onto an interesting shore surface of giant, flat-topped sandstone boulders interspersed with some small areas of fine gravel. Unless the weather has been dry, a stream wanders through the centre of the bay toward its distant mouth.

Suitability for children This place is best suited to adults—particularly adults who love to explore hidden nooks and geologically strange crannies. Older, sure-footed children may enjoy accompanying their parents to this unusual shore, but they will have to have adventure in their blood.

Suitability for groups You won't need to worry overmuch about intruding into a closed neighbourhood, since you can easily find lots of space between you and the nearest house. Even so, bring only a few, select nature-loving friends or family members here—and make sure they understand what they are likely to find.

View Most of your viewing megabytes will be taken up observing the features of this strange little bay. Photographers and sketchers will have plenty of unusually picturesque fodder to take away with them, but it will all be of foreground and middle ground. The bay is no doubt at its prettiest when the tide is at least partially in, even though less shore is available to wander.

Winds, sun and shade Generally well protected from northwest winds, the bluff is fairly exposed to the southeast winds that are refreshing on a hot day, chilling on a cool day. The morning is by far the sunniest part of the day. By noon, patches of shade start to spread over the bluff and down onto the shore.

Beachcombing This is a spot for a little exploration of an unusual shore, not for striding out over long distances. This enclosed bay is rich with life, so take time to enjoy some of the intertidal species, ochre sea stars, frilled dog whelks, chitons, limpets and littleneck clams among them.

Seclusion You will see two houses, one across the bay toward its outer edge, the other on the same side of the bay and a little behind you. Otherwise, you are likely to have the whole spot to yourself. Do you feel you need a beautiful view spot to ponder a short list of burning issues? Come here, and you are unlikely to be disturbed on your way to illumination.

While you're here . . . It is unfortunate that no access routes lead to the shore where the views from Gabriola are most fascinating—namely around the Flat Top Islands. The one partial exception, and well worth visiting for the clifftop glimpse it gives of this deeply convoluted bit of geography, is the end of Marvin Road, about 800 m east of Dragon's Lane on North Road.

Gabriola: Drumbeg Provincial Park

19
DRUMBEG PROVINCIAL PARK
An isolated and quiet day-use park with a small, pebbly beach and walking trails through woods along a rocky shoreline

Location, signs and parking Trundling off the ferry, drive up the hill and turn right onto North Road, the first road on your right. About half a kilometre later, swing right onto South Road and follow it for roughly 12 km until you come upon Coast Road on your right. About 100 m along, turn down Stalker Road. A few hundred metres along, turn left into Drumbeg Park when you see the prominently displayed provincial park sign. Another few hundred metres along this narrow, forested road will bring you to a circular turnaround and ample parking spot. Signs inform you that both fires and camping are not options. Another, directed at the hound jumping eagerly at your heels, tells you not only that leashes are required, but also that failure to clean up after your dog will cost you $150. Also note the sign showing the location of the outhouses.

Path A wide, level path, about 50 m long, brings you to a small, grassy area with picnicking facilities. Those with walking difficulties should find the path easy. Likewise, those who happen to have a kayak with them and want to paddle along this section of coast will find this a comparatively easy spot to get into the water. Away from the high-current area of Gabriola Passage and yet within the protection of several islands, this is a safe and intriguing place to explore by kayak.

Beach Directly in front of the picnic area, a pebbly beach slopes fairly smoothly toward the low-tide line of slab-like boulders. On either side of this deeply inset little bay, the shore is composed of stratified layers of level stone mixed with areas of pebbles. The uppermost beach of fine, loose pebbles and beach logs makes a comfortable and attractive area for munching your way through your provisions and spending several blissful hours in the company of *Anna Karenina* or your prairie cousins.

Suitability for children If building sandcastles doesn't underpin your child's capacity to be happy on the seashore, then consider this a great place for a beachy outing. The pebbly beach is great for splashing furiously at high tide or, at low tide, for providing a whole menagerie of creatures to befriend. The beach is also unusually rich with skipping stones and magically polished little pebbles. If you value familial harmony, though, remember to pack water shoes and dry clothes.

Suitability for groups This park is large enough and quiet enough that an entourage filling several cars could easily park, and find space on the shore. The presence of facilities is an obvious feature for a large group. The diversity of pleasures, too, some of them involving staying put on the comfortable shore, some of them involving strolling the extensive shoreline and trails, can make this a great place for a family reunion. Still, this is not one of those provincial parks with phalanxes of picnic tables beside a huge beach.

View From its unusual position at the southeast end of Gabriola Island, this little bay allows you to look out past Rogers Reef and Breakwater Island and along the north shore of little-known Valdes Island to the open waters of the southern Strait of Georgia. By walking out of the bay in either direction, you will find that your view becomes even more attractive, dotted with more islands and giving you a glimpse of the narrow passage of rushing water between Gabriola Island and Cordero Point.

Winds, sun and shade When visitors to the beaches on the northwest end of Gabriola are suffering acute cases of gooseflesh during a strong northwesterly blow, visitors here can be broiling. If you like heat, though, don't come here when a southeast wind is blowing. The pebbly beach is sunniest during the middle part of the day, but you can remain in sun by moving along the shore to the left.

Beachcombing Shore walking is one of the great pleasures of this park. The strata of sandstone and conglomerate rock on both sides of the bay are level enough to make walking easy and yet tilted and eroded enough to have you whipping out your camera or reflecting on the forces of geology. Forested paths, mostly parallel to the shore, allow you to choreograph different combinations of shore and forest walking. Be warned, though: some have reported seeing giant hogweed in the park, an invasive species that can produce painful, even chronic, skin reactions.

Seclusion You won't find many provincial parks on the islands that seem as quiet and isolated as this one. You will see other visitors, possibly even scuba divers, all taking advantage of the small-scale versions of nature you find here. If the planets align themselves just right, however, you just might be alone on an unusually attractive piece of shoreline.

While you're here . . . Two access routes allow you to explore the hidden, indented shoreline along the narrow passage between Sear and Gabriola Islands.

1. At the very end of Fenwick Road, a steep and narrow trail runs beside power lines to a deeply convoluted piece of shore beneath some dramatically sculpted banks of sandstone. From here you get an interesting view of most of the narrow channel that, to the north, leads to Silva Bay and the marina there.

2. On Coast Road, between Fenwick Road and Withey Road, look for a path marked by a yellow concrete PUBLIC ACCESS block, directly opposite a garden with a wire fence. This path, about half a kilometre long, leads to the narrow shoreline directly across from Sear Island, a mere 100 m away.

20
STALKER ROAD
A short dirt path onto a mixed shore facing Gabriola Passage, with slabs of smooth sandstone alternating with loose, polished pebbles

Location, signs and parking From the ferry, drive up the hill and turn onto North Road, the first road on your right. About half a kilometre later, turn right onto South Road and follow it for very roughly 12 km until you come upon Coast Road on your right. About 100 m along, turn down Stalker Road and follow it to its end, a little over 1 km along. At the end of the road, you will find a large gravel turnaround area with more space for vehicles than is ever likely to be used. One sign urges you not to block access to the private driveways, another not to camp.

Path A slightly rough, dirt-and-gravel track leads beside a ditch and through bushes only a dozen metres onto the beach. Kayakers could well add this to their list of good spots to get their wee boats into their element with a minimum of exhaustion or fuss. They should, however, make sure they understand the potential dangers of nearby Gabriola Passage. Those with other beaching equipment, and particularly those who are able to put their artistic flair to good purpose, should also be happy with the easy route to a scenic serving of shore.

Beach You might have to do a little lightweight clambering if winter storms have tossed around the many logs of the upper beach. Once on the shore, though, you will find lots of welcoming spots among the pebbles and logs for spreading out your whole kit and caboodle of towels, children and coolers. Head to the left of the trailhead, and you will find some curious spots where you can even use oddly smooth slabs of sandstone as improvised tables. At low tide, bands of pebbles and gravel stretch toward the low-tide line, interspersed with almost flat strata of sandstone.

Suitability for children Not only can you get your little ones easily onto the beach—and off it—but you can also easily set them up for lots of beach play without worrying overmuch about them hurting themselves or your eardrums. The tidal pools and tabletop-like ridges of low rock should act like magnets to most children. Even when the tide is mostly out, they can walk easily to the water's edge—but you may want to make sure that they don't go much beyond it. Be kind to yourself and, before coming, double-check your beach bag for water shoes.

Suitability for groups A small bevy of kindred spirits will shower you with kudos if you lure them down the byways of the remote end of Gabriola Island to this hidden bit of shore. You won't find any facilities, of course, but will find lots of parking, easy access and an unusual, and unusually attractive, little bay.

View Tucked into the shoreline just north of Josef Point, this little bay looks down the vast expanse of the Strait of Georgia past the long northeast shore of Valdes Island. Smaller bits and pieces decorate the waterscape—little Kendrick Island and several low-tide reefs off Valdes, and the tip of Breakwater Island, tucked around Gabriola to the north. Although you can't quite see the rushing waters of Gabriola Passage from this bay, you can get a slightly better view by making your way along the shore to your right. The shoreline actually in the passage, however, is probably too steep to allow you to get the closest view.

Winds, sun and shade Don't choose this spot on a cool day if a southeasterly is in the forecast. If, however, the weather people are warning about even a strong northwest wind, come here prepared to feel smug that you will hardly feel a stir of air. Also be prepared to overheat if the day is warm. You won't find even a scrap of shade until at least mid-afternoon, when some maples on your right might give you some welcome relief.

Beachcombing If you've visited Drumbeg Provincial Park in the past and walked along the shore, you may, without realizing it, have found your way to this beach. Lying just around the point of land to the left, the park and its interesting shoreline can be the first section of a much more extensive bit of shore walking. Heading in this direction, you can walk about 1.5 km before the shore becomes uncomfortably narrow.

Seclusion Houses are close by, so you won't want to laugh too raucously at your aunt's elephant jokes. On the other hand, you won't see the neighbours and, thanks to maple trees and bushes, they won't see you.

Gabriola: Surf scoters off northwest Decourcy Road shoreline

21

GRAY ROAD

A drive-on entrance to an extraordinarily flat area of sandstone in the middle of Degnen Bay

Location, signs and parking Trundling off the ferry, drive up the hill and turn right onto North Road, the first road on your right. About half a kilometre later, swing right onto South Road and follow it for almost 10 km until you see Cooper Road on your right. A mere 50 m down Cooper, turn left onto Gray Road and follow it to its end—or, if you're a little daring, beyond its end and onto a large stretch of sandstone looking more or less like concrete. If you don't drive to the shore, you'll have to park 50 m back at the intersection with Murray Road, where you'll find some space on the shoulder of the road. On a beach log, two signs make vehemently clear that you mustn't even think about collecting your paella ingredients here. The shellfish are contaminated.

Path Because you can drive directly onto the shore, those who have extreme walking difficulties, those who want to go wild with a bad-weather feeding frenzy from the comfort of their car, and those who want to get kayaks as easily as possible onto the shore will all be pleased to discover this spot. Kayakers should note, however, that out of the protected waters of Degnen Bay, the currents of Gabriola Passage can swirl dangerously fast—up to 8 knots at both flood and ebb. Since this spot is used for launching boats, you will have to be careful that your vehicle doesn't block the approach road.

Beach You won't find many beaches like this anywhere—and certainly not on any of the Gulf Islands. Looking for all the world like freshly poured concrete, a large area of sandstone slopes gradually toward the distant low-tide line and some equally flat areas of pebbles. Since Degnen Bay is so well protected from the weather, even the shore on both sides of the access spot is dotted with boats. As intriguing as the beach is, it doesn't have any good spots for picnicking, or even lolling tentatively about.

Suitability for children Children might have a hard time even recognizing that they are on a beach, given how level and smooth it is. Still, they could hardly find an easier surface to run about on, and, on an incoming tide, to wade and splash safely—if they don't mind water that can be a little nippy.

Suitability for groups Quite apart from the fact that parking is a major difficulty for more than a couple of cars, only a small group of birdwatchers, photographers or artists would want to come here. Lovers of the unusual and photographable, however, really will want to put this spot on their personal maps.

View This is a spot for viewing foregrounds and middle grounds—not great distances. Most immediately eye-catching are the shores of this deeply indented, roughly Y-shaped bay. Dotted with boats, some on the shore, some anchored, some moored at the public wharf on the opposite end of the bay, the scene is full of life and colour. Treeless islets and reefs in the middle of the bay are backed by the heavily sculpted northern end of Valdes Island on the other side of narrow Gabriola Passage. Sketchers and photographers will appreciate the complex patterns of overlapping landforms and passageways.

Winds, sun and shade Completely sheltered from northwest winds, this bay is also largely protected from most southeast winds. The lack of shade on the upper beach will be of little account to most visitors, since few are likely to install themselves there.

Beachcombing Wandering the intertidal zone is one of the great pleasures of this intriguing spot. Head to the right and explore toward the end of the bay, where the sandstone strata becomes more irregular. Be aware, however, that the land adjoining the point is a First Nation reserve, and around this point the shore is steep.

Seclusion You are unlikely to find anyone using this access spot other than the occasional local resident launching or retrieving a boat. Still, this whole bay is crowded with little houses and boats.

22

SPRING BEACH DRIVE
A wooden staircase at the end
of a quiet cul-de-sac to an
unusual south-facing beach
with a varied shorescape

Location, signs and parking Roll off the ferry, drive up the hill and turn right onto North Road, the first road on your right. About half a kilometre later, turn onto South Road and follow it for almost 10 km until you see Price Road. The simplest, but not the shortest, route through the subdivision you are entering is to take Price Road about 800 m to a T-junction with Islands View Drive, and turn right. After about 600 m, turn left onto Grilse Road. After about 150 m, you will come to a T-junction onto Spring Beach Drive. Turn left and follow it to its end, about 200 m along. Here you will find a large asphalt turnaround with parking for several cars.

Path Unless the invasive Himalayan blackberries have not been held in check, you should see a narrow gravel path cut through them. About 50 m along, you will come to two sets of wooden stairs. Just a little weathered, they have been surfaced with asphalt tiles and provided with a handrail to add to their security, especially in wet weather.

Beach This odd beach has scatterings and patches of just about everything. Probably the most conventional—and comfortable—part of the shore is just to the left of the steps. Here you will find a few weathered logs under some overhanging willow bushes and a strip of coarse sand and pebbles, just about perfect for a sun-baked bit of picnicking or a full-on chat-fest with your long-lost half-sisters. Be warned, though—this part of the beach is subject to accumulations of seaweed and small chunks of driftwood. If the tide is low, you will find rough gravel, a few swarms of large boulders and, depending on the tide, some large tidal pools. Farther along the shore to the left, giant, weirdly sculpted chunks of sandstone stand against a bank of leaning firs.

Suitability for children If you have come here for an adult-oriented afternoon of sun and seclusion, don't fear that your children will be bored.

Still, you would be crazy not to bring sturdy water shoes and a change of clothes, supplemented with a truly delicious picnic, if you want to coexist happily with your child. Even then, you might hesitate to bring the most wobbly and easily damaged children. The barnacles and boulders in some places can be aggressive.

Suitability for groups This is much too constricted an area for more than two or three families. For that size of group, however, this unusually warm and secluded spot could be a good choice, particularly if their primary interest is soaking up sun, view and the latest gossip, rather than dashing about the shore.

View Always attractive, the view is especially striking in the spring, when the mountains of Vancouver Island are at their snowy best. Because you're tucked into a shallow bay, your view is primarily to the south across Pylades Channel and the chain of islands leading your eye into the distance—Link, De Courcy, Ruxton and Pylades. You may be most interested in picking out De Courcy Island, not just because Pirates Cove Marine Park is located on its southeast end, but also because it is the site of the infamous cult of Brother Twelve in the late 1920s. The high, forested ridges of Valdes Island stretch away on the northwest side of Pylades Channel.

Winds, sun and shade Feeling a little chilly in spite of the sun? Head to this beach during the afternoon, and you just may bake your socks off. Significantly protected from most winds, this little shadeless bay faces into the sun. Break out the sunscreen and sun hats.

Beachcombing This protected and diverse shore is rich with intertidal life. Choose a very low tide, and you might be able to find giant multi-legged sun stars, leafy hornmouths and blennies. You can also make your way along the shore to the right for a considerable distance. Still, don't select this beach over others if extensive shore walking is your idea of a proper visit to the beach.

Seclusion While this little bay is located more or less in the centre of a heavily developed subdivision, the beach itself feels wonderfully secluded. Lovers of seclusion might wish to send a few thoughts of gratitude to thick trees and high banks.

While you're here . . . If you are driving northwest along South Road away from Spring Beach Drive, you will have the chance to visit three different spots, all providing some attractive and interesting opportunities for more beach exploring.

1. Where South Road first comes close to the shore, you can pull over by the concrete barrier and find a short path through periwinkle onto a pleasant part of the south-facing shore. Here you will see broad tidal flats and interesting tidal pools. If you have one of the maps that show the narrow triangle of land just north of here to be waterfront parkland, don't be misled. Currently, that land is thick with bushes.

2. About 100 m northwest of the point where South Road leaves the shore, if you look carefully, you will see a small path heading through trees and, if you search, a yellow concrete block saying PUBLIC ACCESS. This trail leads to a beautiful view spot and bench at the top of a complicated set of staircases down the high bank. This staircase is closed because it needs repair, but, with any luck, will be open by the time you visit. The broad, level shore is mostly flat sandstone with clusters of boulders.

3. Opposite Stokes Road, you will see a little country graveyard. If you park by the mailboxes, you can walk toward the shore and come to a broad but fairly steep trail angling down the bank to a shore with a little bit of everything. Generally level and dotted with boulders, the shore here can be used for pleasant picnicking or for beginning several kilometres of shore walking.

23
EL VERANO DRIVE
A busy launching spot on a fine pebble beach in the middle of False Narrows

Location, signs and parking After your ferry ride, drive up the hill and take the first road on your right, North Road. About half a kilometre later, turn onto South Road and follow it for about 7 km. At an open grassy area, El Verano Drive forks off to the right. Take it for about 400 m, until you see a wide opening between houses with a broad paved route to the clearly visible shore, about 75 m away. You will probably see at least a dozen cars parked on either side of this paved section if you come during the summer, but you should have no difficulty finding a spot for yourself. Beside this parking area, signs ask you to help protect Gabriola's groundwater and to steer clear of toxic shellfish if you know what's good for you.

Path This is a popular launching spot for small boats, because you can drive right to the edge of the pebbly beach—and, as a bonus, the pebbly beach slopes steeply enough that the water is never far away, even at low tide. Be aware, though, if you are a kayaker: the currents here, in False

Narrows, can reach over 4 knots. Check your current tables and/or stay close to the shore, where the current is least strong. Those without kayaks will, of course, find this an easy place to get quickly onto the shore for a photo shoot or even a little heavy-duty sunning.

Beach The fine pebbly beach S-curves past the access point. Usually without beach logs, it nevertheless has an upper shore of coarse sand and pebbles that can be an attractive place for sitting if kayakers aren't already occupying it. This looks like an enticing place to swim, since the seabed drops fairly steeply off over a smooth pebbly bottom. Beware, though, because the current running past can be more than a little nippy.

Suitability for children You won't find many beaches close by that are quite so appealing for wading, splashing a little more than is reasonable, and searching out beautifully polished pebbles. While the surface of the beach could hardly be safer for little ones, parents should be wary of the currents and the generally cold water. Because you will find it so easy to get to and from the beach, you may wish to come here for a short bit of exploration rather than an extended visit.

Suitability for groups This is about as good a spot as you can find for launching a whole armada of kayaks. It is not, however, a good place for a group of picnickers or sunbathers—in part, because it so much appreciated by so many kayakers.

View Dominating your view is the low, park-like shore of Mudge Island, only 200 m across False Narrows. Looking east down the narrows, however, you may be able to pick out a bit of De Courcy Island, once infamous as the location of a cult run by the notorious Brother Twelve. More striking are the high crests of Valdes Island extending far into the distance.

Winds, sun and shade Remember the sunscreen and sun hats. Although breezes can blow up and down the shoreline, this shadeless spot can become toasty hot on a still summer afternoon.

Beachcombing Though neither steep nor rugged, the shore in both directions is narrow and thus not well suited to easy walking. If the tide is low, however, you can make your way in either direction and, within little more than 100 m, find large tidal flats, rich in snails and bivalves.

Seclusion Gabriola Island probably has other spots that are even less secluded than this one, but you would be hard-pressed to find them. Houses crowd forward along the shore, across the road and on both sides of the parking area. In addition, if the weather is at all reasonable and the time of day is right, you are likely to be sharing the shore with others, many of whom will be in the process of getting craft into or out of the water.

24
FERNE ROAD
A roadside grassy field with two picnic tables and a gentle slope to a gravel beach on False Narrows

Location, signs and parking With your short ferry ride behind you, drive up the hill and take the first road on your right, North Road. About half a kilometre later, turn onto South Road and follow it for about 7 km. The first point at which it comes alongside the shore, you should see Ferne Road on your left and a broad gravel road on your right curving a few metres into a large beachside parking area. At the end of this parking area, several signs on a cluster of maples admonish you "absolutely" not to light fires and to beware of toxic shellfish. On a rough grassy area, you will see two picnic tables.

Path Those who have come to Gabriola Island with the express purpose of paddling its waters might be thrilled to find such a convenient place to get their craft onto the beach, but they will be best off when the tide is at least partway in. If it's not, head for nearby El Verano Drive. Because you can virtually park on the shore, this is a good place to come if you're treating your kindly neighbour with recent hip surgery to a seaside visit.

Beach Most distinctive about this gravel beach is that it is covered with shards of barnacle-covered brick, from, as you might guess, a former brickworks. At low tide, about 100 m wide, the barnacle-and-gravel shore slopes gradually toward the low-tide line. To the left of the picnic area, the tidal flats become even wider. While the uppermost bit of shore immediately below the grassy area is reasonably attractive as a place to assume the full lotus position, or just flop, most visitors are likely to prefer the grassy area and picnic tables.

Suitability for children Since this is a such a handy—and generally warm—picnic spot, families may well want to stop here, even though the beach doesn't offer what most children like best. With lunch taken care of, all children will naturally make a beeline for the shore—and the water. Easy to explore and riddled with squirting and squelching shore life, the beach can entertain all children if they are the least bit curious. Provide them with tough water shoes and expect them to get wet, and you will all drive away from this beach happy.

Suitability for groups Limit your herd to two or three cars, and you will find heaps of parking space and decent picnic opportunities. In addition, you won't experience a trace of anxiety about invading a congested neighbourhood, since you aren't even within singalong distance of the closest house. Do be aware, however, that your group won't find public washrooms here.

View The Harmac pulp mill isn't most people's idea of a viewing gem, but from this angle and distance, it makes a fairly discreet intrusion into your view up Percy Anchorage and Northumberland Channel. Besides, you will probably find most interesting the high, forested shore to the west of this spot and the equally forested mound of Mudge Island only a few hundred metres away.

Winds, sun and shade If the day is cool on the north or west of Gabriola Island, set your sails for this beach. Though a northwest wind can be a little fresh here, this is an island hot spot. In the afternoon, since you won't find any convenient shade, you might find yourself sizzling.

Beachcombing Most of the best beach walking can be found in the immediate area and at low tide. While you can make your way fairly comfortably to your left along the shores of False Narrows, just east of this access the shore is fairly narrow.

Seclusion Although this spot is next to a densely settled development to the east and, to boot, is just off a fairly busy road, you will be surprisingly unaware of locals—and they of you.

While you're here . . . For a completely different kind of shoreline close to here, head northwest a short distance on South Road and turn left along Wharf Road. It ends at Green Wharf, an attractively located spot beneath steep banks. You will see here lots of "commuter boats" belonging to the lucky folk who have houses on Mudge Island, a short distance across Percy Anchorage.

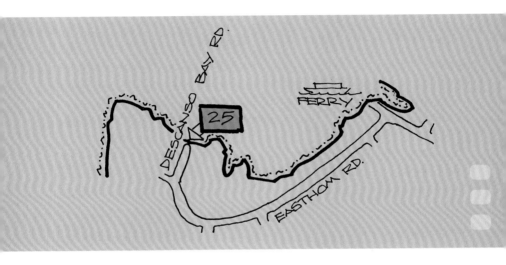

25
DESCANSO BAY ROAD
Within easy walking distance from the ferry terminal, a nearly perfect little beach of polished pebbles looking across Descanso Bay toward the Malaspina Galleries

Location, signs and parking Heading uphill from the little ferry, take the first right, Easthom Road, and carry along for a little over 1 km. Descanso Bay Road on your right goes about 200 m to the end of the road and a constricted gravel turnaround area. Two driveways lead from near the end of the road, but you will find room for a car on either side or, for a short period, right at the end of the road, overlooking the shore.

Path At the end of this gravel strip is a conveniently located park bench and a waste bin. Only a metre or so above the shore, the top of the bank slopes gradually, making this an excellent spot for launching kayaks and getting immediate access to the spectacular sandstone cliffs tucked around the point to the left. Otherwise, you may be pleased that you can be ensconced in your car enjoying a picnic while foul weather lashes at your windows. Those with walking difficulty will also find getting onto the shore a breeze down a little foot ramp, but they may prefer to take advantage of the park bench overlooking the shore.

Beach About 50 m wide, this lovely little bay of loose, shiny pebbles is bounded on either side by ragged sandstone outcroppings. A few beach logs scatter the upper shore, but some of the space is taken up with dinghies belonging to locals. Your options for setting up base camp for an afternoon's seaside pleasure are thus a little limited, but only a little. The lower part of the shoreline, some 50 m away, is mostly large broken rocks. While the beach is best for exploring at low tide, it is prettiest at high tide. High tide is also by far the best time to get those toes wet, or, in hot weather, the whole shebang. Enjoy your swim.

Suitability for children In spite of the absence of sand, this beach has much to recommend it as you sort through your mental criteria for what you want most on your afternoon with the children. You may be thinking about ease of access to and from the car, of safe, warm swimming possibilities at high tide, and of opportunities for climbing over interesting rock outcroppings at low tide. You may also like a beach where a mid tide converts some of these outcroppings into a little islet suitable for a mini Robinson Crusoe. Put all of these together, and you just may want to head for Descanso Bay Road.

Suitability for groups A carload of discreet family members will thank you for bringing them. Those living on either side of this access point will not thank you if you are visibly or volubly invasive.

View From this southwest side of Descanso Bay, you will be looking mostly across and into the bay itself, about 500 m wide at this point. You will, however, be able to make out two points of low, cliffy shoreline extending out of the bay. The one farther away happens to be Malaspina Point, the location of the well-known landforms called the Malaspina

Galleries. If your eyes wander into the open straits, you will also see a small slice of the Coast Mountains and the distinctive lumpy cone of southern Texada Island.

Winds, sun and shade Southeast winds can riffle the water here a little, but this beach is generally protected from those winds. On a hot day you will be happy that you are freshened by any wind from the northwest, even more so because you won't find so much as a morsel of shade at any time of day. Forget the sunscreen, sunglasses and sun hat at your peril.

Beachcombing You may well enjoy walking along the shore to your right, since you can round the rocky headland and find yourself on the extensive tidal flats of the adjoining bay. The long, narrow ridges of the sandstone strata there make for some intriguing investigation. Walking farther than this becomes uncomfortable, though, and walking in the opposite direction, to your left, rapidly becomes nigh on impossible.

Seclusion Visitors don't usually come to this spot, but some locals do. Witness the dinghies on the beach. In addition, houses are clearly visible on either side of this access road—though not beyond it. You will hardly feel in the middle of a crowd, but you will feel exposed, no matter what you do.

Gabriola: Entrance Island Lighthouse

PART 2 Denman Island

DENMAN ISLAND HAS BY far the most familiar shoreline of any of the islands in the Salish Sea. Anyone who has driven Highway 19A between Courtenay and Bowser will have spent significant parts of that trip looking across Baynes Sound at the forested banks and shores of this large island. Many of these drivers will also have taken the little ferry from Buckley Bay, often using Denman Island more or less as a transit route from the western ferry terminal to the eastern one to reach Denman's more popular sister, Hornby Island. Take heed, though. If you haven't made plans to interrupt your beeline from terminal to terminal, you are missing out on some beautiful and little-visited pieces of shoreline. Warm-water swimming, long shore walks and splendid views, particularly toward the mountains of Vancouver Island, are among Denman's best features. With few outcroppings of solid rock except toward its southeast end, this is an island of broad intertidal zones of pebbles and gravel. This feature has made the shores of Baynes Sound among the best oyster farming areas on Canada's west coast—and, many insist, the world. Those looking for "secret beaches" won't find huge numbers, but they will find enough lovely spots to more than justify their stop here. Beach seekers will have to be determined to hunt down well-hidden little trails but will be rewarded with equally well-hidden beaches.

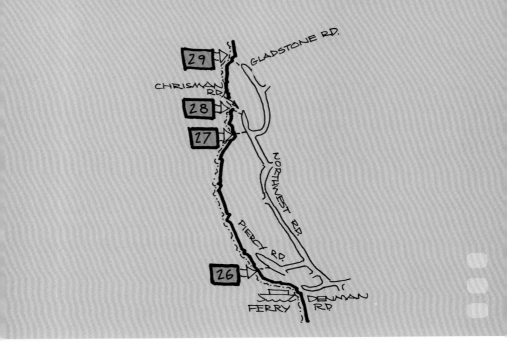

26
PIERCY ROAD
Within walking distance from the western ferry terminal, a path through a grassy field and down a bank to a pebbly upper shore

Location, signs and parking On foot, by bicycle or in a vehicle, head the 400 m up Denman Road and turn left at Northwest Road for another short stretch. Once you turn left onto Piercy Road, you will see that it leads downhill toward the shore and then swings right to run parallel to the coast. About 200 m along this section, you should see a grassy field with a path running straight toward the shore.

Path Once across the field, the path angles down the bushy bank and then drops down some venerable dirt-and-plank steps to a small grassy area by the shore. Here you will see a weathered picnic table just a few steps from the upper beach.

Beach The upper part of the beach is probably the most attractive part of the shoreline here, a gentle slope of coarse sand and crushed shell lined with a few convenient beach logs. Low tide exposes about 100 m of gravel and some areas of solid-rock slab, the most prominent of which sports a red-and-white navigational light. Visitors to this beach should respect the oyster farm.

Suitability for children At high tide, when the oysters are securely tucked away underwater, this is a welcoming spot for a picnic, a search for shell treasures and a warm-water splash. Because the shore faces southwest and because the tidal flats are extensive, a high tide in the afternoon can be deliciously warm. You might want to put a cap on decibels when you consider that neighbouring houses aren't very far from the beach.

Suitability for groups While this is not the place to seek for a large group gathering, if you are touring the island with half a dozen cyclists or a car full of fellow quilters, you will find enough space for a decadently sun-baked picnic. Except for the two tables at different points on the land, don't expect facilities.

View You are close enough to the ferry that you can see the slip along the shore to your left. Primarily, though, your eyes will be directed across the 2 km of Baynes Sound and the compact sequence of high points that

Denman: Piercy Road

make up the Beaufort Range. With a map in hand, you may be able to pick out most prominently, from south to north, Mount Apps, Mount Henry Spencer, Mount Stubbs and Mount Chief Frank. If you happen to be here as evening closes in, cross your fingers for a surreal sunset.

Winds, sun and shade Most prevailing winds run roughly parallel to the shore, scooting up and down Baynes Sound, though you are most likely to be chilled by southeast winds. In fact, an afternoon can become baking hot. If you are gasping for a little shade, you can walk up the slope to find the willows and maples screening a ramshackle picnic table.

Beachcombing This whole side of Denman Island, largely pebbles, gravel and gently shelving rock, makes for easy and pleasant walking. Do be aware, though, that you should respect the farmed oysters busily growing in the centre part of the intertidal zone. At the very least, keep to the uppermost bit of shore.

Seclusion This beach access is located in the midst of a strip of beach-front houses. The chunk of land currently still public is large enough that you are far from the lap of the neighbours. Be aware, though, that proposals have been made to use this land for seniors' housing.

27
CHRISMAN ROAD—SOUTH
A fairly steep trail down a forested bank to a secluded, gradually sloping shore of gravel and boulders

Location, signs and parking Once you have made your way up from the ferry ramp about 400 m and turned left on Northwest Road, your mission is to stay on this road for about 6 km, in spite of some surprising corners. Where Northwest Road takes a 90-degree dive to the right, watch out for the signpost for Chrisman Road, leading straight ahead. At this corner, find a spot to tuck your car onto the grassy shoulder. Here, and en route to the shore, you will see no fewer than three different signs telling you that you mustn't, under any circumstance, even think about starting a fire.

Path This is not a path for the unsteady members of your family. A fairly rough user-made trail, it winds over a small ditch and drops a little awkwardly almost 15 vertical metres.

Beach The gradually sloping shore, at low tide about 75 m wide, is composed of patches of pebbles, gravel and rounded boulders. Not quite in a natural state, the shore bears the signs of an oyster farm. Along the uppermost shore, tire tracks are noticeable in the compacted gravel. Elsewhere, careful lines of rocks are evidence of this local industry, bent on producing the world-famous "Fanny Bay Oysters" grown throughout Baynes Sound. Sadly, though, recent reports have indicated that Baynes Sound has become too acidic for oysters to spawn naturally.

Suitability for children Only rough and tough little explorers will enjoy facing the challenge of the steep trail. Since the shore is not great for picnicking and not suitable for exploring the tidal flats, you are better off taking your children to the nearby access at the north end of Chrisman Road.

Suitability for groups While this spot is well worth visiting, it would have to be a small group with specialized interests and abilities. Your average picnickers are better off elsewhere.

View The view is one of the glories of this spot. Shutterbugs and neo-Emily Carrs will not want to miss the opportunity for some striking compositions, particularly if they arrive during the spring, when the mountains of the Beaufort Range are deep in snow. In the morning the sun's rays dramatically pick out the contours of the crags. Equally picturesque are the curving treed shoreline to the left and the shorefront boathouse to the right.

Winds, sun and shade Because of the slight indentation of the shoreline at this point, it is significantly protected from the strongest winds, especially those from the northwest. During the morning, though the shade from the large firs can make the upper shore gloomy, by late morning and during the afternoon this coast is basted with as much sunshine as the sky can dish up.

Beachcombing The shore here is easily walked, as it is around the entire north end of Denman Island,. You should, however, respect the oyster farm and keep to the uppermost shore.

Seclusion For some, it will be the combination of splendid views and utter solitude that will bring them here—and keep them here for as long as it takes to solve the world's problems or think about nothing whatsoever.

28
CHRISMAN ROAD—NORTH
A broad, well-prepared path down a wooded bank to a gradually sloping shore of pebbles and crushed shells

Location, signs and parking Make your way up from the ferry on Denman Road 400 m and turn left onto Northwest Road. Stay on this road for about 6 km, being careful where Northwest Road takes a sharp left. Watch for the signpost for Chrisman Road leading straight ahead as Northwest Road takes a 90-degree dive to the right. About 200 m along, the road comes to an end in a turnaround. Here you will see a red-and-yellow sign making sure you fully understand that fires on the beach are verboten.

Path A carefully prepared dirt path has been cut into the slope, dropping about 12 m down the wooded slope. If the path happens to be muddy, you may find the heavy rope looped from several large trees is useful, but under normal conditions you should not need it.

Beach The trail ends between some large shorefront firs overhanging traces of a First Nation midden. The most appealing part of the beach is the first half dozen metres of crushed white shell and fine pebbles. Dotted with a few very old beach logs, this gently curving shoreline makes an appealing area for sinking deep into baking rays or a meaty novel. As part of an oyster farm, the shore is crossed with faint tracks from a service vehicle. Farther down the gravel shore, some 100 m wide at low tide, you can see other evidence of oyster culture.

Suitability for children Probably the best beach for children on the west side of Denman Island, this spot is also best visited at high tide. With the barnacles and razor-sharp oysters of the main part of the shore deep under the turquoise waters, you and your child can use the large sandy and pebbly shore as home ground for all the thrashing and splashing you like. The upper part of the beach is also good for creating fantasy castles and race-car tracks. Two reminders, though: you will have a bit of a trot back to the car if you forget anything, and you might have a less relaxed visit than you want if you forget water shoes.

Suitability for groups While a minor horde should go to Fillongley Provincial Park, a clutch of good friends or duty-bound family members can be comfortably arranged for an afternoon's salty pleasures. Plan to arrive at high tide, however, when the shore is prettiest and when you don't need to herd your guests away from the oysters on the lower shore.

View Because this spot is at the southern end of a long, concave section of shore at the northwest end of the island, your gaze is naturally directed along the tapering shore and, about 9 km away, toward tiny Sandy Island (aka Tree Island). Against the sky, the Beaufort Range leads to barely visible Courtenay and Comox. Like the few other beach access spots on this western side of Denman Island, this one can be a perfect place to view a blazing sunset.

Winds, sun and shade You will feel most wind from the northwest here, refreshing on a hot day or chilling on the other sort of day. It may be particularly welcome on an afternoon when the sun beats directly on the shore and the slightly overhanging firs offer only a little shade.

Beachcombing Since your eyes lead you in that direction anyway, you may be tempted to undertake the trek to the northwest tip of the island. If the tide is low, you can even walk the kilometre of tidal flats out to Sandy Island—and beyond. Read your tide tables well, though, and come prepared with proper footwear, sun protection and so on.

Seclusion Although few houses have been built in this area and most are at the top of the heavily treed bank, one house immediately left of the trailhead is virtually on the beach. You are unlikely to see other visitors at this spot, but you will not exactly feel you can have a secret tryst with mother nature.

29
GLADSTONE WAY
The northernmost access on Denman Island, a gradually sloping pebble-and-boulder shore within walking distance of the tip of the island and Sandy Island

Location, signs and parking Make your way up from the ferry on Denman Road 400 m and turn left onto Northwest Road. Stay on this road for about 8 km. Pass the signpost for Chrisman Road, leading straight ahead, as Northwest Road takes a 90-degree dive to the right. Gladstone Way, forking to the left off Northwest Road, ends in a huge gravel turnaround with a single gated driveway. Here you will see two signs, one saying WALKWAY and the other putting paid to any misconstrued plans for a beach-fire singalong.

Path A wide, level path beckons from a stand of small firs. Sloping gradually toward the shore, the dirt path becomes a little rutted at one point, though a potentially handy rope has been put in place beside one section of the path. The path ends in a pretty grassy patch with a few logs and a short drop onto the upper beach.

Beach If you arrive at low tide, you will see more than 400 m of tidal flats stretching before you, much of it covered with flat areas of shale and dotted with clusters of large, irregular boulders. By far the most conventionally pretty part of the beach is the first dozen metres, where a slope of crushed shell, coarse sand and fine pebbles makes a beckoning place for polishing off a novel, a picnic or a conversation.

Suitability for children Like other beaches on the west side of Denman Island, this one is probably best suited for children at high tide. Crabs, starfish, frilled dog whelks and other shore favourites are plentiful even at a mid-tide level. At high tide, though, when the water is warmest and the water's edge is sandiest, the opportunity for perfecting the dog paddle is at its peak. Even without swimming, the attractive area of uppermost beach is perfect for burying father's feet or decorating mounds of sand with pretty pebbles and butter clam shells.

Suitability for groups Given the huge parking area and the comfortable upper shore, a minor herd could have a great picnic and sunbathe here without worrying about overcrowding a small residential area. The lack of facilities and the tromp from the car should be factored into your plans, however.

View Probably the most eye-catching part of the view is the curving sweep of shore leading to the island's northern tip and, beyond, tiny Sandy Island (aka Tree Island), a provincial park off the northern tip. The rounded peaks of the northern end of the Beaufort Range taper down toward the low land around Comox Lake, while the higher peaks of Strathcona Park form the skyline farther north. Facing more or less west, this can be a perfect spot for viewing a psychedelic sunset.

Winds, sun and shade Shady during the first part of the day, the temperature here can evolve from a simmer to a full rolling boil during a hot, still afternoon because of the lack of shade. Largely protected from southeast winds, this northwest-facing shore can be fanned or buffeted by a northwest blow.

Beachcombing At almost any tide, you can make your way along the shore for about as long as you like, though should confine your tromping to the uppermost shore when you pass oyster farms. One of the most enticing bits of shore walking anywhere among the Gulf Islands is the one to Sandy Island. Obviously, you'll have to make sure your ability to read tide tables is up to scratch. Choose a very low tide, however, and you can walk the kilometre-broad stretch of tidal flats out to Sandy Island—and much farther, if you are game for the adventure. Most of the way you will be walking on pebbly shore, configured into strange mounds and ridges at some points. Make sure you've studied your tide tables before going out to the island!

Seclusion Although you are not exactly miles from the nearest house, you will find yourself close to experiencing a sense of perfect seclusion.

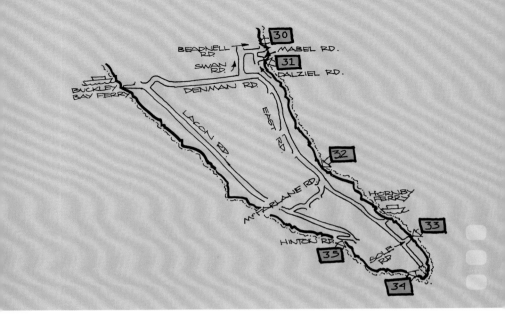

30 FILLONGLEY PROVINCIAL PARK

A large area of forest next to a long, level beach with tidal pools, gravel and sand

Location, signs and parking Rumble off the ferry and make your way across Denman Island via Denman Road, the direct route to the Hornby Island ferry. About 4 km along, turn left onto Swan Road and, after about 700 m, turn right down Beadnell Road, following the blue-and-white provincial park sign. You can drive straight ahead, practically onto the shore, or turn left into the large parking lot. Various signs point out where you may not park overnight, though the park does have 10 campsites—usually full in summer. If you are planning to demonstrate your marshmallow-roasting skills, you will have to go elsewhere. Beach fires are not permitted.

Path Those with walking difficulties or toting little family members and the food to feed them will be pleased with the few steps necessary to reach the beach, but might have to be a little careful in the loose, pebbly sand. Note the location of several picnic tables and the rustic washrooms before going directly to the shore.

Beach The whole upper shore area has a wonderfully beachy feel, with a large area of sun-baked loose sand dotted with patches of beach grass and weathered logs. The slope of coarse sand and pebbles just below beckons sun worshippers to spread-eagle their afternoon into oblivion. If you arrive at low tide, nearly 300 m of pebbles, tidal pools and sand separate you from the water's edge. Turn left if you prefer a little less extensive beach.

Suitability for children If you've promised your children a day at the beach as a reward for holding still at the dentist's office, this is probably the spot on Denman Island most likely to please them. The nearby parking, the facilities and the opportunities for building castles of sand, shells and seaweed should be everything they need to satisfy their beach cravings. Water shoes, or at least crocs or flip-flops, are a good idea, particularly if swimming, skimboarding or kite flying are on the agenda. If the tide happens to have submerged the best places for running games, note that you can find a grassy field in the park (formerly a lawn bowling pitch for the early settlers).

Suitability for groups This is by far the best spot on Denman Island for a horde of raging granddads or a convention of kindergarten graduates. The easy directions from the ferry terminal, the parking space, the facilities and the large beach and park should please just about any group.

View The Mount Geoffrey Escarpment, the high point of Hornby Island roughly 3 km distant, dominates the nearby skyline. Across the northern Strait of Georgia, however, the unlovely scars of mining on Texada Island stand out a little more than you will like.

Winds, sun and shade If breezes, walloping winds or anything in between are stirring up the straits, you will feel them on this shore. Winds don't generally blow directly onto the shore, however, and if you want to reduce the number of goose pimples, moving up the beach should give you a little shelter behind logs. If you become baking-hot, you can find a little shade behind some of the fledgling shorefront firs that dot the upper beach, but most of the beach is sunny throughout most of the day.

Beachcombing Strap on your day pack, tighten up your water shoes and head out for as long a beach walk as suits your temperament and your stamina. Sloping gradually and dominated by gravel and pebbles, almost all of Denman Island's east coast is enticing and easy to walk.

Seclusion This is a much-loved provincial park—though never a crowded one. In fact, most summer visitors seem to head straight for Hornby Island, bypassing even Denman's most appealing beach.

31

MABEL ROAD
A level, loose gravel path through beach grass and a large accumulation of beach logs to wide tidal flats of gravel and tidal pools

Location, signs and parking You can follow the signs to Fillongley Provincial Park most of the way. This means crossing Denman Island on Denman Road. About 4 km along, turn left onto Swan Road and, after about 700 m, turn right down Beadnell Road. Toward the end of the road, turn right onto Dalziel Road and about 150 m later, left onto Mabel Road. At the end of the road you will see a gravel area and two large boulders on either side of the short path to the shore. The only sign posted here puts a damper on those who were planning to spend a night camping on the beach. Take heart. The provincial campsite is a few minutes away.

Path Level, wide and only a few dozen metres long, this path is a breeze for most visitors, but it isn't quite as easy as it looks. The loose pebbles and coarse sand might be a bit of a challenge for those with walking difficulties or those struggling with beach paraphernalia.

Beach The large upper beach is thick with beach grass and massed logs. The strip of shore immediately below the logs is appealing as a spot for sprawling indolently or devouring rapaciously. At low tide, 300 m of shore separate you from a cooling dip. Composed of areas of tidal pools, gravel, boulders and sand, the shore stretches a considerable distance in both directions.

Suitability for children Safe and full of play options, this a good beach for almost every child. Choose low tide for flying kites, throwing Frisbees or wading through tidal pools of tiny toe-tickling fish and crabs. Choose high tide if you most want to encourage a thorough soaking. No matter what the tide, though, this beach has enough foot-shredding barnacles that forgetting water shoes could be a minor tragedy.

Suitability for groups While the beach itself is huge, the parking is limited and many neighbouring houses are close by. If you have a group, choose the provincial park just a few minutes away. There your group will have lots of parking space and all the facilities anyone is likely to need.

View Because this beach is near the northernmost end of a long concave section of the island's northeast shore, you can see many, many kilometres along the shore, almost to its southernmost tip. A mere 2 km of water separate you from Hornby Island and the exposed bluffs and forested ridges of the Mount Geoffrey Escarpment.

Winds, sun and shade A windy day on the Strait of Georgia usually translates into a windy day on this beach. From some westerly winds, you will be slightly sheltered. The spot is equally exposed to sun. Go carefully through the checklist of sun protection gear, clothes and lotions You'll need everything on the list.

Beachcombing If ever there was an island made for beachcombing, Denman is it, and if ever there was a spot on that island where beach-combing tempts, this Mabel Road access is it. Although you can walk as far as your heart desires in either direction, walking north will probably be most satisfying, especially along isolated stretches of the coast beneath high sandy banks.

Seclusion Understandably, this is a popular residential chunk of the island. On either side of the access spot, houses perch in a phalanx, ready to soak up as much view as their windows will absorb. On the other hand, if you walk far out onto the tidal flats, you are unlikely to meet more than the occasional seagull.

32
EAST ROAD
A roadside parking area with easy access to a large mixed shore of pebbles, tidal pools and conglomerate rock

Location, signs and parking One way of reaching this spot is simply to follow the main route toward the Hornby Island ferry, but it is easier to find if you first turn right onto Lacon Road about 1 km from your entry spot to the island. Roughly 6 km later, turn left onto McFarlane Road. At a T-junction and the end of this road, approximately 3 km along, turn left onto East Road. The spot you are looking for is a wide, bare pull-off on the sea side of the road, about 200 m from McFarlane and opposite a house numbered 4021. Several cars could fit into this spot, but you are unlikely to have company if you park here. The only sign posted warns you that overnight parking or camping are not on. Because, in fact, you can park more or less at the edge of a little bank overlooking the shore, this is an enticing view spot for car picnicking if the weather has taken it upon itself to turn nasty.

Path More or less from the centre of the parking area, a rough dirt track leads down to the shore about 2 m below. While the path is straightforward going for most, those with walking difficulties may prefer not to risk slipping but instead take refuge on the convenient log bench beside the path.

Beach The uppermost part of the beach, backed with thickets of tall beach grass and almost empty of convenient logs, is the most conventionally pretty part of the beach. With its comfortable slope and graceful curve along the shore, this area of loose, fine pebbles is an inviting place for picnicking or pondering. The rest of the beach, dropping almost

Denman: East Road

200 m to the low-tide line, is anything but conventional. The middle part of the shore, a broad swath of compressed pebbles, is cut across with huge tidal pools and low ridges of conglomerate rock.

Suitability for children While it is hard to predict how children will react to an unusual beach, this is a beach with no significant hazards, plenty of warm water and lots of potential diversions for certain subspecies of children. Low tide is probably best for the curious and hyperactive. High tide is best for convenient and warm-water hijinks. While not crucial, water shoes will keep to a minimum the likelihood of your needing to practise first aid on little feet.

Suitability for groups Though this is not exactly a congested neighbourhood, it is a neighbourhood nevertheless. Parking and shore space are ample, but not enough to make a visit by more than a dozen folk a good idea.

View This beach is near the south end of a long section of concave shore. You can see virtually the entire northeast coast of Denman, or at least as far as Fillongley Park. Across Lambert Channel, the distinctive ridge of Mount Geoffrey runs above much of the shore of Hornby Island.

Winds, sun and shade Both northwest and southeast winds cheerfully whoosh back and forth along this section of coast. A slightly elevated ridge of rock to the south creates a minor wind block and thus provides some protection from an unwelcome southeasterly.

Beachcombing Come with resilient footwear, and you can set off in either direction for as extensive a shore walk as you like. The shore is composed of low ridges of sedimentary rock interspersed with tidal pools and patches of small rock. Because East Road runs close to the shore for many kilometres, you can easily arrange a pickup or shuttle.

Seclusion This is a quiet spot, but it is not a secluded one. Close to a road that channels ferry traffic in both directions and close to several houses perched along and across that road, this shore is as exposed as you are likely to find outside a park.

33
BILL MEE PARK
Picnic facilities and access to a remote section of conglomerate shoreline, as well as a top-notch launching spot for boats

Location, signs and parking Follow the traffic and signs from the western ferry terminal to the eastern one, which connects to Hornby Island. This means crossing Denman Island on Denman Road and turning right onto East Road. About 7 km later, when you reach the turnoff for the Hornby ferry, keep ahead for another kilometre on East Road until, at a sharp corner, you see Sole Road and the sign for Bill Mee Park on your left. Less than 100 m down this road, you will see a large gravel turnaround area, a welcoming sign, washrooms and picnic tables. One sign provides information on launching, another forbids fires and yet another asks you not to molest shore life—a tidbit to be passed on, perhaps, to your five-year-old.

Path You won't find many more professionally engineered launching ramps anywhere. If you have come here with your loyal kayak, you can drive to the water's edge behind the protection of twin breakwaters. You can otherwise use this spot to make your way easily onto an attractive and unusual piece of shoreline.

Beach Although you will see a small pebbly area on either side of the concrete ramp, you will probably be most tempted to find a route to the water over the boulders of the breakwaters. If lunchtime has rolled around and you have a handy supply of sandwiches, you may find the picnic tables are beautifully situated, providing welcome alternatives to perching on the wild undulations and crests of the conglomerate shore.

Suitability for children If you are looking for a convenient picnic place with tables and washrooms, this spot has clear advantages over more isolated and undeveloped ones. Once here, most children can enjoy exploring their way along the shore. If your sole purpose for an afternoon's outing is to find a place for children, however, you and they will be happier elsewhere.

Suitability for groups A few friends wanting an unconventional and beautiful picnic location may well enjoy the handy waterfront tables and other facilities. Big groups, however, or ones expecting to idle some hours away on a comfortable beach should go to Fillongley Park.

View The most striking visual feature from this spot is the high escarpment of Mount Geoffrey, a wedge-shaped hill 300 m high, on Hornby Island. Since Lambert Channel is only about 1.5 km wide at this point, you can pick out Ford Cove.

Winds, sun and shade As the positioning of the two breakwaters suggests, one on either side of the launching ramp, wind and the accompanying waves can come from both directions. Since the high trees behind the shore can cast considerable shade during the afternoon, be prepared to be cool on a windy afternoon.

Beachcombing Unlike most of the shoreline around Denman Island, this part of the coast is largely irregular, shelving conglomerate. Walking along the shore, particularly to the south, is thus interesting but does occasionally require a little spryness. For the first few hundred metres, the shore at low tide is almost 100 m wide but narrows considerably as you continue south. You can also walk north, but the ferry terminal for Hornby Island doesn't do wonders for your sense of wilderness wandering.

Seclusion A few houses dot the treed shoreline above the low bank. On the whole, though, this is a quiet and secluded part of the island.

34 BOYLE POINT
PROVINCIAL PARK
A trail through old-growth
forest to clifftop views of
Chrome Island lighthouse,
and side trails to the shore

Location, signs and parking Although two main routes lead to the south end of the island and Boyle Point Provincial Park, the shorter begins with a right turn onto Lacon Road about 1 km from the western ferry. Roughly 6 km later, turn left onto McFarlane Road. At a T-junction, approximately 3 km along, turn right onto East Road. A little over 4 km later you will arrive more or less at the road's end. You can't help but see the sign for the park and ample parking area. Note the location of the handy pit toilets.

Path About 1.5 km long, the wide and largely level trail leads through an old forest with some impressive firs to the major lookout over Chrome Island lighthouse. A side path en route leads to another lookout, Eagle Rock. While you will see signs warning you to keep to the main path, you will also see that well-worn paths lead to various points on the sedimentary rock shore.

Beach As you walk toward the southern tip of the island, you will see a small side path leading to the right. Those intrepid souls who are happy to climb down more than 20 m onto the shore will find themselves on so-called Betty's Beach. An attractive upper shore, about 100 m long, drops to tidal flats more than 200 m wide at low tide and covered with tidal pools.

Suitability for children This is not a park for those with stubby little legs and uncertain balance. It is, however, an exciting spot for those children old enough to stride out and enjoy high viewpoints without hurling themselves down steep banks.

Suitability for groups Needless to say, a few cars of kindred spirits looking for a short but spectacular walk will find lots of room and probably lots of seclusion. Make sure you've warned your group that they will regret not bringing a camera.

View Above all, this is a spot to visit for its views. Different seasons and different times of day produce dramatically different views, so you will want to return—and return. The most iconic view is that of Chrome Island, but notice the unusual perspective you get down the east coast of Vancouver Island and the southern straits. If you can time your visit just right and arrive during a herring spawn in early spring, you will have splendid views of well-fed eagles and sea lions, along with cormorants, ospreys and, of course, gulls.

Winds, sun and shade Since most visitors don't come for the beach experience, sun and wind won't make much difference. Those who go to Betty's Beach, however, will find the spot generally well protected and, in the afternoon, nigh on baking. From the view spot, a strong southeast wind and its accompanying waves will add zest to your already spectacular view.

Beachcombing Beachcombing will not be high on many visitors' list of interests. Those who do decide to make their way down to the shore will find plenty of foreshore to explore, particularly along the southwest coast. The northeast coast is much steeper and broken into large chunks. For a rare adventure, comb through your tide tables until you find the extremely rare occasions when the tide drops enough that you can walk all the way out to Chrome Island lighthouse—with or without a little wading.

Seclusion Because the park is tucked away at the end of the island and because most visitors head straight for Hornby Island, you are unlikely to clap eyes on many other visitors.

35
HINTON ROAD
The only easy access to the large tidal flats of Denman Island's southwest coast

Location, signs and parking After a short but pretty ferry crossing from Buckley Bay, head uphill from the ferry terminal on Denman Road. Less than 1 km along, turn right onto Lacon Road. Very roughly 8 km along this coast road, look for Hinton Road angling back sharply and delivering you quickly to a large gravel turnaround area virtually on the shore. This spot is used by operators of an oyster farm, and their trucks drive directly onto the shore. You, however, may not. Note that other signs forbid beach fires and overnight parking. Particularly important at this spot, perhaps, is the warning not to damage or remove oysters at this oyster tenure.

Path Kayakers will be interested in the fact that they can drive right to the upper shore. They will, nevertheless, have to be very careful with tide tables. Arrive at low tide and not only will you be unwelcome, since you would have to tread over oyster beds, but you will also face 300 m of tidal flats. Those with walking difficulties or mammoth picnic hampers should, however, be pleased with the ease of getting to the upper shore.

Beach Most visitors will be primarily interested in the splendid upper beach of crushed shell and fine pebbles. With just the right slope and just the right number of sun-bleached logs dotting the gentle curve of the shoreline, this south-facing beach is perfect for soaking up rays, views and a full dose of peace and quiet. At a very high tide, too, this is a good place for a cooling dip, especially since the water that has crept up over 300 m of sun-heated shore can be bathtub warm.

Suitability for children Since children should not disturb the oysters plumping themselves up for distant gourmands, they should concentrate

Denman- Hinton Road

on mounding up piles of sand in the uppermost part of the beach. At high tide, however, with water shoes and a change of clothes, making watery mayhem will be too tempting to resist.

Suitability for groups Two or three cars' worth of beach buddies can easily be accommodated here for a comfortable, scenic and well-protected picnic. Do prepare them, though, for the fact that they will find not a trace of a facility.

View You won't see many other spots that give you a similar perspective on Vancouver Island's mountains and, in particular, Mount Arrowsmith. Baynes Sound, separating Denman Island from Vancouver Island, is about 2 km wide here and narrows to less than 1 km at low tide where the tidal flats extend from Mapleguard Point far into Baynes Sound. As evening approaches, this is a perfect viewing spot for a sunset filling the sky behind the Beaufort Range.

Winds, sun and shade Although this west-facing spot is not completely protected from any of the most common winds, it can be very hot during a summer's afternoon when only a northwest breeze is stirring the air. The lack of shade can make this spot blistering.

Beachcombing If you keep to the upper beach, well off the oyster farm, you can bite off as much shore walking as you can chew. Although the shore narrows considerably on either side of this spot, it is easily walk-able for many kilometres, but easiest if you head north.

Seclusion You will be aware of one shorefront house about 100 m to your left. Occasional houses punctuate the shore, but on the whole you will see few others and be seen by even fewer.

PART 3 Hornby Island

JUST ABOUT EVERY ONE of the islands in the Salish Sea is a favourite for someone, yet Hornby Island probably has more passionate devotees than any other island. Reaching this island requires some planning and patience, especially during summer months, when the first of two ferries you must take, the one to Denman Island, can be overcrowded. In some ways, Hornby Island seems a little out of place geographically. Composed almost entirely of sandstone and conglomerate rock, swathed in a sun-baked aura of arbutus and Garry oak, Hornby seems like a "southern" Gulf Island that has drifted north from its moorings. Some of the popularity of the island arises from the fact that its most striking areas, far from being "secret," are big public parks. The provincial parks of Mount Geoffrey, Tribune Bay and Helliwell, each distinct from the others, each large and welcoming for visitors and each stunningly beautiful, are all well known and much visited. These, along with Whaling Station Bay, account for virtually all of the shore visits to Hornby Island. While you really, really do want to visit all of these places, you will be missing out on many memorable shore experiences if you explore no further. Carved into smooth undulations alternating with otherworldly bulges, large areas of this sandstone shore make for interesting shore walking. Finding the routes to the less well-known spots around the coast isn't always easy, but in many cases, once you've found the route, you can drive virtually onto the shore. Thus, in addition to its other features, this island is a great one to visit if you want to get to the shore with as few steps as possible. Those with kayaks, impatient children and infirm relatives will want to make a beeline for the Buckley Bay ferry terminal on Vancouver Island, the gateway to this lovely island.

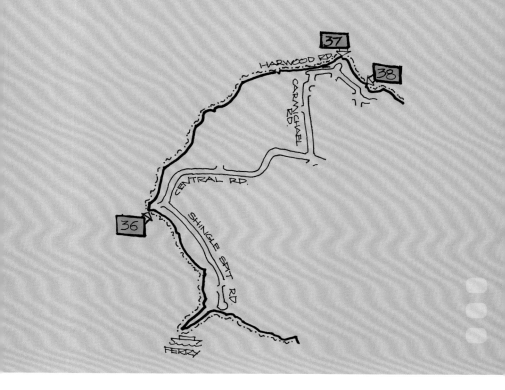

36
PHIPPS POINT
Shorefront parking at a
promontory with a disused
jetty, gravel beaches and
sandstone ridges

Location, signs and parking Drive from the ferry along Shingle Spit
Road for about 2.5 km until you see a sharp curve in the road to the
right and the road sign for Central Road on the left. Turn left and follow the road about 200 m as it descends a high bank and delivers you
to a shoreside turnaround area and parking for about three cars. The
only sign here, issued by the Ministry of the Environment, announces
this to be the site of an oyster lease and forbids destroying or removing
oysters. Don't even think about it.

Path You could hardly design a better spot for those with walking difficulties to explore a little seashore. From the parking area, it is possible to walk above the beach along a disused jetty extending 75 m from the shore into deep water. Getting onto the shore on either side of the jetty is also a breeze. Kayakers should also like this spot, since even at low tide they can easily reach the water. Needless to say, the shorefront parking and the wide sweep of view from its position on the convex shoreline make this a superb spot for a car picnic when driving rain has chased you from the beach.

Beach Extending around the curve of this promontory, known as Phipps Point, this beach has lots of diversity. Picnickers and sun lovers will want to seek out one of the sections of upper beach with coarse sand, pebbles, broken shell and handy beach logs. On this varied beach, however, ridges of sculpted sandstone alternate with stretches of gravel—and the oyster beds that you shouldn't disturb. While low tide exposes only about 50 m of shore at the tip of the promontory, on either side of the promontory it uncovers more than 200 m of rock and gravel.

Suitability for children All children can safely and conveniently toddle or cavort around this spot. The most active and nimble will have the most fun, though. The rock ridges, jetty, logs and sandy upper beach are almost guaranteed to stimulate such children for several hours of good fun. The proximity of the car is clearly an asset when sudden crises or demands arise. Partly because of the sensitive nature of the oyster lease and partly because of the shore itself, plan to come when the tide is at least partly in.

Suitability for groups While the shore itself has heaps of room for a group, and while the chances of disturbing neighbours are small, parking near the shore is difficult for more than two or three cars. In addition, of course, the spot has none of the facilities most large groups need.

View The view is one of the splendours of this spot, in part because of its location on a promontory. Prominent among the many scenic pleasures vying for your attention are the ridges of the Mount Geoffrey Escarpment; the high buttresses of the Beaufort Range behind Denman; the sand cliffs at Denman's north end; and the long curve of shoreline along Hornby's northwest coast.

Winds, sun and shade Few spots give you so many options of exposure to, or protection from, sun and wind. One shore of the promontory is exposed to the northwest, the other the southwest. A cluster of large shorefront arbutus provides patches of shade throughout much of the day, though evening shade can be scarce.

Beachcombing If you are careful to stay off the oyster beds, you can walk for many glorious kilometres along gently shelving shoreline. Long-distance walkers will probably be most interested in turning right, where the coastline is the most varied and scenic.

Seclusion While this is not exactly a wilderness area, you will feel well away from the few houses near here, especially if you wander along the shore to the right and settle down on the upper beach there.

While you're here . . . Consider visiting a lovely, secluded section of shoreline with a sandy upper beach, reached via a wooded path about 150 m long. About a kilometre along Central Road, turn down Savoie Road and follow it to its end, about half a kilometre later, in a small turnaround area outside a private gate. The dirt path leads from the left side of the turnaround, dropping a little steeply toward the shore down a bank about 10 m high.

Hornby: Phipps Point

37

GRASSY POINT

A striking promontory of low,
level seaside meadows above an
extensive shore of conglomerate
ridges and declivities

Location, signs and parking Drive along Shingle Spit Road for about
2.5 km where, at a slight jog, the main cross-island road changes name
to Central Road. A little less than 3 km along this twisting road, take
a sharp left onto Carmichael Road, and follow it along its S-curving
route to its end, about 1.5 km later. Turn right onto Harwood for about
300 m until you see the road sign for Gunpowder Trail on your right.
On your left you will see a brightly coloured hand-painted sign saying
GRASSY POINT. You will also see a gravel track leading to a shorefront
turnaround about 100 m past another, professional sign saying GRASSY
POINT COMMUNITY PARK.

Path If you have parked on the shoulder of Harwood Road, your walk
to the shore is along a grassy path through a sea meadow sprinkled with
a few low firs and bushes. En route you will see two park benches with
lovely views over the sea meadows, in mid-May carpeted with camas lilies
and larkspur. If, however, you park at the end of the gravel track, you are
vitually on the beach and perfectly situated for a car picnic or, at mid to
high tide, launching a kayak.

Beach The first thing you will notice on this beach is the fascinating
conglomerate rock. Typical for this section of Hornby is the remarkable size of the rounded volcanic stones embedded in the sandstone.
While most of the shore itself is low, irregular bumps and curves, the
uppermost shore is inset with small curved bays of loose gravel and
convenient beach logs. The beach most suited for picnics or sunbathing
is immediately in front of the turnaround, though this beach partly
lies in front of private property. The wonderfully open and meadowy
exposure of the whole promontory is guaranteed to encourage you to
stay—and stay.

Suitability for children While adults are more likely to savour this unusual beach than children, the shore is well enough suited to charging about and exploring that most children should be easily entertained here. Since low tide exposes more than 100 m of shore, including two nearby reefs and several tidal pools, most sure-footed children will find lots to explore.

Suitability for groups Although both the grassy area and shoreline are expansive, this spot is best for only a small group. In fact, you can be almost guaranteed that a small group of seascape and wildlife lovers will be immoderate in their enthusiasm over this beach. Keep in mind that there are no facilities and you are within yodelling distance of houses on either side.

View Because this is a promontory, you can see along great swaths of Hornby's north and east coast. A little less happily, you will discover that this is probably the best place to view the giant mining scar on Texada Island's southwest coast. You can easily ignore that, however, and cast your eyes to the apparently empty horizon where, in fact, Savary, Hernando and many other islands spread across the northern straits. If your timing is right, you just might catch a technicolour sunset over the mountains of Strathcona Park.

Winds, sun and shade Although you can find some protection from a southeast wind, you can find none from a northwest blow. Likewise, no trees grow along this low shore to provide shade on a sunny day.

Beachcombing While the conglomerate rock can be a little rough underfoot, the shore in both directions is wide and level enough that explorers can begin a major or minor expedition here. Walking in both directions provides shifting views and a surface of generally wide, gently shelving sedimentary rock and gravel.

Seclusion One of the pleasures of beginning a walk along the shore is that once you have gone more than a few hundred metres past the houses dotting the wooded banks, you will find about as much peace and quiet as the waves and gulls will allow you. Grassy Point itself, though, can be a favourite spot for a few locals—but rarely more than a few.

38
HIDDEN COMMUNITY PARK
Paths down a forested slope to an upper beach of fine white sand and logs, extending to a smooth, level surface of sandstone

Location, signs and parking Drive along Shingle Spit Road for about 2.5 km where, at a slight jog, the main cross-island road changes name to Central Road. A little less than 3 km along this twisting road, take a sharp left onto Carmichael Road, and follow it to its end about 1.5 km later. At this T-junction, turn right onto Harwood Road for about 600 m. Keep an eye out for a grassy opening in the vegetation and a small green sign saying HIDDEN COMMUNITY PARK. You will find parking space for a few cars along the road or the rough grassy area. The sign is vehement about not camping but otherwise just makes a generalized request to help maintain the park.

Path More than one path leads to the beach, each about 50 m long and dropping gradually about 10 m en route to the shore.

Beach You will emerge from under tree boughs to see a minor logjam and a pretty beach of fine white sand. Unusual for the island is the concrete firepit ring in the centre of this sandy section. Aside from a patch of high wild grass to one side, the sandy section leads directly into a striking tabletop surface of fine-grained, nearly white sandstone. Well over 100 m wide at low tide, this surface is dotted with little tidal pools and, near the low-tide line, is increasingly covered with seaweed.

Suitability for children Your children will have to cope with a bit of an uphill trail on returning from the beach. They will also have to be the kind of children who have enough imagination that they can enjoy the diversions of this unconventional beach. For the sandbox crowd, the upper beach is well suited to mounding sand into tractor tracks, and the logs are great for executing feats of daring and imagination. The tidal pools and crea-ture-crammed crevices of the lower part of the beach beg to be explored.

Hornby: Hidden Community Park

Choose an incoming tide on a hot afternoon for your own private water park, as the water creeps around the formations and over the smooth sandstone.

Suitability for groups While this is designated as a park, don't choose it with expectations of finding park facilities. If your group knows what to expect and comes prepared, though, the lack of facilities should not discourage you. A dozen or so visitors can easily be accommodated at this capacious and isolated pretty spot.

View From its position on the north coast of the island, the park looks out on the empty spaces of the northern strait and, to the east, almost the entire 50 km length of Texada Island. The real charm of this park as a view spot, however, arises from the fact that it is at the base of a small bay. The high wooded banks and treed promontories, particularly on your right, are especially appealing.

Winds, sun and shade Reasonably well protected from southeasterly storms, this little bay is fully exposed to every breeze, wind and gale from the northwest. The uppermost part of the beach is in shade through most of the day, but the sandy upper beach is large enough that you can easily spread out your beach blanket in full sun throughout the day.

Beachcombing Like most spots on this side of Hornby Island, this is a good one to explore at low tide or, even better, to use as a launching point for a major tromp along the mostly level shelves of sandstone. One satisfying destination is Tralee Point, about 2 km to your right. Grassy Point, about half a kilometre to your left, is a good destination for a more restrained and contemplative stroll. For a real adventure, though, head to Collishaw Point, 3 km to your left, and prepare to be amazed by the huge expanse of low-tide sandstone formations extending almost a kilometre to the northernmost tip of the island.

Seclusion The park more or less lives up to its name. "Hidden" from all but one bank-top house, this largely untouched bit of shoreline exposes houses only if you walk to the low-tide line and look far along the shore.

Hornby: Cormorants by ferry terminal

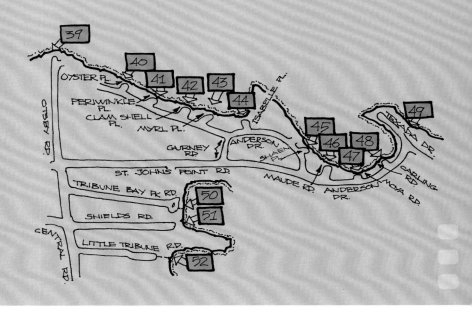

39

OSTBY ROAD

A long forest trail zigzagging down a high bank to a remarkable shore of smooth, flat sandstone with areas of large, rounded boulders and tidal pools

Location, signs and parking Drive along Shingle Spit Road for about 2.5 km where, at a slight jog, the main cross-island road changes name to Central Road. After about 7 km, when you come to a crossroads, turn left onto St. John's Point Road. Carry on around the huge tree that sits in the middle of the intersection. Take Ostby Road, which begins on the other side of the tree, to its end. Pull over onto the shoulder where you see a sign forbidding overnight parking and camping.

Path You will probably be thrown off a little by the impression that the end of the road morphs into a private drive. This impression is actually correct—up to a point. Walk a few metres ahead, and you will be rewarded with a well-used dirt trail leading off to the left. The trail leads through attractive open woods of salal, swordferns, cedar, fir and maple as it zigzags down a high bank. Potentially slippery at a few points, the pathway is bordered in the steepest places by handrails. You would obviously want to engage in some heavy-duty weighing of pros and cons before guiding a friend or relative here who has difficulty walking or is in poor physical condition.

Beach Like the shore at many spots on Hornby Island, it is here composed of mostly level sandstone, patches of rounded boulders and tidal pools. To describe the beach in these terms, however, is misleading, because those elements are particularly beautiful here. The upper beach in particular, with clustered logs and smooth, almost white sandstone, is an appealing spot to picnic or spend an afternoon reading and absorbing more sun than is good for you.

Suitability for children If your children have sand and only sand in mind as you set off for the seashore, you clearly won't want to bring them here. Otherwise, they could find few more attractive and enticing places to investigate. Easy and safe to traverse, yet well supplied with scuttling, clinging and oozing creatures, the shore and its tidal pools should keep most children thoroughly entertained. For wading and splashing, even swimming, come at or near high tide.

Suitability for groups Any group you shepherded here would have to know that they were coming to a place with no facilities and no soft beach sand in which to flop languorously. Otherwise, as long as they are careful with their parking, a dozen or so people could easily be accommodated at this little-populated and spacious chunk of shore.

View Because it is situated at the head of an open, north-facing bay, this access spot looks out primarily on the large expanses of the northern Strait of Georgia. Treed promontories frame the view, one nearby, the other tapering to the north.

Winds, sun and shade Reasonably well protected from southeast winds, this little bay welcomes with open arms every waft or gale from the northwest. While you can find shade during the middle part of the day, as the afternoon progresses you will have to move closer and closer to the bank if you want to keep cool and protected.

Beachcombing Like most other spots on this section of Hornby Island's north coast, this one is a good starting point for beginning a major shore trek. At the same time, though, it is an enticing shore to explore in leisurely fashion—easy to traverse, yet diversified.

Seclusion Though you are not quite alone here, you may well have the impression that you are. The high banks and enthusiastically verdant growth will do everything to create a sense of isolation from crowds.

40
OYSTER PLACE
Level, road-end access to a small bay dominated by a huge tidal pool surrounded by level expanses of conglomerate rock

Location, signs and parking Head along Shingle Spit Road for about 2.5 km where, at a slight bend, the main road changes name to Central Road. After about 7 km, when you come to a crossroads, turn left onto St. John's Point Road and carry on 1 km to another intersection. Continue on St. John's Point Road to the right. Roughly 2.5 km along, turn left onto Gurney Road and follow it to a T-junction about 150 m later. Turn left onto Anderson Drive for a little under a kilometre, where you will see a sign for Oyster Place. Attached to the signpost is another sign telling you that you may not park overnight or camp. When you drive to the end of this road and realize that you can park with an attractive view of the shore, you might realize why visitors in camper vans just might find this an appealing spot to roost.

Path Since you need take only a few easy steps to the upper shore, you might consider this to be a good spot to launch kayaks. Up to a point you would be right, but only if you plan a launch in or around high tide. Otherwise, you will be facing a long haul to the distant waterline.

Beach Unusually for this part of Hornby's coastline, this little bay collects more than its fair share of beach logs. Below this appealing area for improvised seats or picnic spots, the shore is largely smooth gravel. Were the shore to stop there, it would be unremarkable. It doesn't. Instead, what you see in front of you is a shore feature you may have seen nowhere else. A gigantic tidal pool, some 75 m across and 50 m wide, almost completely fills this little bay. The crest of the rock on the other side of this huge pool, just about at the high-tide line, is covered with a stubble of salt-tolerant vegetation.

Suitability for children If you make sure your children are properly shod, you could bring them here on a cool day when sandy cavorting isn't appealing. Exploring the tidal pool would no doubt end up with a lot more than just wet feet, so be prepared.

Suitability for groups Like the other access spots on this bit of coast, this one has the space for a bevy, but neither the facilities nor the attractions that the average group has in mind for a day at the beach. Keep this spot in mind for a small group of fellow ramblers or photographers. You can almost be guaranteed that they will never have heard of the spot and yet will be intrigued by what it offers.

View The prettiest and most sketchable part of the view is probably the immediate foreground. The banks of logs, the treed promontory to your right and the high ridges of conglomerate rock, looking strangely like concrete, are the most eye-catching parts of your view. Come at a mid to high tide, when the water flows around some of these ridges, for the most picturesque take on the intertidal rock formations. If your eyes do drift across the expanse of open water, you will recognize the entire shore opposite to belong to the mighty Texada Island.

Winds, sun and shade The small promontories on either side of this shallow bay may provide a little shelter from the winds, but, for good or ill, you are likely to feel wind, whether in the form of a refreshing breeze or a chilling gale.

Beachcombing You will find it hard to resist wandering around the lumps and bumps of this remarkable bit of shore. Be aware, in addition, that this is a good starting point for long beach walks, most of them over writhing configurations of solid conglomerate rock and sandstone, varied with occasional patches of gravel and pebbles. Low tide obviously provides the best choice of routes, though the lower half of the beach is generally steeper and slippery with seaweed.

Seclusion The access is situated in a developed section of the coast, so you will be aware of several houses peering from the trees along the generally low bank. Visitors, however, rarely make their way here—or even know of its existence.

While you're here . . . An additional 200 m along Anderson Drive will bring you to Geoduck Place, a short, dead-end road with a pretty view over a section of sculpted and irregular shoreline most easily accessible from Oyster Place.

41
PERIWINKLE PLACE
Easy access to a quiet, low and level section of the island's undulating northern coast of conglomerate rock

Location, signs and parking Head along Shingle Spit Road for about 2.5 km where, at a slight jog, the main cross-island road changes name to Central Road. After about 7 km, when you come to a crossroads, turn left onto St. John's Point Road and carry on 1 km to another intersection. Continue on St. John's Point Road to the right. Approximately 2.5 km along, take Gurney Road on your left and follow it to a T-junction about 150 m later. Turn left onto Anderson Drive for about 400 m. Here you will see the sign for Periwinkle Place along with a sign forbidding overnight parking or camping. This little-used gravel road ends within a few metres of the shore behind a few logs and a section of salt-tolerant vegetation. Parking is easy here, mostly because you are unlikely to find any other cars.

Path It is difficult to say how far you need to walk to get onto the shore, simply because the upper shore slopes so gradually that the supra-tidal zone merges almost indiscernibly into the intertidal zone. You will pass

Hornby: Periwinkle Place

patches of logs, polished gravel and salt-tolerant vegetation as you walk toward the water.

Beach It is hard to find a beach anywhere with such an indistinct uppermost shore, blending as it does into the landforms above the tide. A few patches of logs make reasonably welcoming perching spots, but the beach is otherwise not hugely appealing as a picnicking spot. Once you have made your way past the bits of salt-tolerant vegetation, you will see that the shore of largely conglomerate rock slopes gradually toward the low-tide line, about 100 m away.

Suitability for children This is a safe piece of shore, easily explored by even very small children. A few tidal pools, home to starfish and sculpins, will act as magnets to many small children—but not all. This is a good spot to enjoy for its unusual features, not for swimming, picnicking or water play.

Suitability for groups You can easily bring several cars here without feeling that you are invading a closed community. Since you will find no facilities and few places for comfortable picnicking, though, you will win kudos as a group leader by bringing only those who are interested in poking about a strange piece of shoreline or undertaking a full-whammy shore walk.

View Framed by a picturesquely weathered fir, the perspective along the shoreline to your right is an especially appealing combination of head-lands and trees. Across the northern Strait of Georgia, the lumps and bumps of Texada Island, some 20 km distant, seem to blend into the mainland behind.

Winds, sun and shade The winds that blow up and down the strait also blow across this shore, though largely parallel to it. Except by the little shorefront fir, most of this shore is without a trace of shade all day long.

Beachcombing Like several other access points along this stretch of coast, this is an excellent one from which to begin a significant bit of shorefront exploration. Head to your left, and you can walk for several kilometres, much of it on wave-worn strata of sandstone and conglomerate rock.

Seclusion The access road ends close beside one house. Although houses dot the shoreline in either direction, they are well spaced, and this whole area is little visited.

42
CLAM SHELL PLACE
A low, exposed promontory of weathered grass overlooking a lunar shore surface of eroded conglomerate rock and giant tidal pools

Location, signs and parking Drive along Shingle Spit Road for about 2.5 km where, at a slight jog, the main cross-island road changes name to Central Road. After about 7 km, when you come to a crossroads, turn left onto St. John's Point Road and carry on 1 km to another intersec-tion. Continue on St. John's Point Road to the right. Roughly 2.5 km along, turn left onto Gurney Road and follow it to a T-junction about 150 m later. Turn left onto Anderson Drive for about 150 m until you see the sign for Clam Shell Place and another telling you not even to think about camping or parking overnight. Unusually for Hornby Island, too, you will see a warning from the Department of Fisheries about the (lethal) dangers of paralytical shellfish poisoning. After all, this is "Clam Shell Place."

Path Far from having to stagger down a steep path, you can drive right onto the low rock outcropping. Like a rounded concrete ramp, it merges gradually into the upper shore. Kayakers can obviously get their craft easily onto the shore, but if they are wise, they will use this as a launching spot only at or near high tide. If you are caught out during wretched weather, this is one of the best spots on the island for being able to nibble on a car picnic in full view of the ocean. Winter, when the tide is usually in during the day and when waves from the southeast can create a minor furor, can be a particularly good time for a car picnic.

Beach Somewhat like the beaches at some other spots accessible from Anderson Place, the one here is little short of bizarre. Eroded into strangely shaped crests and troughs, the surface, largely of conglomerate rock, seems a little like a paved lunar surface. A particular large declivity to the left of the access point creates a kind of inlet at mid tides and a huge tidal pool at the lowest tides. A small cluster of logs and beach grass on a raised bit of shore jutting out to the right could make for an inviting and unusual picnic spot.

Suitability for children If you prep your children well, and possibly tempt them with a few crunchy treats, you can make an unusual event of your exploration of this shore. The walking is secure, slippery only near the low-tide line. The hunt for chitons, limpets, frilled dog whelks and many other shore treasures can add to the fun. Even so, you should realize, as your child very quickly will realize, that a visit here is not a visit to a normal "beach."

Suitability for groups The beach has sufficient space and sufficient parking that you can bring a few cars packed with eager explorers. It will have to be eager explorers, however, who will want to come here, not your average basker.

View Although the point of access is on a small promontory, most of the shore is concave in either direction. The result is that your view is framed by perspectives up and down a small section of Hornby Island's north coast. Across 20 km of open water, Texada Island, by far the largest island in the Strait of Georgia, covers almost the entire range of your view.

Winds, sun and shade If there is wind out there, there is wind in this bay. If there is sun in the sky, there is sun here.

Beachcombing Beachcombing is probably the chief draw of this place. Come equipped with sturdy shoes, camera, water bottle and the rest, and set out for an intriguing exploration of many kilometres of shoreline. For maximum isolation and the least interrupted walking, head left, possibly arranging a pickup at the Ostby Road access or, if you are truly ambitious, at Grassy Point.

Seclusion While the end of the access road seems almost to be in the front yard of a neighbouring house, this is an uncongested part of the coast. You can see the occasional house, but not many. As for fellow beachgoers, most won't drift here from the public parks or Whaling Station Bay.

43
MYRL PLACE
A drive-on access to a peculiar, extensive shore of conglomerate rock and tidal pools

Location, signs and parking Drive along Shingle Spit Road for about 2.5 km where, at a slight jog, the main cross-island road changes name to Central Road. After about 7 km, when you come to a crossroads, turn left onto St. John's Point Road and carry on 1 km to another intersection. Continue on St. John's Point Road to the right. Roughly 2.5 km along, turn left onto Gurney Road and follow it to a T-junction about 150 m later. Turn left onto Anderson Drive for about 75 m until you see the sign for Myrl Place and another sign squelching any scheme you might have had to set up your tent or settle in with your Kozy Kamper Kween. Follow the narrow gravel road about 75 m until you decide the road stops and the shore starts.

Path You can drive right onto the upper shore. This is the place to weather a storm while snugly sipping steaming drinks, or to get your kayaks easily onto the shore. You will be either frustrated or a gluttor. for punishment, however, if you arrive with your kayaks when the tide is out. The water, at low tide, is a full 200 m away.

Beach By any standards except, perhaps, those of Hornby Island, the beach is strange. In fact, you might do a double take until you realize what appears to be weathered concrete is, in fact, conglomerate rock. Undulating in waves and long, low crests, this dark-grey rock stretches about 200 m to the low-tide line. At various low points and in varicus pockets, you will see patches of rounded gravel and tidal pools. Intriguing to look at and explore, the beach has no particularly inviting picnic spots, at least not where the access road ends. In a pinch, you can find a comfortable roosting spot on some of the nobbly bits or on one of the weathered logs nearby.

Suitability for children If you—or, more to the point, your children—think of this as an interesting piece of geography to explore rather than a beach, then you will find this a safe and child-friendly place to wander and peer. Although the lowest part of the shore is a little seaweed-slippery, it is generally level enough that even there, wandering is easy. Water shoes will make negotiating the shallow tidal pools a breeze.

Suitability for groups Clearly, a herd of bovine picnickers and baskers will not be pleased if you guide them here. If you are part of an outdoors or walkers' club, though, you can provide a novel break from the usual forest park walks by starting an exploration here.

View Expansive and uncluttered, your view from here is partly up the northern end of the Strait of Georgia, but, for the most part, it is dominated by the high, undulating flank of Texada Island. To your right, a few hundred metres away, your view is framed by the pebbly bay at the end of Isabelle Place beach access.

Winds, sun and shade Bring a windbreaker if the day is cool and a northwest wind is up to its usual tricks. Even a southeast wind can whisk a little uncomfortably along this shore. If the day is hot, however, you will be pleased that the shore is exposed to these cooling winds. The upper part of the shore collects some patches of shade during the afternoon, but the shoreline is low and the trees are fairly sparse.

Beachcombing You could do much worse than make this the starting point of a full-on beach walk to your left. You will tromp over a few gravelly beaches, but most of your walk will take you over a wide, generally solid shelf of conglomerate or sandstone rock for several kilometres. Tralee Point is about 3 km away and Grassy Point another 3 km beyond that.

Seclusion You can glimpse a summer house on either side of this access road and others along this entire stretch of shore, but "glimpse" is the operative word. Most locals laudably prize the Garry oaks, arbutus and firs that grow along this low, exposed shore.

44

ISABELLE PLACE

A broad grassy track to a north-facing bay with pebbly upper shore, a huge tidal pool and sandstone outcroppings

Location, signs and parking Not quite the shortest way, but certainly the simplest, begins with a drive along Shingle Spit Road for about 2.5 km, where, at a slight jog, the main cross-island road changes name to Central Road. After about 7 km, when you come to a crossroads, turn left onto St. John's Point Road and carry on 1 km to another intersection. Continue on St. John's Point Road to the right. Very roughly 3 km along, it merges with Anderson Drive. Take a hard left onto Anderson Drive. About 400 m along, spot the sign for a house numbered 7370 and, immediately opposite, the gravel road, Isabelle Place, leading toward the shore about 50 m away. At the end of the road, you will find room to park and a sign telling you that, as at other similar spots on Hornby Island, overnighters are verboten. At the same time, note that this is an attractive spot to park, with only a slightly restricted view of the sea, and therefore one to keep in mind for a car picnic if the weather gods have delivered rain.

Path Only a dozen or so metres long, the wide path leads past salal and high grass down dirt steps. The post-and-rope installation can help if the path seems a little daunting. Kayakers could easily manage their vessels here but will probably want to come at, or near, high tide.

Beach Situated at the base of a bay about 150 wide, the upper beach is a slope of fine, loose gravel curving for a considerable distance in either direction and punctuated with a few logs. Low tide retreats almost 200 m to reveal a complex beach with a little bit of everything. Here you will find an area of soft sand, a giant tidal pool, a patch of rocks and, most interesting, a high outcropping of layered sandstone extending across much of the bay.

Suitability for children Many children can be happy here, particularly if they are nimble and easily switched into exploration mode. The upper slope of pebbles is a comfortable spot for grit-free picnicking. The rest of the beach has not only diversity of slope and shore type, but also hundreds of crevices, nooks and pools harbouring strange and exotic sea creatures. At high tide, this is a good swimming beach, but everyone will be happiest if the least stoical members of your family wear their water shoes.

Suitability for groups Although this spot is more or less in the middle of a neighbourhood, the houses are sufficiently well spaced that a small—and civilized—group wouldn't run roughshod over the sensibilities of locals. Keep in mind, though, that your group won't find facilities here. Forewarned is . . . forewarned.

View You will not be alone if you find that your view-spotting eyes don't stray much beyond the middle ground. To your left, the low wooded slopes above the sandstone shore frame your view. To your right, the higher chunk of weathered sandstone stratum cuts across any view you might otherwise have up the northern straits. Still, you can see, some 20 km distant, the northern end of Texada Island and, alas, its gigantic mining scar.

Winds, sun and shade Almost fully protected from the huffing and puffing of a southeasterly blow, this little bay doesn't have even a straw house's worth of protection from winds from the northwest. If you need shelter from the sun, you will have to bring your own. Although you can find a little shade during the first part of the day, this low exposed shore has none in the afternoon.

Beachcombing You can begin a long shore walk in either direction from here. Broad sandstone shelves for much of the way give you good footing and yet diverse features to admire. Don't dash off for distant horizons, though, until you've taken time to peer curiously at the creatures and crevices within this area.

Seclusion Don't expect to be alone, either with your beloved or with mother nature. The few locals you can expect to find, however, will not interfere with your enjoyment of the peculiar pleasures of this peculiar spot.

45 SHAEN PLACE— WHALING STATION BAY
A waterfront parking spot leading to a wide area of beach grass, level sandstone and tidal pools—and to the main beach of Whaling Station Bay

Location, signs and parking First head along Shingle Spit Road for about 2.5 km, where the main cross-island road changes name to Central Road. After about 7 km, when you come to a crossroads, turn left onto St. John's Point Road and carry on 1 km to another intersection. Continue on St. John's Point Road to the right. Very roughly 3 km along, it merges with Anderson Drive. Take the sharp turn left, and about 75 m later, right onto Shaen Place. On the road signpost you will see a sign putting paid to any unlikely plan you might have to spend the night here in your camper van. Another large and complex sign, especially designed for the four access routes to Whaling Station Bay, welcomes you but reminds you to be on your good behaviour in various ways, some obvious, some not. Don't light fires without permission and don't let Lassie run free or despoil the beach. Some—we all hope—less frequent visitors are told not to bring their horses or carve up the sandstone. The sign also helpfully tells you the location of the nearest public facilities.

Path You can drive more or less to the end of this sloping road, and, if the road happens to be empty, park in full view of the shore of Whaling Station Bay. Kayakers and car picnickers might be particularly interested in this feature but should also note that a considerable chunk of foreshore lies between them and the waterline.

Beach The first part of the shore is a strange mixture of shore types. Nearly level, this area is reached only by very high tides. It comprises tall shore grass, dry smooth sandstone and sandy gravel. Indeed, when the tide is nearly high, little islands and raised areas appear above the water. Immediately to the right of this area, a small sandy beach, separate from the main part of the bay, is overlooked by a private house. Most visitors, of course, will want to make a beeline to the stretches of low-tide sand. Notice as you go, though, that the sloping section of sandstone can be treacherously slippery—but, with its tidal pools, also very interesting.

Suitability for children If you have little scuttling children who find remaining upright a bit of an issue, you are probably best off going to the accesses to the beach at Carling Road or Moya Road. Otherwise, this spot has some real advantages over either of those spots. First, you can set up home base on one of the nobbly bits of smooth sandstone without finding that your children seem bent on adding sand to your sandwiches and scalp. Second, you may just well find that when your children have finished dashing around the sandy beach, they will want to settle down for some heavy-duty exploration of tidal pools and rock crevices. Indeed, this part of the sandstone shore is much richer in life than the sandy part of the beach.

Suitability for groups Most access routes to this gorgeous hunk of beach are popular enough with locals that bringing a group of any size would not be a good idea. This comparatively little-used route, however, might be suitable for two or three cars to unload themselves and their beaching gear.

View Located near one end of the nearly circular Whaling Station Bay, this spot looks primarily back along the treed shore around the bay. The comparatively narrow window of view outside the bay is across the northern part of the Strait of Georgia toward the northern half of Texada Island and, beyond, the mountains behind Powell River.

Winds, sun and shade You will feel both northwest and southeast winds here, though the former considerably more than the latter. As for shade, if you need protection from the sun—and you probably do—you will have to bring your own.

Beachcombing You would be well outside the norms of average beaching behaviour if you didn't want to walk, saunter or scamper across the 200 m of beach. If this experience merely sets you up for more ambitious exploring, you can venture your way along the shore for many kilometres. If you come here more than once, you might choose to go in one direction one day and the other direction another day, even making your way to the right over the broad and diversified shore as far as Helliwell Park.

Seclusion This part of the bay is much less popular than the others, but it is hardly secluded. Among other things, as you will notice, you are well within the sightlines of several shorefront houses, poised to look askance if you toss aside the decorum of civilization.

While you're here . . . About 150 north along Anderson Drive, Roselyn Place leads a short distance to a lovely viewpoint from the top of a small but steep sandstone bank.

Hornby: View over Denman from Mount Geoffrey

46 MAUDE ROAD— WHALING STATION BAY

An unusual upper shore composed of a long, level shelf of smooth sandstone, bordering the west end of Whaling Station Bay and its expanses of near-perfect sand

Location, signs and parking From the ferry terminal, head first along Shingle Spit Road for about 2.5 km until the point that the main cross-island road changes name to Central Road. After about 7 km, when you come to a crossroads, turn left onto St. John's Point Road and carry on 1 km to another intersection. Continue on St. John's Point Road to the right. Very roughly 3 km along, it merges with Anderson Drive. About 100 m along Anderson Drive, you will spot a single signpost with three signs, one identifying the road as Maude Road, others indicating that this is a beach access and that you shouldn't even think about camping or parking overnight. You can park on either side of this short, rough bit of road, but don't be surprised if most of the spots are already taken and you need to park along the shoulder of Anderson Drive.

Path Unlike the other access routes to this beach, this one requires a little hoofing, first down a sloping dirt track past a little beachfront shed, then across an area of high beach grass, and finally onto a flat slab of sandstone. In all, though, you need to tote what or whomever you are toting only about 20 m, and the surface is easy.

Beach The main part of the beach, and the main reason for coming here in the first place, is the gorgeous expanse of fine, packed sand that fills the 200 m long beach and, at low tide, is about 200 m between high- and low-tide lines. What distinguishes this access spot from the others at the end of the bay, though, is the long smooth slab of sandstone along the uppermost shore. If you choose this sand-free zone for laying out your beachware and munchables, not only can you enjoy grit-free egg sandwiches, but also you can get quick and easy access to the lower part of the sands. If you are after a swim at mid to high tide, this can be an attractive and convenient launching platform into the deeper water of Whaling Station Bay.

Suitability for children Because the sandstone strip of the upper shore drops a half metre or so first onto a small area of rocks bordering the sandy beach, small children might be happier at one of the other, more level access spots at Carling Road or Moya Road. For other children, though, this can be a great place to set up camp outside the loose sand and still within easy reach of all of the romping, running and digging that children have foremost in their little beach-loving minds.

Suitability for groups In principle, you could come here with a small group and find lots of space both to picnic and to wander. In fact, though, this can be a popular spot for locals, so parking can be congested. You are best off, therefore, coming with only a small group and being prepared to move to another spot if the parking here is too tight.

View From this side of Whaling Station Bay, the main view outside the bay is directly across the northern Strait of Georgia, some 20 km wide at this point, and onto the huge scar of the mining operation on Texada Island. Otherwise, your view is of the nearly circular shores of the bay itself and its low forested shoreline punctuated with houses.

Winds, sun and shade If the day is a little chilly anyway and a northwest wind is howling its way down the straits, you might regret this choice of spots. Otherwise, expect lots of sun and lots of warmth on this exposed, shade-free shoreline.

Beachcombing After you've finished barefooted jogging through the crystal-clear wavelets, you may have a yen for a bit more exploration. You can, in fact, walk for many kilometres along the mostly level shore on both sides of the bay. However, you should wear shoes appropriate to a shore walk with some rough surfaces and wet spots. Tralee Point, roughly 4 km to the west, makes a good destination for the committed walker.

Seclusion A quick glance will reveal that you are in sight of many houses, some overlooking this bit of shore, and more sprinkled around the bay. In addition, the large beach itself is almost certain to be also sprinkled with other beach-lovers. The key word in both cases, though, is "sprinkled." You won't be alone, but you also won't be in anything approaching a crowd.

While you're here . . . You would be doing a disservice to yourself not to carry on a little farther down Anderson Drive to Helliwell Road and the short distance to the parking lot for Helliwell Provincial Park. Probably the most visited spot on Hornby Island after Tribune Bay, this large, forested park is exceptional for its magnificent clifftop walks with views down the Strait of Georgia and over Flora Islet. However, the section of trail along the northern coast does allow access to low areas. You will find some pretty and protected pebble-and-rock bays and low rocky headlands that often include middens, some of them evidently once much used. At low tide, it is possible to walk over 300 m out along an irregular sequence of spits and reefs almost to Flora Islet.

47 MOYA ROAD—
WHALING STATION BAY
Level, easy access to the central part of the fine sandy beach in Whaling Station Bay

Location, signs and parking From the ferry, follow the signs toward Tribune Bay Provincial Park—though that is not your destination. The route involves going along Shingle Spit Road for about 2.5 km, where the main cross-island road changes name to Central Road. After about 7 km you come to a crossroads. Turn left onto St. John's Point Road and carry on 1 km to another intersection. Continue on St. John's Point Road to the right. Very roughly 3 km along, it merges with Anderson Drive. About 500 m along Anderson Drive, look for signs saying MOYA ROAD, BEACH ACCESS and NO CAMPING OR OVERNIGHT PARKING. Other signs show where you can't park. Another large sign, specifically made for Whaling Station Bay, has multiple messages. Some, like the ones telling you not to bring horses or carve on the sandstone, are unlikely to affect your planning. Others, telling you that your favourite hound must be leashed and that you may not light fires without permission from the fire chief, could. Be aware that the only public washroom is located at the Carling Road access near the east end of the beach.

Path The short, flat gravel road ends virtually on the shore behind a patch of knee-high beach grass. The path, between two large boulders, is only a dozen or so level metres to the sand. If the day has turned nasty and you have an overstuffed picnic hamper, this is a good spot to console yourself with a cozy car picnic complemented by a sea view.

Beach Almost as perfect as Tribune Bay, and about half the size, the beach at Whaling Station Bay at low tide is a nearly circular stretch of fine, grey sand, about 200 m in diameter. Curiously, the beach has only a few logs for picnic props, but it does have a wide stretch of dry, sugary sand perfect for laying out towels and treats.

Suitability for children If you've promised to reward your room-tidying children with a day at the beach, they will feel well rewarded if you choose this spot. As you load up the family car, feel free to include just about every piece of beaching paraphernalia in your arsenal. This is the kind of shore where everything from masks, snorkels and skimboards to buckets and spades can be well and thoroughly used.

Suitability for groups This narrow, short access road with its limited parking is often chockablock with cars. While you can find a little parking on the shoulder of Anderson Drive, don't plan to come here with more than one or possibly two other cars. Instead, head to Tribune Bay Provincial Park, with its capacity to handle a cast party for the *Titanic*.

View The undulating skyline far in the distance beyond the mouth of the bay is the northern end of Texada Island. This fairly limited window on the world of the waters beyond the bay is largely the result of the nearly circular shape of Whaling Station Bay. Thus you see mostly the curving treed shore hyphenated with little houses. Most distinctive is the bare rocky promontory on the east side of the bay framing the whole sweep of the shore.

Winds, sun and shade If you're planning a beach day on Hornby Island, make a special point of checking the marine forecast. Unless the day is hot, a strong northwesterly can do an impressive job of creating goose-flesh on this beach. If the folk on the beach of nearby Tribune Bay are ducking for cover from a southeasterly, however, you may be roasting here. The heat of the beach in the afternoon is amplified by the fact that most of the shade cast by the shorefront firs disappears in the afternoon.

Beachcombing Almost every visitor will want to wander barefooted through, around and over the expanse of compacted, fine sand. If you want to explore beyond the bay, you can stride for kilometres in either direction but will probably find most appealing the walk leading toward and beyond the left side of the bay. Obviously, you will need shoes, though crocs or flip-flops might be enough for a shoreline dominated by undulating slabs of smooth sandstone broken by pebbles and gravel bays.

Seclusion A favourite spot with locals and, to boot, located in the middle of a thoroughly developed little subdivision, this beach is not even slightly secluded. You may, however, be disappointed if you arrive expecting to find beach crowds to admire the results of your efforts in the gym.

48 CARLING ROAD— WHALING STATION BAY

Probably the most convenient access route to the magnificent sandy beach of Whaling Station Bay

Location, signs and parking Bustle off the ferry and straight ahead on the shore-hugging Shingle Spit Road for about 2.5 km. At a slight jog to the right, the main cross-island road changes name to Central Road. Stay on this road for roughly 7 km until you come to a crossroads. Turn left onto St. John's Point Road until, almost 1 km along, you come to another crossroads. Continue right along St. John's Point Road. Very roughly 3 km along, it merges with Anderson Drive. About 700 m along Anderson Drive, look on your left both for the Carling Road sign and a green-and-white BEACH ACCESS sign. At this point you will also see a sign trashing your plans for overnight parking or camping. Farther along this short dirt road, you will see a pit toilet tucked into the bushes and a sign of instructions and prohibitions. Along with the fairly predictable instructions to keep dogs leashed and clean up after them, and to check with the fire chief about fire regulations, is the surprising—but welcome—prohibition against horses. You will also see a sign unique to Hornby Island and this bay in particular—not to carve in the sandstone!

Path Along with the outhouse, the feature that many will find most attractive about this particular approach to the beach is that you can drive within a few metres of the shore. Not only can you, therefore, get all those squirming children and overloaded picnic totes onto the shore easily, but you can also, during miserable weather, come here for a cozy little car picnic.

Beach The beach of perfect, silver sand at Whaling Station Bay is surpassed only by that at Tribune Bay. At low tide, it stretches for about 200 m along the shore and 200 m toward the waterline. A broad strip of sugary loose sand covers the uppermost beach, but, oddly, is lined with very few beach logs. While the water can be reasonably warm at most tides, choose high tide if you are looking for the warmest swim.

Suitability for children It is difficult to imagine many more perfect beaches for most children than this one. The particular pleasures will vary with the tide, of course, but the most common pattern for a summer's afternoon is for warm waters to rise during the course of several hours, inundating teetering sandcastles to the accompaniment of shrieks and mad scrambles. Older children can exhaust themselves skimboarding at the tide line, and the littlest children can splash happily in the bath-warm water of the few large tidal pools.

Suitability for groups While just about any group will find lots of space on the beach itself, they will not find lots of parking space or lots of space between shorefront houses. The conclusion? Take most groups to nearby Tribune Bay Provincial Park—unless a southeast wind is making life wretched there and you really need the protection. If you do come to Whaling Station Bay with a few cars' worth of fellow beach-lovers, use Carling Road as your access spot since you have access to an outhouse here.

View One of the unusual features of this bay is that it is narrower across its mouth than across its middle. The result is that from most points, and especially this one, your view is mostly of the shores of the nearly circular bay. A thick forest dotted with houses lines the shore for most of this circle, while a picturesquely bleak promontory—Cape Gurney, also laden with houses—juts partway across the east side of the bay.

Winds, sun and shade Unlike Tribune Bay, which is almost completely sheltered from a northwest wind, Whaling Station Bay can be thoroughly buffeted by this wind. Also unlike Tribune Bay, however, this beach is well protected from a southeast wind. In fact, given the proximity of the two beaches, you could hardly ask for a better-designed set of windy day choices. You can easily sprawl in the sun's rays throughout most of the day, but the uppermost beach is shady during the first half of the day.

Beachcombing While walking within the bay itself is fairly limited, if you want to go for a tromp, don a pair of shoes and set out along the low sandstone shelf in either direction. Probably, however, you will find the walk leading along the shore to the left the easiest going.

Seclusion This beach backs up against a dense little development. You will be aware of houses and, possibly, their occupants of you, no matter where you turn, though most of the houses here are nestled among trees. As for fellow beachgoers, however, most of them head straight for . . . Tribune Bay—most, but not all.

49
TEXADA DRIVE
A little-used grassy track to a large expanse of level, mixed shore on the exposed northeast coast, separated from Whaling Station Bay by Cape Gurney

Location, signs and parking Trundle off the ferry and straight ahead on the shore-hugging Shingle Spit Road for about 2.5 km. At a slight jog to the right, the main cross-island road changes name to Central Road. Stay on this road for roughly 7 km until you come to a crossroads. Turn left onto St. John's Point Road until, almost 1 km along, you come to another crossroads. Turn right to continue on St. John's Point Road. Very roughly 3 km along, it merges with Anderson Drive. When Anderson Drive comes to an end at Texada Drive, turn left and, as you approach, 100 m along, keep your eyes peeled for a road-width track, often overgrown with grass, leading to the right. Although you could risk driving partway down this rutted track, you are best off simply squeezing onto the narrow shoulder of Texada Drive to begin your exploration.

Path About 50 m long, this level track is an easy walk past a few clusters of bushes dotting an increasingly open grassy area. Anyone except those with the most extreme walking difficulties will find this an easy stroll, at least most of the way. Depending on how enthusiastic previous visitors and winter storms have been, you might have to push your way through some knee-high beach grass and climb over a few logs.

Beach This is a curious bit of shoreline, something of an acquired taste, but for those into exploration mode, certainly worth checking out. Areas of salt-tolerant vegetation on the left merge into a broad patch of compacted gravel. Farther to your right, low, mostly level slabs of sandstone are dotted with a few giant boulders and at least one large tidal pool. At low tide, about 150 m of this odd and diverse shore lies between you and the water's edge.

Suitability for children Most children will cheerfully throw a holy fit if you bring them here instead of adjacent Whaling Station Bay. If, however, you stop here as part of an afternoon's package that includes the neighbouring sandy beach, older, curious children will actually find a much greater diversity of shoreside treasures here than on the sandy tidal flats. The lack of cliffs or difficult areas to traverse also makes this spot suitable for a family wander.

Suitability for groups Only a few friends who share a love of diversity and a curiosity for seeing as many facets of Hornby Island as they can would be interested in coming here. In any case, the parking is limited and the space between neighbouring houses not great.

View To your right, roughly 15 km away, you can pick out the low, bumpy skyline of Lasqueti Island's northern tip. Directly in front, about 20 km of open water separates you from the higher and much larger Texada Island. Unfortunately, you get a clear view of the huge scar from the mining operations there. If you are looking for Powell River, you won't see it because, from this angle, it is tucked behind Texada.

Winds, sun and shade This is probably one of the most generally exposed spots on Hornby Island, in part because of the lack of many large trees, in part because it is on a piece of coast where most winds meet nary an impediment as they scoot up and down the Strait of Georgia.

Beachcombing Shore walkers will find this a great place to begin a 2 km exploration of the broad, oddly configured sandstone intertidal zone that extends all the way to Helliwell Park and St. John's Point at its southeast tip.

Seclusion Almost no visitors come to this spot. Witness the thickets of untrampled beach grass. While several houses are built along this strip of shore, none of them crowds close to the strip of access land.

50 TRIBUNE BAY PROVINCIAL PARK

The best-known beach on Hornby Island, considered by many the most beautiful beach of the Salish Sea

Location, signs and parking With your car stuffed with beach paraphernalia, head from the ferry along Shingle Spit Road for about 2.5 km. At a slight jog in the road, continue along the main cross-island road now called Central Road. Stay on this road for roughly 7 km until you come to a crossroads. Turn left onto St. John's Point Road, and after about 500 m, you will see the sign for Tribune Bay Provincial Park. Turn right, and another 500 m will bring you to a huge, doughnut-shaped parking area. En route you will notice various signs telling you, among other things, that dogs must be on leashes, alcohol is forbidden and fires are even more forbidden. You will also notice side paths leading toward picnic tables, a picnic shelter and washrooms, all of which may prove to be key in making your stay here the memorable occasion you have been trying to orchestrate.

Path A broad level path leads toward the shore, descending through an area of loose sand as you approach the upper beach of logs. The path is manageable for those with walking difficulties, but the easiest route to a nearby sandy beach is at Little Tribune Bay.

Beach Wind up for enthusiastic exclamations as you dig out your bathing suits, cold chicken salads and sunblock. Nearly a kilometre long and 300 m from upper beach to low-tide line, this almost flawless expanse of fine, silver sand is jaw-droppingly beautiful. Even at low tide, it is one of the warmest swimming beaches in the Salish Sea, and, at high tide, can become almost bathtub warm.

Suitability for children You won't be able to find any beach anywhere that is more likely to rocket your little ones into a stratosphere of beachy bliss. The practical conveniences of this large public beach, along with its acres of sand, logs and warm water, are a recipe for a whomping good afternoon.

Suitability for groups By far the best spot on either Denman or Hornby Island for a mammoth food, sun and sand fest, this park has everything. Do be aware that, while your Elvis Imitators Convention may not camp here, they will find a large commercial campsite within walking distance of the beach. Also be aware that not all the public facilities are beside the entrance to the beach. A trail runs parallel to the beach through an open area to more facilities.

View While virtually all other large sandy beaches on the Salish Sea have broad views, this beach is remarkable for the way the view of the Strait of Georgia is framed by promontories. The high, heavily forested shore on the north side of Tribune Bay curves out of sight to St John's Point, the location of another, equally remarkable must-see, Helliwell Provincial Park. The much smaller but equally pretty peninsula at the right end of the beach separates Tribune Bay from another charmer in the world of sandy beaches, Little Tribune Bay.

Winds, sun and shade While almost all other large sandy beaches in the Salish Sea are exposed to the sometimes chilling effects of northwest winds, that at Tribune Bay is almost completely protected. Not so, however, from a southeast wind. These generally chillier and more unpredictable winds funnel straight into Tribune Bay. The protection from most winds, along with the lack of shade, can make the whole beach a little bit of an oven. If you don't have your own protection from the sun and heat, you can find shade among the large firs but will have to move well back from the beach.

Beachcombing Everyone who visits this beach walks, jogs or cartwheels along the water's edge for the full length of the bay. Not everyone, but many, intrigued by the convolutions of the smooth sandstone promontory at the right side of the bay, will venture out and around this easily walked chunk of geography. Once on the other side, shore walkers will find Little Tribune Bay, almost but not quite as beautiful as Tribune Bay itself, but offering the option of a little nude sunbathing and swimming.

Seclusion This is one of the most natural-feeling large public beaches on the Salish Sea, thanks, in large measure, to the almost complete lack of private buildings within sight. It is, however, the least "secret" beach in the Northern Gulf Islands. Unless you come during wretched weather or mid-winter, you will not be even remotely alone.

51 SHIELDS ROAD— TRIBUNE BAY

A broad level path through well-pruned bushes to the sculpted shelf of undulating sandstone and tidal pools at the south end of Tribune Bay

Location, signs and parking Trundle off the ferry and straight ahead on shore-hugging Shingle Spit Road for about 2.5 km. At a slight jog to the right, the main cross-island road changes name to Central Road. Stay on this road for roughly 7 km until you come to a crossroads. At this point, oddly, Central Road is also the name of the right turn onto the crossing road. Your mission is to drive straight through the crossroads onto Shields Road until it ends about half a kilometre later in a large gravel turnaround area. A hand-lettered sign on a tree firmly instructs you to banish all thoughts of starting fires.

Path About 30 m long, this broad, level gravel path leads past a wildly spray-painted outhouse and through a lane-like thicket of trimmed bushes. The last few metres before you reach the sandstone shelf are through soft dry sand. In spite of the slightly unstable footing here, those with walking difficulties may find this access to the large beach on Tribune Bay to be easier than the one from the main park.

Beach Many are understandably immoderate in their enthusiasm for this beautiful beach. About 700 m long and, at low tide, 200 m wide, this perfect expanse of silver sand curves gracefully along the head of a deeply inset bay. Shields Road access brings you just beyond the end of this beach to the base of a promontory of sandstone. Underfoot you will find a broad expanse of gently undulating rock, patches of sand, tidal pools and remarkably shaped lumps of sandstone. For picnicking, you can choose either the uppermost beach with its patches of logs or the middle part of the beach with its lumpy natural picnic tables of sandstone.

Suitability for children Some experienced parents will find this access better than the main one through the park. Avoiding the sand, you can set up camp in a sandstone nook and yet easily venture toward the stretches of sand where most children will go berserk with water wings, spades and skimboards. One of the beauties of this spot is that you can arrive at any tide and still have lots of warm water for swimming yet sand for scampering. In addition, the whole playground of the sandstone shelf invites dozens of other options, most of them involving climbing over imagination-stirring formations or combing through tidal pools of skittering fish and crabs.

Suitability for groups While the largest groups will, sensibly, want to go to the nearby provincial park, some groups, knowing the advantages of this approach to the same beach, might prefer this route, assured of good parking, access to an outhouse and more space than they will know what to do with.

View One of the features that make this beach in the running for the most beautiful in the Salish Sea is the largely untouched headlands and bluffs of grass and forest that frame both sides of the view. To the north, high bluffs curve out of sight well into Helliwell Park. To the south, a much shorter and lower promontory is similary beautifully treed. Almost inevitably, your view will be sprinkled with dozens of pleasure boats moored in the bay.

Winds, sun and shade No other large, sandy beach in the Salish Sea is as well protected from a northwest wind, the most common wind during the kind of sunny weather when you are likely to treat your children or yourself to a day at the beach. If you happen to choose a day with a southeast wind, however, take consolation in the fact that your kite will be well supplied with wind and that you won't find much shade cooling you more than you want. On a very warm day you can find some shade, especially during the late afternoon, near the uppermost part of the beach.

Beachcombing Only the most indolent, overfed or rheumatic will be able to refrain from beach walking. The dilemma most will face is whether to yield first to the temptation to walk, jog or leapfrog your way along the enticing long beach to your left or to explore the bizarre configurations of sandstone rising out of the easily walked shore to your right. Out of sight, but wonderful to visit, is Little Tribune Bay, a surprisingly short distance around this southern promontory. Clearly, any reasonable shore-goer will—no, *must*—walk in both directions.

Seclusion Unless you arrive when the rest of humanity is asleep or huddled away from bad weather, you will find others somewhere at Tribune Bay, though not necessarily at this access spot. On the other hand, you will never find it crowded and, because the bay is free from massive residential developments, you will feel deliciously immersed in a breathtakingly gorgeous corner of the natural world.

52
LITTLE TRIBUNE BAY
A beautiful stretch of sand with patches of boulders and mounds of beach logs, popular with both nudists and non-nudists

Location, signs and parking Beetle your way off the ferry along Shingle Spit Road for about 2.5 km. At a slight jog to the right, the main road changes name to Central Road and turns inland. After roughly 7 km, you will come to a crossroads. At this point, oddly, to stay on Central Road, turn right. A mere 200 m later, turn left onto Little Tribune Road, a rough road of about 300 m, ending in an irregular gravel area with parking for several cars on either side. In wretched weather, when you don't need to worry about blocking the way onto the shore for fellow nudists, you can even park almost on the shore, in full view of whatever crashing and thrashing a southeast storm is dishing up. The only sign here is aimed at those who would park between 11 p.m. and 7 a.m. and thus have their car "impounded." Note for future reference the handy outhouse tucked into the bushes.

Path This is by far the easiest and shortest access to a sandy beach on this side of the island—or it is if winter storms haven't created a chaotic logjam along the uppermost beach. You can manage a brace of kayaks into the water here, but, unless you choose high or mid tide, will get more of a workout en route to the water than on it.

Beach Whether you consider the term "Little Tribune Bay" to be appropriate or not depends on whether you are thinking of the strip of sandy beach or the whole bay. The sandy section merges into a broad intertidal expanse of flat sandstone and loose rocks. Less than half the length of the larger beach, and not quite as wide at low tide, the 300 m of sand are also a little more embellished—or, at least, lined with areas of rock and boulders. No other beach on Hornby Island collects as many logs on its upper beach, trapped at the head of the bay by winter storms from the southeast. Although this is considered the nudist beach of the island, you won't feel out of place if you decide to limit the extent of your . . . suntan. In fact, you are likely to be in the majority.

Suitability for children Unless you are worried about having to explain some basic principles of human anatomy, you could hardly do better in choosing a wonderful beach spot for just about every watery or sandy shenanigan your children have in their repertoire. Bring buckets, spades, Frisbees, skimboards or just a lot of hyperactivity. The close proximity to the car and even the presence of the pit toilet give a practical spin to this wonderful spot. One word of caution, though: on an incoming tide, some of the toe-stubbing boulders can be hidden by the warm turquoise water. Move down the beach to your left to minimize the number of unwelcome encounters with the unwelcome barnacle and consider bringing water shoes, for the most part unnecessary at this beach.

Suitability for groups For a full-on swarm of relatives, go to the nearby provincial park at Tribune Bay. For a more intimate group, you might well prefer this beach for its comparative quietness. Although the outhouse is the only facility to help with the practicalities of having a group, you certainly will find enough space that you needn't feel you are unfairly crowding into an already crowded area.

View If you come here after having been to Tribune Bay, you will be struck with how much more exposed and weathered this bay feels. Instead of thick forests and enclosing promontories, you will see grassy fields dotted with some houses and clusters of wind-battered small trees. Because the mouth of this bay is so wide here, too, you may notice that you seem to be able to see forever down the full fetch of the Salish Sea.

Winds, sun and shade Whether refreshingly welcome or icily unwelcome, the northwest winds that blow on most of Hornby's beaches can scarcely be felt here. On the other hand, even the tiniest trace of a southeast wind, not to mention a perfect storm, are not even slightly moderated before reaching this shore.

Beachcombing Build beachcombing into your plans, and you won't regret it. Obscured by the small treed promontory at the left end of the sandy beach, Tribune Bay lies a short distance in this direction. The walk there past and over surreal sandstone formations is memorable—and photographable. More ambitious explorers can head to their right and make their way over generally easy shore the several kilometres to Sandpiper Beach.

Seclusion Although a few houses dot the shoreline, you are spared the cheek-by-jowl crowds you might expect at such a beautiful piece of waterfront. In addition, the houses are set back enough that you will hardly feel in their front yards. On the other hand, this is a popular spot, though mostly with locals and never with hordes.

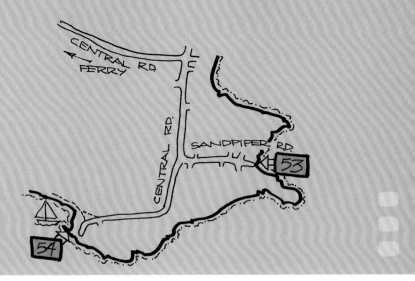

53

SANDPIPER BEACH

A small grassy park and
sandy beach surrounded
by astounding expanses of
sandstone strata

Location, signs and parking From the ferry, head along Spit Road for
about 2.5 km. Where the road heads inland, it changes name to Central
Road. Stay on this road for roughly 7 km until you come to a crossroads.
At this point, oddly, in order to stay on Central Road, take a sharp right
turn. About 2.5 km along, turn left onto Sandpiper Road and follow it
to its end at an open triangular junction with Porpoise Crescent. You
will see a gravel track leading a short distance off the road into a small
parking area surrounded by a split-cedar fence. Half a dozen cars can fit
into this spot easily but you're unlikely to see many others. Here you will
see a sign telling you that, no, you may not camp or park overnight, and
another announcing this to be Sandpiper Community Park.

Path A new crushed-gravel path leads directly ahead from the parking
lot, a few dozen metres down a slope toward the beach. Those with

walking difficulties should find this path easy going, unless their knees are really acting up.

Beach Arrive at high tide, and the beach will seem attractive and unremarkable. You will see an appealing shore of coarse sand and pebbles sprinkled with logs. Arrive at low tide, and you will see a beach such as you are unlikely to have seen before (unless you are familiar with Mayne Island.) A small but appealing lower area of sand immediately in front of the park yields to a huge low-tide expanse of tilted sandstone strata, creating writhing ridges and tidal pools to the low-tide line some 300 m away.

Suitability for children This is a great beach for children of almost all stripes. Unless the little ones need a huge expanse of sand, they will find diversions aplenty. Building sandcastles or raceways in the sandy part of the beach and swimming in generally warm water at high tides are the most conventional pleasures. The strange rock formations and tidal pools will appeal to just about any curious and adventurous child.

Suitability for groups Local groups occasionally use either the grassy field or the shore itself. Don't be surprised if you see a yoga group, for example, greeting the morning sun. With its grassy field and perfect picnicking beach, this spot would suit a small group that prefers a quiet neighbourhood to a large public park. A group interested in exploring the bizarre rock formations of the shore at low tide will be particularly happy to know about this spot.

View The most immediately interesting part of the view is the coastline in both directions. Framed by Downes Point on the right and Dunlop Point on the left, the bay also faces across Tribune Bay to Helliwell Provincial Park, which covers much of St. John's Point. Across about 20 km of open water, the undulating forms of Lasqueti Island are visible on a clear day.

Winds, sun and shade Whether you welcome a cooling wind or dread a chilling one, do expect to feel anything a southeast wind can whomp up. If a northwest wind is churning up the straits, however, you are unlikely to feel much of its cooling effects. While the sun hits the shore most directly during the first part of the day, the lack of shorefront trees means that you will be in full sun throughout the day unless you provide your own shade.

Beachcombing Choose low tide, wear strong shoes and enjoy exploring the uneven strata of the tidal flats. At the lowest tides, you may even be able to reach the reefs off Dunlop Point. If you are still energetic and curious, you can walk all the way to Tribune Bay. If you also feel logistically spry, you can arrange a shuttle or pickup from the park there.

Seclusion Although this park is in the middle of a development, you won't see shorefront houses for a considerable distance on either side of the access path. Because of the dinghies and canoes that locals store here, though, you won't feel even remotely isolated. At the same time, you just may not see or be seen by a single, solitary soul.

54
FORD COVE
A harbour with access to two shores, one a gravel beach good for launching kayaks, the other an undulating sandstone shelf with striking formations

Location, signs and parking From the ferry, head along Spit Road for about 2.5 km. Where the road heads inland, it changes name to Central Road. Stay on this road for roughly 7 km until you come to a crossroads. At this point, to stay on Central Road, take a sharp right turn. About 6 km brings you to the end of the road at Ford Cove. Since this is a public dock with a few shops, it has a large parking area.

Path If you have come here to launch a kayak at the only launching spot for quick access to this part of the coast, you will find a road-width slope of crushed gravel immediately to the right of the wharf. For access to the more popular sandstone shelf, most visitors use an improvised bit of bank beside one of the shops.

Beach Kayakers, beware: the beach to the right of the breakwater stretches nearly 100 m to the low-tide line. While the first few metres are composed of flat, smooth sandstone, the main part of this shore is fairly compact gravel all the way to the low-tide line. On the south side of the breakwater, facing Lambert Channel, the beach is a fascinating version of Gulf Islands sandstone, with smooth undulating waves sprouting Martian protuberances and dotted with tidal pools. Picnickers might want to make a timely visit to the coffee shop here and spread out their shoreside nibblefest among a cluster of the inviting bumps on the shore.

Suitability for children This is far from the kind of shore most children have in mind when you announce that you are going to the beach. Still, most children, even fairly wobbly ones, could have a rollicking good time wandering among, climbing over and peering into the imagination-stirring lumps, bumps, crevices and pools of the sandstone part of the beach. Only the most shore-wise children, however, will be able to descend the fairly steep lower shore to reach the water's edge.

Suitability for groups This is probably not the kind of place to organize a major picnic to welcome the new bride to the family. It is, nevertheless, exactly the kind of place to bring two or three cars' worth of friends in exploration mode. You will find plenty of parking for your kindred spirits and plenty of space along the shore.

View One of the interesting features of this distinctive spot is the perspective it gives on the landmark Mount Geoffrey Escarpment, which drops steeply to the water between Ford Cove and the ferry terminal, about 3 km along the coast. Across Lambert Channel, about 1.5 km wide at this point, is the wooded shore of Denman Island. Perhaps most striking, though, is the view past the south end of Denman, which includes Chrome Island lighthouse and the mountains around Horne Lake on Vancouver Island. Sunset lovers should register the fact that this is one of the best spots on Hornby Island for these spectacular light shows.

Winds, sun and shade All species and subspecies of wind funnel up and down Lambert Channel, but Ford Cove, with its skookum breakwater, is well protected from the waves that accompany the winds. In any case, the shore to the right of the breakwater is considerably less windy, if less enticing, than the outer shore. As for shade, you'll find almost none except during the first part of the day, and only then if you tuck well up toward the upper shore.

Beachcombing Shore explorers and walkers of all sorts may well want to seek this spot out for its distinctive opportunities for memorable walks.

Some will want to walk the Shingle Spit Trail through Mount Geoffrey Escarpment Provincial Park (go to nearby Euston Road to gain access to the two higher trails). The more adventurous can make their way along the fascinating shoreline between here and the ferry terminal, about 3 km away. The real gem here, though, and hidden away from all except those who have been tipped off, is the shore walk to the left of Ford Cove. Comparatively narrow and steep near the waterline, the sandstone shore begins to broaden about half a kilometre along. By the time you reach Norman Point, about 1 km away, you find yourself at an extraordinary chunk of shoreline. Completely isolated from any other public access, the dramatically warped configurations of sandstone at this corner of Hornby Island extend to almost 500 m at low tide and stretch for 1.5 km before the shore suddenly narrows and becomes steep.

Seclusion This busy little cove is very far from being secluded—at least in the normal sense. Since, however, it is literally the "end of the road" without many other destinations along this road, it is far off from the main tourist destinations on the island. Shore walkers, of course, can easily plunge themselves into complete seclusion.

Hornby: Mount Geoffrey Escarpment shoreline

55 MOUNT GEOFFREY ESCARPMENT SHORELINE

Approached from the ferry terminal, an amazing shoreline of lunar conglomerate formations punctuating a sequence of small gravel coves

Location, signs and parking There is no road map for this beach because it is next to the ferry terminal. This is an excellent destination for those who would like to leave their car on Denman Island. Foot passengers to Hornby Island can combine a visit to the Mount Geoffrey Escarpment Provincial Park trails overlooking Lambert Channel with an exploration of this little-visited piece of shoreline at the base of the escarpment. Drive or walk away from the ferry until, about 50 m along the road, at the beginning of the hill, you see a gravel road heading off to the right. If you are driving, you can park along the shoulder here or drive the 150 m down this road to a small turnaround area beside a breakwater and a launching ramp suitable for kayaks. Near the beginning of this gravel road is the sign and trailhead for the trail to Ford Cove that runs along the base of the escarpment. From the end of the gravel road, you will find it easy to make your way onto the pleasant gravel beach next to the ferry terminal. Much more interesting, though, is the section of shore beyond the breakwater, reached by a clear path, a dozen or so metres long.

Path Don't stop on this pleasant but ordinary and exposed gravel beach, but carry on at least as far as the first rocky crest.

Beach Depending on how far you wish to walk in order to choose the perfect spot to tuck yourself away, you can find several enticing options. Patches of boulders, solid outcroppings and spectacularly weird conglomerate bumps are varied with some lovely little gravel coves lined with logs. Comparatively narrow by Hornby Island standards, the shore doesn't become steep until about half a kilometre along.

Suitability for children Not the most obvious choice for the littlest children, this shoreline could be great for children who are nimble of foot and mind. You can spin your visit primarily as an investigation into the Martian landscape, complete with plans to scale as many of the bumps as possible. Alternatively, you can simply find the first attractive nook to spread out your fodder and other beach ware, don water shoes and get as wet as quickly as possible.

Suitability for groups Go to one of the large public parks if you are primarily interested in providing the most comfortable, conventional and capacious site for your group. If you want a quiet and unconventional beach, you can easily come here without even the remote possibility of disturbing locals or feeling cramped.

View Across Lambert Channel, your view is predominantly of the low, undulating landforms of Denman Island. Behind Denman, however, you can pick out the high points of the Beaufort Range on Vancouver Island—Mount Clifton, Mount Chief Frank, Mount Stubbs and so on.

Winds, sun and shade Both northwest and southeast winds waft or bluster their way up and down Lambert Channel. If the day is cool, though, and you want protection, you can almost certainly duck out of wind's way. If you come during the afternoon, on the other hand, you will be hard-pressed to find shade. Basted, broiled and baked, you might be grateful that the cooling water is so close by.

Beachcombing Although this is one of the most interesting pieces of shore on Hornby Island, it is not the easiest to walk after the first half kilometre or so.

Seclusion Partly, perhaps, because it is so close to the ferry terminal, and partly because most visitors are inclined to head to one of the big parks, few seem to make their way to this fascinating piece of shoreline. Don't be surprised if you can make small talk only with the local gulls.

PART 4 **Quadra Island**

⭐ **QUADRA ISLAND STRETCHES ALMOST** the whole length of Discovery Passage, which runs north of Campbell River along Vancouver Island's coast. It is not just one of the Gulf Islands but part of an archipelago of islands, including Cortes, often called the Discovery Islands. Quadra typically puts out its tourist bumph under that appealing name. In fact, Discovery Passage is a key characteristic of the island. This narrow waterway funnels not only all of the deepwater ships heading north and south along the coast but also the fast-moving currents. Although some of the strongest tidal rapids in British Columbia run past the shores of Quadra Island, the southern, most settled end of this large island is far distant from the drama—and danger—of these waters. It is this south end of the island where almost all of its publicly accessible beaches can be found. The short and conveniently scheduled ferry ride from Campbell River across Discovery Passage arrives at this south end, too, adding to the incentives to discover this Discovery Island's beaches.

Although the stereotypical large, sandy beach is not a Quadra feature, the island is blessed in other ways. First, it must rank first among all of the islands for walkers. Not only does the easily accessible but often secluded shore extend for endless kilometres, but also several forested paths run next to wilderness shoreline. Add to that the views of mountains and islands from Quadra Island's shores, views many consider the best in the entire Salish Sea, and you may want to put Quadra high on your list of favourite islands.

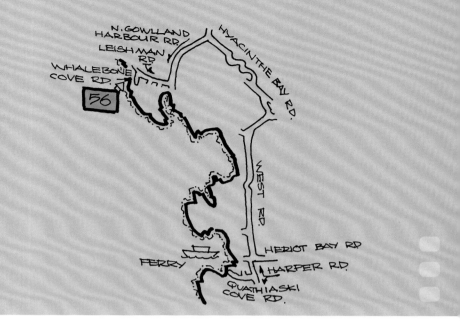

56
WHALEBONE COVE ROAD
The only open access on the west coast of Quadra Island north of Quathiaski Cove, good for shorefront parking and launching kayaks

Location, signs and parking Upon making your way uphill from Quathiaski Cove, turn left onto Harper Road for a little under half a kilometre, right onto Heriot Bay Road, then almost immediately left onto West Road. After roughly 5 km, turn left onto Hyacinthe Bay Road for a little over 4 km until the junction with North Gowlland Harbour Road on your left. Between 3 and 4 km along this road, you will see Leishman Road on your right. Just before the end of Leishman Road, about 1.5 km along, you will see, clearly signposted, Whalebone Cove Road angling back and downhill 100 m to the shore.

Path You will find yourself in a capacious gravel turnaround area, sepa-rated from the upper beach only by a few sparse little trees and a level chunk of wild grass a dozen or so metres wide. From here, getting yourself or your kayak onto the shore is clearly a breeze. Wise kayakers, though, will want to check current and wind conditions, since Discovery Passage can be treacherous.

Beach You will find yourself at the head of a little cove with high rocky banks on either side. The beach, some 50 m wide and extending about 50 m to the low-tide line, is cut through by a small stream. Mostly even and covered with gravel, the beach also has a few clusters of larger rocks and boulders. Unusually, almost no logs have made their way against the upper shore. A small dock belonging to a neighbouring house extends into the bay, and a boat or two is often anchored in front of the beach.

Suitability for children You don't need to worry much about the next generation coming a slippery cropper on this level shore. Children will be kept most busy by floating convoys of driftwood down the little stream, collecting colourful clamshells, or disobeying parental orders to keep feet dry. On the whole, though, this is not the kind of beach you would seek out to reward your child's good behaviour at the doctor's office.

Suitability for groups In some practical terms, especially those involving room for parking and distance from neighbours, this beach is suitable for a group. It is only if a group is toting kayaks or needs a spot for a shorefront car picnic during foul weather that they would feel properly rewarded in coming here.

View From this point on the west coast of Quadra Island, you are north of the main part of Campbell River, some 2 km across Discovery Passage. Thus your view is primarily of a few scattered residences and bits of light industry but, above and behind the city, rise the peaks of Strathcona Park. Because this is the only deep-water channel between the Strait of Georgia and Johnstone Strait, your view is likely to include lots of boat traffic, from tiny fishing boats to giant freighters and even Alaska-bound cruise ships.

Winds, sun and shade If you have come here after visiting the beaches to the north and east off Hyacinthe Road, you will be astounded at how dry and sun-baked the shore here feels after those densely forested coves and bays. Morning is somewhat shady on this south-facing bay, but the afternoon can be stifling, especially if the only breeze on offer is from the northwest.

Beachcombing Most of the beach walking you are likely to do here is a bit of strolling along the intertidal area. If you are really curious and determined, though, head to the right around the point for a view into the little bay to the north. Just out of sight and a short distance south are the Copper Cliffs, plunging not only into the water but far below it. A favourite spot of scuba divers, this underwater "wall" is particularly rich with current-fed sea life.

Seclusion The only reason this access road exists is that developers have created a subdivision here and along the Copper Cliffs. Though you will see only a few houses and probably no other visitors, you won't feel even remotely that you are in a wilderness area. Just so you know.

Quadra: Shellalligan Pass Trail

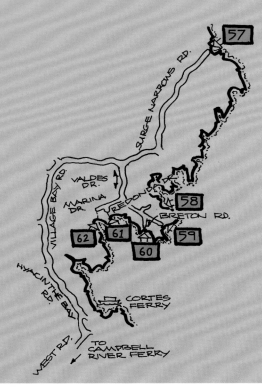

57 HOSKYN CHANNEL
LANDING COMMUNITY PARK
The most remote beach on
Quadra Island and the beginning
of the Surge Narrows shoreline
trail, beside the island's most
protected kayak-launching spot

Location, signs and parking The drive to this shore is long and bumpy.
Those who want to explore Surge Narrows Trail or launch their kayak
here are the most likely to go the distance. Settling in for a scenic drive,
head uphill from Quathiaski Cove, turn left onto Harper Road for a little
under half a kilometre, right onto Heriot Bay Road for 200 m, then left
onto West Road. After roughly 5 km, turn left onto Hyacinthe Bay Road
and keep ahead almost 22 km, as it changes first to Village Bay Road and
then, for the last rustic 5 km or so, Surge Narrows Road. At the end of

the road just past a lodge—oriented to kayakers—you will come across two parking lots, one near the beginning of your descent, one close to a launching ramp. Both are almost certain to be crammed with cars. It won't take you long to realize why you're are not alone, and, indeed, why you would want to bring your kayak here. This is by far the most protected launching spot for exploring the Discovery Islands and Desolation Sound. Most of the other spots closer to Heriot Bay are generally good but require crossing exposed water where, if a southeasterly storm comes up, life might be just a little too interesting.

Path The compacted gravel road drops fairly steeply to the shore so that, even at low tide, you and your trusty kayak can get easily to the water. Near the upper shore, several dinghies await better days. An additional well-built trail with a few gravel-and-board steps leads around a treed knoll to an aluminum walkway and a small floating dock.

Beach This is not even remotely the kind of beach where you want to linger or picnic, though at low tide it is well supplied with squidgy and scuttling creatures. Covered with barnacle-encrusted gravel, it drops smoothly toward the nearby low-tide line.

Suitability for children Children who have been cooped up in the car will be happy to throw a few rocks and lovingly torment a few crabs, but they are unlikely to want to stay here long.

Suitability for groups This is a spot primarily for kayakers and walkers, though curious view seekers should also be intrigued at this unusual spot. You might want to carpool because, even though the parking areas are quite large, you could have more competition than you want.

View Before heading out on your walk or your paddle, make sure you take time to wander along the short path to the right of the launching area and drink in some of the splendid view. The high bluffs of Quadra's northeastern shore curve to a point behind which the strong currents of Surge Narrows churn back and forth four times each day. Three small islands, Peck, Sturt and Gospel, in that order, nestle in front of the much larger and higher Maurelle Island. Across the broad stretch of water to your right, another large island, Read Island, tapers toward the north and the narrow gap, Whiterock Passage, separating Read from Maurelle

Island. Behind the passage, the high and usually snow-clad peaks of the Coast Range provide a dramatic backdrop.

Winds, sun and shade Though some winds funnel along Hoskyn Channel, it is well away from the full blast of most prevailing winds. Most who come to this spot are not likely to care about sun or shade. For the record, though, the whole area is generally shady, especially along Surge Narrows Trail.

Beachcombing While the opportunities for shore walking are virtually nonexistent, the opportunity for walking parallel to the shore and onto the shore is as enticing as the newly constructed trail leading from this spot. About an hour's walk, some of it fairly strenuous and taking you about 150 m above sea level, delivers you to a rocky shore by Surge Narrows. Come when the current is at its strongest and you can witness the peculiar forces at play in these tidal rapids.

Seclusion Although the spot is crowded with cars, you are unlikely to see many people about. On the trail itself, prepare to be surprised if you see a single solitary soul in this area of barely touched wilderness.

58
SHELLALLIGAN PASS TRAIL
A network of forested trails, including one to a protected pebbly bay and another around a rocky headland

Location, signs and parking The journey—and it is a journey—to Valdes Drive begins with the route from Quathiaski Cove toward the Cortes ferry. After toodling uphill from Quathiaski Cove, turn left onto Harper Road for a little under half a kilometre, right onto Heriot Bay Road for 200 m, then left onto West Road. After roughly 5 km, turn left onto Hyacinthe Bay Road for about 5 km until the junction with Village Bay Road. About 8 km later, turn right onto Valdes Road for about 4 km until you see a sign for the Shellalligan Pass Trail and a narrow dirt track. You can also approach from another signposted track off Village Bay Road but will have farther to go down a rough track. You could choose to park on Valdes Road, but, unless your car is particularly low slung or unless the track has been eroded, you should be able to ooze slowly just over 1.5 km along this track to a small parking area.

Path Although the trail system is, roughly, a figure of 8, to get to an attractive beach most quickly, keep more or less ahead and to your right, where you will see a clear, wide path through alder leading directly to the shore, about 100 m distant. In fact, if you are trying to begin a kayak tour around the top end of Read Island and a southeast storm is battering all of the launching spots between Heriot Bay and here, you could trek your kayaks to this protected beach and its access to increasingly protected water.

Beach The uppermost strip is probably the most attractive part of the beach. About 75 m long, this curving shore of pebbles and small gravel is lined with just the right number of logs rather than the hundreds that you will find on most beaches near here. The tide drops almost 100 m, revealing a small patch of wet sand and other areas of gravel and pebbles.

Suitability for children This is probably the most convenient beach for small children in the whole nest of beaches reachable from Village Bay Road. Although they will have to walk a little distance from the family-mobile, they will find a well-protected, gently shelving beach with no greater obstacles than the ever-pesky barnacle. Still, you would be wise to bring water shoes along with your usual arsenal of beaching goods. While the beach is usable at all tides, those children intent on getting as wet as possible, as conveniently as possible, will be happiest at high tide—when the beach is also most attractive.

Suitability for groups This is a remote and completely undeveloped beach. Keeping in mind the limited parking, if you have a small group in mind that would enjoy this kind of beach, you can come confident that you won't be forcing your way into a congested spot.

View Because the bay is fairly narrow and deep, much of your view consists of the picturesquely rugged and forested headlands on either side of the bay. Across Hoskyn Channel, about 2 km wide at this point, you will see the heavily forested crests of Read Island.

Winds, sun and shade Morning is the sunniest part of the day, and the left side of the beach the sunniest end of the beach. On the other hand, the right side of the beach is most protected from winds.

Beachcombing This is a great place to choose if you would like to combine walking with lolling. Instead of strolling along the beach, however, you will be walking along trails, or, at least, marked routes. Some of the most awkward sections, around the rocky headlands and far above the shore, are the most scenic. In fact, the first section, along the headlands to the left of the beach, allows you the best close-up ocean views. If you do the full loop, some two or three hours long, you will come across two smaller beaches, but much of your walking will be some distance from the water. In addition, you will have to complete the loop by walking along a forestry service road.

Seclusion This is a remote spot but a favourite with locals. All this means is that you are likely to have the opportunity to shoot the breeze with an occasional dog walker and otherwise have the place entirely to yourself.

59
VALDES DRIVE
A storm lover's and geologist's paradise, with shorefront parking on a south-facing rocky bay

Location, signs and parking The beach at the end of Valdes Drive, one of a fascinating cluster accessible from Village Bay Road, begins with the route from Quathiaski Cove toward the Cortes ferry. Thus, after heading uphill from Quathiaski Cove, turn left onto Harper Road for a little under half a kilometre, right onto Heriot Bay Road for 200 m, then left onto West Road. After roughly 5 km, turn left onto Hyacinthe Bay Road for about 5 km until the junction with Village Bay Road. About 8 km later, turn right onto Valdes Road for almost 8 km. Since you can drive virtually onto the shore, you are unlikely to experience much uncertainty about finding the beach. You will see two instructive signs, unusual for Quadra, one forbidding fires, the other forbidding overnight parking and camping.

Path Once you've learned that you can drive practically onto the beach, you would be more or less right in deducing that even unsteady walkers can easily get onto the shore—but not completely right. The distance is short, but the logs are many that heap themselves against the uppermost shore. When you see the large CABLE sign on a tree, you'll understand why the dirt road goes all the way to the shore.

Beach The beach is fascinating but hardly conventional. Because it is located on a contact zone between igneous rock and limestone, the outcroppings combine colour in striking variations. Some of the rock, indeed, is said to be marble, and tales of lime kilns and sinkholes hidden among the trees are rife in the area. The beach itself, though, is composed of irregular patches of large, rounded boulders, other patches of small rocks, a large tidal pool and outcroppings of solid rock. At mid to high tide, this would be a reasonably good place to launch kayaks, as long as you don't mind a bit of a stumble over the logs and boulders.

Suitability for children Small children would probably need more rescuing from slips and crashes than you would find conducive to a relaxed beach experience. Older children, however, will need little encouragement to run amok. As long as they don't expect sand and are occasionally fuelled with chocolate chip cookies, they will find everything they need for imaginative and soggy frolicking.

Suitability for groups This is not the kind of spot the average group would have in mind if you promise them an afternoon at the beach. If, however, you want easy parking and lots of shore space with a splendid view, you could do a lot worse than provide two or three cars' worth of long-lost cousins with an intriguing beach experience. Facilities, of course, simply don't exist.

View Both the foreground view of this unusual bit of shore and the background view are crammed with picturesque details. Because the shore is concave at this point, your view is framed by rocky, treed headlands. On your left a string of reefs, exposed at low tide, leads out to the Breton Islands. The centre of your view is the open horizon down the Strait of

Georgia and, on the right, Rebecca Spit. Photographers' alert: you will have a hard time restraining yourself!

Winds, sun and shade Because the beach faces south and is backed by a stand of enthusiastic firs, the right end of the beach starts to become shady shortly after noon. Thus you can determine the amount of shade you want simply by moving along the beach. You aren't quite so lucky with winds. If your friendly weatherperson has predicted a strong southeast wind, then you just might want to hunker down elsewhere. If, however, it is a northwest wind kicking up a fuss, you won't feel a thing at this beach.

Beachcombing Although you won't find this a good place to stride freely, you can find it a good place to explore curiously. Come at low tide and you will no doubt feel drawn to the shore to your right and the arching spit linking two high-tide islets. Locals head along a trail to the left through the woodlot to reach a wonderfully isolated beach at the head of the next bay.

Seclusion To add to the menu of attractive traits, the sense of isolation will rank high for those who like to commune only with nature or with their fellow adventurers.

60
BRETON ROAD
A level path to an isolated pocket cove tucked in between high headlands on Open Bay, good for launching kayaks

Location, signs and parking Though the distance from the ferry is great, the rewards of finding several adjacent beaches are far greater. From Quathiaski Cove, turn left onto Harper Road for a little under half a kilometre, right onto Heriot Bay Road for 200 m, then left onto West Road. After roughly 5 km, and well before the Cortes ferry terminal, turn left onto Hyacinthe Bay Road for about 5 km until the junction with Village Bay Road. About 8 km later, turn right onto Valdes Road for almost

6 km, until you see Breton Road on your right. Another half kilometre will bring you to a kind of fork. The main gravel track swings left, and a dirt track leads straight ahead. Park on the broad shoulder here.

Path Your route to the shore lies between these two larger tracks immediately to the left of the sign indicating the right branch to be private. Although the track to the shore is wide, even and only gradually sloping, it does have one hazard—but only for those wearing shorts and sandals. The hazard? Stinging nettles! You may want to collect some for your dinner while simultaneously contributing to the ease of those following you to this shore.

Beach A little wedge-shaped cove narrows to a tiny, rocky beach, a mere 20 metres wide and bordered by steep rocky outcroppings. Like other south-facing beaches along this part of Quadra, it is mounded with wave-battered driftwood. Since the tide never retreats very far, and since the surface, though rocky, is easily passable, this is a good spot for getting a kayak into the briny.

Suitability for children To get your children to the shore, you will have to teach them the perils of the dreaded nettle. In addition, you may find the attractions of the beach too limited for most children to bother bringing them here. If you are coming here anyway in search of solitude yourself, however, and can throw the odd peanut-butter cookie in the direction of your good-tempered and curious children, you can expect a little reprieve as they toss rocks, hunt for crabs and starfish and commandeer log galleons.

Suitability for groups You wouldn't need to worry about adding to the congestion of an already congested beach if you sought out this isolated spot. Despite the accommodating parking, however, this is the kind of odd beach to visit when your own soul needs a little refurbishing, not the kind of beach that will please the rabble.

View You will feel more embraced by this little cove than perched on the edge of a vast view. Framed by two short headlands of steep rock, the perspective out of the bay is toward Rebecca Spit and the empty stretches of the entire Strait of Georgia.

Winds, sun and shade In spite of the enclosed feeling of the little cove, it is exposed to the southeast winds but, unsurprisingly, completely shielded from winds from the northwest. If you want to bask, bake or broil, come here during the middle part of the day. Otherwise, expect some generous swaths of shade.

Beachcombing The shoreline on either side of the cove is, more or less, precipitous—especially to the right. If you are determined to explore and are willing to do some rock climbing, you may be encouraged to know that, totally out of sight from this beach, but within 200 m in either direction, you will find attractive beaches tucked into deep bays.

Seclusion The chances are good that you will have this spot entirely to yourself, notwithstanding the dwellings you can glimpse through the alders.

61
REDONDA DRIVE
A remote wilderness bay with a rocky little beach and mountains of driftwood

Location, signs and parking Although getting to this spot requires a fair amount of driving, much of it through near-wilderness conditions, not only is the route beautiful, it also rewards you with opportunities to visit several different beaches close to each other. The first part of the journey is one with which most island visitors will be familiar—the well-signposted route to the Cortes ferry. From Quathiaski Cove, turn left onto Harper Road for a little under half a kilometre, right onto Heriot Bay Road for 200 m, then left onto West Road. After roughly 5 km, and well before the Cortes ferry terminal, turn left onto Hyacinthe Bay Road for about 5 km until it merges onto Village Bay Road. About 8 km later, turn right onto Valdes Road for over 4 km, right onto Marina Drive for about half a kilometre and left to the end of Redonda Drive. Here you will see a grassy turnaround area with plenty of room for your now well-seasoned car.

Path At first you may not spot the path, but persevere. Look to the left of the turnaround and you should see, partially obscured by salal, the beginning of a twisty, sometimes rocky, but generally clear trail. Much of the way, you will be next to a split-cedar fence and thus be reassured that you are on the right track. Though not steep, the trail can be a little tricky for those not steady on their feet.

Beach You will first be struck by how much driftwood can be crammed into such a small area. The additional fact that so much of this driftwood is small broken bits can lead you to muse about the strength of the winter storms that thrash straight into this bay from the exposed southern waters. Covered mostly with large rocks, the little bay, some 75 m wide, is bounded on either side by steep headlands. At low tide, when the water retreats about 75 m, a band of attractive and welcoming sand is exposed.

Suitability for children This is perhaps not a great place to bring very small children. The slightly tricky trail, the driftwood barricade and the bouldery beach can all be a little challenging. If you are going to visit here, your children—even sure-footed children—will be happiest if you come at low tide when the sand is exposed. Children and sand? Beat that combination, if you can.

Suitability for groups It is hard to imagine what kind of group, other than a small band of fellow searchers of the far-flung, would want to come here. You will find plenty of parking and plenty of space, but hardly the kind of shore sought out by the average group.

View What gives this spot its special atmosphere is that it feels both exposed to the elements yet set deep into the end of a sequence of bays. When you consider that the larger bay from which this particular little bay is separated is called Open Bay, you will realize that you may be not the first to notice that combination of sensations. Steep, rocky shores extend in both directions, though tucked just out of sight around the headland at the right side of the beach is another publicly accessible beach at the end of Marina Drive.

Winds, sun and shade As the driftwood—and its battered condition—suggests, this bay is open to the full whammy of southeastern winds and waves washing up the Strait of Georgia. From northwest winds, however, it is completely protected. Facing largely south, it can be toasty warm during the first half of the day but becomes increasingly shady during the course of the afternoon.

Beachcombing You may well want to do a little beachcombing in the purest sense—that is, poke around in the driftwood to see what interesting bits of flotsam have found their watery way to this shore. Except for wandering across the beach at low tide, though, you will want to confine your explorations to the rock-bordered beach.

Seclusion Although this beach very much has the feeling of a wilderness beach, it is not, in fact, wilderness. A few lovers of isolated shores and deep forests have built both in the woods to the right of the access spot and among the trees on the rocky peninsula to the left of the beach.

While you're here . . . On your way here, you might want to break your journey with two stops of interest:

1. A little under 2 km along Hyacinthe Bay Road, look for Endersby Road and drive the short distance to its end. A small path runs parallel to a fence, bringing you to a beautiful and unusual view spot looking on Heriot Island. Unfortunately, the bank is too steep to allow you shore access without going onto private property.

2. Roughly 3 km along Hyacinthe Bay Road, where two drives fork off the road, a broad track S-curves down a high, treed bank toward a protected bay and interesting views into this innermost part of Hyacinthe Bay.

62
MARINA DRIVE
A stunningly beautiful and isolated sandy beach set deep into a heavily treed bay and bisected by a small creek

Location, signs and parking Because this is the close sister to the beach at the end of Redonda Drive, and because the directions for getting here are so elaborate, refer to those directions to find your way onto Marina Drive. Instead, however, of turning onto Redonda Drive, carry on straight ahead for another 100 m or so until you come to a turnaround.

Path You will see a road-width track leading into the forest and partially blocked by two large rocks. You will also see, attached to an alder partway down the path, a colourful, hand-lettered sign asking you to cooperate with the locals in removing litter from the beach. Don't let the easy beginning of the trail lull you into believing your unsteady family members can negotiate the rest of it. Well over 100 m long, the trail becomes steep and rocky as it approaches the shore. Small children, however nimble, might need some hefting and steadying.

Beach Those who have visited the wild west coast of Vancouver Island will be surprised at how closely this beach, on the relatively protected Salish Sea, resembles the pocket beaches common along the shores of Vancouver Island open to the Pacific Ocean. The thickets of wave-thrown logs, the rounded rock outcroppings and the expanses of coarse sand are three ingredients. Add to that the thick spruce forest, the dark rock headlands and even the creek winding down the beach, and you could swear you've been transported to the Island's west coast. About 125 m wide, the beach at low tide exposes about 200 m of sand and tidal pools. A curious feature of this shore is that as the tide comes in, it submerges the middle part of the bay first, leaving temporarily high and dry a slope of coarse sand along the left side of the shore. Do be aware, before you go bounding across the beautiful stream to explore the salt meadow and forests there, that except for the narrow access strip, the whole area at the head of the bay is First Nation land.

Suitability for children If it weren't for the challenges of the access trail, this would be a nearly perfect spot for children. For older children, for whom the tricky parts of the trail might seem a lark, this is a great destination. The clever and well-prepared parent will have a backpack for the treats and towels to dole out as your soggy and sandy child scampers back to home base. The majority of children will probably most enjoy low tide, but even at high tide, when paddling and swimming are better, the beach can't help but please any children worth their salt.

Suitability for groups As with children, so with groups. If the trail isn't a concern, as it needn't be for most, then you can bring two or three cars' worth of kindred spirits, secure in the knowledge that you won't be squeezing into a congested neighbourhood and that you'll be treating them to a gorgeous spot. Remind them, though, that this is a wilderness beach. Those who need facilities should go to Rebecca Spit Park for their group outing.

View From the public end of the beach, the nearly enclosed view adds to the sense of being tucked away into a piece of untouched nature. You will see only the high, forested headlands jutting into Open Bay, except for a narrow slot opening toward Rebecca Spit.

Winds, sun and shade As you might guess from its geography, storms from the southeast give this bay a thorough thrashing, though the access path opens to the more sheltered end of the beach. Northwest winds skirt the beach completely. While early morning is rather shady, the rest of the day doles out the sun generously. If you're roasting beyond a turn, however, you can usually find some shade behind some of the rock buttresses.

Beachcombing Some essential part of your being is sadly lacking if you don't feel compelled to wander along the edge of the stream and out to the water's edge. Still, this is a beach for enjoying what you have rather than going a-questing for more.

Seclusion You will have the impression that you are in an oasis of pure wilderness. While this impression is generally well founded, one house is visible in the distance along the west shore of Hope Bay. You should be aware of two more, tucked away into the forest and accessible by Redonda Drive.

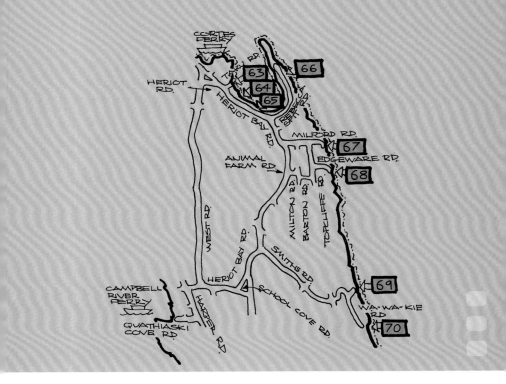

63

TAKU ROAD

A gravel shore in the protected waters of Drew Harbour, good for launching kayaks

Location, signs and parking The simplest method of finding your way here is simply to follow the signs for the ferry to Cortes Island. Otherwise, from Quathiaski Cove Road, turn left onto Harper Road for a little under half a kilometre, right onto Heriot Bay Road for 200 m, and left onto West Road. As you approach Heriot Bay, roughly 6 km along, turn right by the little shopping plaza onto Heriot Road, and immediately right again onto Heriot Bay Road. Taku Road, your destination, is the first left turn, about 100 m later. Simply drive the short distance to the end of Taku Road. You will have to be a little careful with your parking in order not to block cars driving into and out of the resort at the end of the road.

Path At the very end of the road is a small patch of grass with a well-worn, nearly level path along its right border. Those with walking difficulties or balancing a colourful kayak or two will find it a breeze getting this far, but will have to be a little careful negotiating the clutter of logs that are usually pressed up against the upper shore.

Beach Composed largely of gravel, but with a few patches of boulders and the occasional tidal pool, the shore slopes evenly toward the low-tide line. The slope is perfect for launching kayaks, since it is gradual enough that you don't need to worry overmuch about slipping and yet steep enough that, even at low tide, the waterline isn't very far away. The little breakwater located just to the left of the beach guarantees that the shore is well protected from northwest winds, but it is actually there to protect boats at the docks from southeasterly waves blowing across Drew Harbour.

Suitability for children If you are waiting for the ferry to Cortes Island, this is good place to bring your hyperactive children. Within walk-ing distance from the ferry line-up, this spot is well protected and yet welcoming enough for both small children and their more rambunctious larger siblings. If you have been far-sighted enough to bring water shoes and dry things, you can let the kids loose to create watery havoc, knowing that the water of Drew Harbour can become pleasantly warm.

Suitability for groups The spot is much too confined and much too close to neighbouring dwellings to make it good for more than a family or two. Remind yourself that nearby Rebecca Spit Provincial Park is huge.

View Some will find the foreground clusters of docks and fishing boats picturesque. Others—perhaps not. Everyone, though, is bound to be intrigued by the middle-ground view, since about 600 m across Drew Harbour rises the long narrow shoreline of Rebecca Spit and its park. Beyond, above the forests of the spit and to the north, you can see the striking shapes of islands and mainland mountains. Just to the left of the spit, your eye will be caught by a distinctive mountain, sometimes called, appropriately, The Cowboy Hat or Dog's Tooth, but officially (and more hilariously) called Mount Doogie Dowler, after a pioneer of Heriot Bay.

Winds, sun and shade As the presence of the breakwater suggests, even though Drew Harbour is indeed a perfect natural harbour, southeast winds can get a little overenthusiastic during a blow. Even northwest winds can be felt here, but mostly parallel to the shore rather than onto it. Shade covers most of the shore in the afternoon, but the lower beach is in the sun throughout the day.

Beachcombing This is almost the northern end of a gradually shelving, gravel-and-rock shoreline that extends not only all around Drew Harbour and Rebecca Spit, but, remarkably, around the entire southern tip of the island. By turning left, you can make your way into Heriot Bay, with its ferry terminal and inn. By turning right, you can easily walk along the gravel upper beach around as much of Drew Harbour as you like.

Seclusion This is one of the mostly heavily settled areas of the island. Few, however, seem to know about this access to the shore. Even though you are right beside a resort, you will probably see few others here.

While you're here . . . If you would like a concrete launching ramp for your kayaks and secure (but paid) parking, turn left onto Antler Road just before Heriot Bay and make your way the short distance to the public ramp and docks there. Come prepared with lots of coins if you plan to leave your car parked for very long.

Quadra: Mount Doogie Dowler and Rebecca Spit

64
HERIOT BAY ROAD
Roadside access to a protected shore of pebble and gravel in the centre of Drew Harbour

Location, signs and parking From Quathiaski Cove Road, turn left onto Harper Road for a little under half a kilometre, right onto Heriot Bay Road for 200 m, and left onto West Road. As you approach Heriot Bay, roughly 6 km along, turn right by the little shopping plaza onto Heriot Road, and immediately right again onto Heriot Bay Road. About 1 km along, where the road runs next to the shore, you will see a broad section of shoulder, spacious enough for several cars to park but without any directional or instructional signs.

Path From this shoulder, you will spot an irregular but well-used path dropping the 2 m to the shore. While most visitors will have no problem with this path, it would be awkward for those recovering from knee operations or manoeuvering tiny legs.

Beach This section of Drew Harbour is mostly fine gravel with a few patches of pebbles and, lower down the beach, some areas of barnacle-covered chunkier gravel. With an intertidal zone about 100 m wide, the shore sweeps smoothly away in both directions. You will find a few logs dotting the uppermost shore, including some areas, tucked under overhanging maples and willows, where you can feel virtually isolated from the nearby road.

Suitability for children Once down the slightly tricky path, children can be set free to scamper freely with little likelihood of their stumbling across treacherous obstacles. The water of Drew Harbour can become deliciously warm, especially near the end of the incoming tide cycle. Water shoes are crucial, as much for your peace of mind as your child's unbloodied feet.

Suitability for groups Since you are so close to Rebecca Spit Park at this point, carry on with your group to the similar beach there rather than stop at this much more restricted spot.

View It is the view that makes beaching here in some ways more appealing than at Rebecca Spit Park. Facing across Drew Harbour as you are, and directly opposite the treeless section of the spit, you can see not only the entire graceful sweep of the curving shore but also the treed undulations of Rebecca Spit and the towering peaks of the Coast Mountains beyond.

Winds, sun and shade Virtually all winds—whether chilling or refreshing—fan this shore, though indirectly. If you position yourself high among the maples and willows, the first half of the day is sunniest. Otherwise, you can find buckets of sun all day long.

Beachcombing One of the main attractions of this spot is the opportunity it gives you to begin easy strolling along the generally firm and only slightly irregular surface of the gradually sloping shore around Drew Harbour. One pleasant option is to turn left and walk the 2 km into Heriot Bay, where you can treat yourself at the pub.

Seclusion Although this spot is immediately below the road, and houses crowd the bank above the road, the trees and slopes are configured in such a way that you can easily get into your own little isolated world.

65 HERIOT BAY ROAD STAIRCASE
A wooden staircase to a broad pebbly beach near the head of Drew Harbour

Location, signs and parking For the first part of your quest, your route is almost to the Cortes ferry. From Quathiaski Cove Road, turn left onto Harper Road for a little under half a kilometre, right onto Heriot Bay Road for 200 m, and left onto West Road. As you approach Heriot Bay, roughly 6 km along, turn right by the little shopping plaza onto Heriot Road, and immediately right again onto Heriot Bay Road. About 2 km along, after the road has left the shoreline and curved uphill, your attention will be caught by a colourful hand-painted sign depicting a tangle of local animals and emblazoned with the house number 1386. Park along the shoulder of the road.

Path A newly surfaced, crushed-gravel drive leads steeply toward the shore. Where this drive curves to the right, you will see a skookum set of elevated wooden stairs, complete with solid handrails. Pause to enjoy the magnificent view and maybe snap a hundred photos before descending the 17 stairs to the beach.

Beach Toward this end of Drew Harbour, the nearly level gravel shore is, in some places, curiously covered with a stubble of low, salt-tolerant vegetation. Overhung with hemlock and cedar, the upper shore has just enough logs and just large enough a patch of fine pebbles to make a welcoming spot for perching. An intertidal zone about 200 m wide at this point broadens to a delta area to the right, where the zone triples in width.

Suitability for children This is not a spot to single out for beach-craving children. At the same time, the beach could hardly be safer and the swimming water at high tide could hardly be warmer. You and the junior set (and, possibly, the locals) will be happier if you drive a few extra kilometres to the nearby provincial park, where the parking, facilities and beach surface are all better suited to a carefree, salty experience.

Suitability for groups Almost all groups will be much happier and much better accommodated at the nearby provincial park. Still, if you have a few birding or watercolourist friends, you won't want to skip this spot. At the right time of year, the rewards of finding your way here for the view can be enormous.

View Not just from the top of the bank but also from sea level, this beach offers generous eye candy for lovers of graceful trees, sweeping shores, forested knolls, overlapping islands, and, of course, towering mountains. You can't do much better than this.

Winds, sun and shade Winds from the northwest can fan the shore, but, in general, this end of the lagoon is well protected. Unless you come during the first half of the day, you will find more shade than you probably want. However, by walking away from the upper beach, you can always find sun.

Beachcombing One of the attractive features of this spot is the beckon-ing expanses of smooth and level gravel shore curving around the entire rim of Drew Harbour. The options for combining shore walking with a return along roads or by car pickup are many.

Seclusion Many lucky folk have decided to build in the subdivision cov-ering this side and end of the harbour. You are unlikely to find more than a few others on the beach, however. Thanks to the thickets of shore side evergreens, you are unlikely either to be seen by locals or feel that you are in someone's front yard.

66 REBECCA SPIT PROVINCIAL PARK

A striking landform with 3 km of shoreline of coarse sand, gravel and boulders, facing into the pro-tected waters of Drew Harbour and across the Strait of Georgia

Location, signs and parking To reach this least secret spot on Quadra Island, from Quathiaski Cove Road, turn left onto Harper Road for a little under half a kilometre, right on Heriot Bay Road for 200 m, and left onto West Road. As you approach Heriot Bay, roughly 6 km along, turn right by the little shopping plaza onto Heriot Road, and immediately right again onto Heriot Bay Road. Between 2 and 3 km along this road, Rebecca Spit Road leads to the left and about 1.5 km later delivers you to the park. You might note the commercial campground just before the park in case you wish to combine a visit to the park with camping. You will find a large, gravel parking area next to a concrete launching pad. Many signs further instruct you about fires, unleashed dogs, paralytic shellfish poisoning, the location of the washrooms and so on.

Path Those with walking difficulties will appreciate the easy, level sur-faces between parking lot and shore, but they will appreciate more the approach to the beach on the inner west side of the spit than to that on the outer east side. The latter, though level, is usually piled high with logs and at most spots is thick with large, loose boulders. Other paths (and biking trails) lead around the whole 1.5 km of the long, narrow spit. Kayakers will find the concrete ramp near the parking lot good for driving almost to the water's edge for unloading. In the past, permission has been granted by park staff to leave cars in the lot for overnight trips even though the park is closed at night, but you might be wise to confirm this arrangement before paddling off to Desolation Sound.

Beach Although this park has no large swaths of fine sand, it does have areas of coarse sand on the upper shore along parts of the harbour side of the spit. Otherwise, the shore on this side tends to be composed of gravel and small rocks, whereas that on the other side combines undulating crests of rounded granite boulders with a few large tidal pools. Although the width of the beach at low tide varies somewhat, in general, it is about 150 m wide on the outer shore and about 75 m wide on the inner shore. Swimmers can find pleasantly warm water on both shores, but, unsurprisingly, the warmest water is on the harbour side and usually around high tide, while the water is still rising.

Suitability for children If your children have their little hearts set on careening barefooted around silky-soft, sandy tidal flats, they will be disappointed. Otherwise they—and you—will be happy with all the activities this kind of large, varied beach can dish up. You will be equally happy that they are in a safe, largely hazard-free beach environment, able to cavort over logs, explore tidal pools, run splashing into the warm shallow water and so on. Did you toss Frisbees and kites into your trunk just in case? The large grassy area near the parking lot is a good place to reward your efforts.

Suitability for groups This park is, unquestionably, the best spot on Quadra Island for the typical large group bent on gossiping, tossing baseballs and overdosing on potato chips and pop. The presence of washrooms, picnic tables, grassy areas, and, above all, space are clearly huge advantages.

View The views are too varied to begin to identify. It is probably enough to say that with the clusters of Discovery Islands, near and distant, the curves of shoreline and forest, the moored fishing boats in the harbour, all topped by the jagged crests of the Coast Mountains, you and your camera can be very, very busy.

Winds, sun and shade As long as sun is in the sky and winds are on the water, you can either expose or protect yourself as much as you like in this huge and varied park.

Beachcombing One of the main attractions of this site is the trail network through and around the treed sections of the spit. The shore itself, though, offers many appealing options for long-distance walking. You will need sturdy shoes and a little determination to walk far over areas of loose boulders. Still, if you are in exploring mode, you can begin a mammoth trek from here and go around the entire south end of the island to the village of Cape Mudge.

Seclusion This is probably the most visited beach spot on Quadra Island. You will have to come during extreme weather to avoid seeing others or being seen. Even during hot, still days, however, you can easily walk your way to a section of shore that even the most demanding guru would find conducive for a bout of heavy-duty meditation.

67
MILFORD ROAD
Secluded shorefront parking on the east coast of the island, suitable for car picnicking or launching kayaks

Location, signs and parking Head away from the ferry on Quathiaski Cove Road, then turn left onto Harper Road for a little under half a kilometre, then right onto Heriot Bay Road. While you need to follow this road for about 6 km, be careful to note that after about 700 m, you need to make a sharp left turn to stay on the road. A little confusingly, you can cut out this corner by turning onto School Cove Road about 500 m along Heriot Bay Road after Harper Road. About 300 m later, it rejoins Heriot Bay Road. Milford Road is a signposted right turn and brings you, after about 600 m, to the water's edge. Because the access allowance broadens by the shore, the gravel roadbed actually swings right and then cuts back parallel to the shore. As long as you avoid the driveways, therefore, you will find lots of parking under some waterfront evergreens.

Path Hop, skip and jump the very few metres to the shore—but prepare yourself for a mighty logjam along the upper beach. Kayakers can be guaranteed a short, level haul from car to the shore, but they should anticipate making their way over these logs and, if they neglect to arrive at high tide, a considerable intertidal area.

Beach The beach here is similar to that at many other points on the east coast of southern Quadra Island. Below the hundreds of pieces of broken driftwood and jams of logs, the shore slopes gradually to the low-tide line about 100 m away. Composed mostly of rounded rocks, many of them covered with barnacles, the shore is also dotted with a few very large boulders.

Suitability for children The last thing you should anticipate for your children is barefooted leaping. Properly shod, however, most children, and particularly those graced with curiosity and energy, will find lots of opportunity to befriend scurrying and squirting creatures living under the rocks, or to clamber around the logs. The ability to park so close to the shore is an obvious advantage, too. Still, this isn't the sort of beach most children would rank high on their list of best-loved beaches.

Suitability for groups This spot lacks the facilities available at nearby Rebecca Spit Provincial Park. However, the considerable shorefront parking and seclusion could tip the balance if you are looking for a venue for your quilters or choir to munch their way through the afternoon while enjoying a ridiculously scenic view.

View View? You cannot do much better than come to this spot, though mostly if you arrive when the mountains are still thick with snow and if you have brought binoculars. If you are island spotting, you can easily pick out Read Island to the north and, across Sutil Channel, part of Cortes Island and the low mound of Marina Island in front of it. With binoculars and a clear day, you can add Dunsterville Islet, the Subtle Islands and even tiny Mitlenatch Island to your list.

Winds, sun and shade Because this section of Quadra Island's east coast runs virtually north to south, winds scoot more or less parallel to the shore. If you have a titch more air conditioning than you want, you may be able to find a little protection between some of the logs. After a generally sun-bathed morning, the shore becomes increasing shady throughout the afternoon.

Beachcombing Properly shod and properly psyched, you can walk many, many kilometres in either direction, but especially to the south. If you turn north, you will discover a curious bit of shore where, for over a kilometre, winter waves have created a raised bar of loose rock running parallel to the upper shore and, in effect, landlocking a huge pool area.

Seclusion Although this access is between two shorefront houses, both are far enough away and far enough back in the trees that you will feel you have the cry of gulls and the wash of waves entirely to yourself.

68
EDGEWARE ROAD
A convoluted route to secluded shorefront parking with a splendid view over Sutil Channel

Location, signs and parking Head away from the ferry along Quathiaski Cove Road, then turn left onto Harper Road for a little under half a kilometre, and right onto Heriot Bay Road. Commit yourself to this road for about 4 km, though about 700 m along, you will need to make to sharp left turn at an apparent T-junction. You can bypass this corner by turning onto School Cove Road about 500 m along Heriot Bay Road after Harper Road. About 300 m later, it rejoins Heriot Bay Road. Turn right onto Animal Farm Road for 300 m, right onto Milton Road, and immediately left onto Barton Road for 300 m. At the T-junction with Topcliffe Road, turn left for about 500 m, then right onto Edgeware Road. A little over 200 m later, you will be smack dab on the edge of the shore. Congratulations—you made it! You will see a sign stating that fires are not permitted—in spite of, or possibly because of, the tons of ready fuel in the form of driftwood and logs.

Path If a storm is churning up Sutil Channel, this is a good spot to arrive with a cozy picnic and witness the spectacle from the comfort of your car. If you are a keen kayaker, you will be pleased that you can get so easily onto the shore. You will be happiest coming at mid to high tide, though, since at low tide, the water recedes a good 100 m.

Beach Mostly composed of rounded rocks and some clusters of larger boulders, the beach here is a continuation of a similar kind of level shore running for several kilometres in either direction. The distinctive feature of this part of the shore is a large tidal pool just to the right of the access road. You won't find nearly as many large logs pressed up against the winter high-water mark here as at some other points along this shore.

Suitability for children If you have the kind of children who are happy to collect treasures tucked into the crevices between rocks, create imaginative chaos with the minor mountains of driftwood on the upper shore, or simply enjoy getting far soggier than (adult) common sense dictates, then you can bring them here for your own pleasure and be sure you haven't denied them theirs. The absence of sand or fine pebbles for roosting spots most restricts its appeal to children.

Suitability for groups You won't find any facilities here, of course, and you won't find the stretches of sand some groups demand. What you will find is seclusion, a great place for strolling along an expanse of shore and a magnificent view. You decide whether your group is suited to this place—and the other way around.

View Like other spots along this coast, this one thrusts as much scenery at you as your capacity to utter "oohs" and "aahs" will tolerate. Because most of the clusters of islands are across Sutil Channel, 7 km at its narrowest point here, you may well want to bring binoculars to savour the details. When the mountains are thick with snow and the air is clear, your notion of the picturesque will be thoroughly challenged. If you happen to be here during a sunset, the white peaks will turn first golden and then a surreal pink.

Winds, sun and shade On the east-facing shore, more or less straight and unbroken by headlands or bays, most winds run roughly parallel to the land, though you will probably feel a southeast wind most directly. Even though the shore behind this beach is low, the trees are tall enough and close enough together that, by noon, shadows start to creep along the beach and lengthen during the course of the afternoon.

Beachcombing Like other spots on the east coast of this southern section of Quadra Island, this one is a good starting point for a major trek. Walking over rounded rocks can require a little technique, but the shore is generally level and poses no threats from incoming tides. You will find enough access spots that you can mastermind a shuttle exchange with other cars.

Seclusion One house is about 50 m away through the trees to the south of this spot, and another 100 m to the north. You will see neither from the shore here, however. At this rarely visited spot, you can expect to get thoroughly reacquainted with yourself—or your visiting great-aunt.

While you're here . . . At the junction of Heriot Bay Road with Smiths Road, you will see a carved wooden sign indicating the beginning of Haskins Farm Trail. About 1.5 km long, the trail descends through attractive second-growth forest, first to an abandoned homestead site and then to an isolated section of rocky shore, many kilometres from the closest house.

Quadra: Alexandra Peak from Lighthouse Road

69

SMITHS ROAD

Easy shorefront access to
the middle of the rocky beach
running continuously along the
east coast of southern Quadra
Island

Location, signs and parking After your short but scenic ferry ride, go with the ferry flow up Quathiaski Cove Road, then turn left onto Harper Road for a little under half a kilometre, and right onto Heriot Bay Road. About 700 m along, in order to stay on this road, you will need to make a sharp left turn at an apparent T-junction. You can also cut across this corner by turning onto School Cove Road, about 200 m before the T-junction, and rejoining Heriot Bay Road a few hundred metres later. About 2.5 km from the beginning of Heriot Bay Road, turn right down Smiths Road. Toward its end, about 3 km along, this road hairpins and ends in an exposed gravel area near the shore. Currently, this gravel area is rather chewed up with the tracks of graders, but no doubt this is a temporary situation. The fact that you will see a sign forbidding camping or overnight parking suggests that some have brought their camper vans where they are not wanted.

Path Neither vertical nor horizontal distance stands between your trusty car and the shore. In fact, until winter storms toss logs and firewood back into the cleared area created by the graders, access to the shore is even easier here than at the other spots on this section of coast. Because of its exposure and position, this is an excellent place from which to look out on a bout of howling weather from the warmth of your car. Kayakers will obviously find getting their kayaks onto the shore to be a piece of cake. Getting to the waterline, about 100 m away at low tide, is easier if you head slightly to the left.

Beach The beach here is part of the wave-smoothed shore of rounded rocks that runs for many kilometres along this section of Quadra Island's east coast. Just to the right of the access area, however, the shore is much wider than elsewhere and creased with undulations that create a few large tidal pools. Up to the point where the exposed uppermost shore is covered with driftwood, it is distinctly more pebbly here than both farther north and farther south.

Suitability for children Don't select this spot over others if you want a comfortable beach for a toddler. Older children, however, and especially those generously endowed with curiosity, imagination and more energy than they know what to do with, will find plenty of space, pools, logs and, of course, water. You really, really don't want to forget tough little water shoes—flip-flops or even crocs won't quite do the job.

Suitability for groups You will find space in abundance for cars and beach-lovers. Still, in its current churned-up state, the spot is unlikely to appeal to many.

View While the view is similar to that from the access spots farther north on this coast, particularly of the stunning array of mainland crags and peaks, you will see more of the islands to the south. Marina Island across Sutil Channel is the closest, while Cortes looms behind it. Farther south, you should be able to pick out Hernando Island and tiny Mitlenatch Island.

Winds, sun and shade Unlike the other access spots along this stretch of shore, this one is more or less fully exposed to the sun throughout the day. Both common winds blow roughly parallel to the shore rather than directly onto it.

Beachcombing Not many visitors will have the enthusiasm—or the sturdy shoes—to undertake a major trek along this extensive stretch of shore. Any visitor with even a trace of wanderlust or curiosity should turn right along the beach at low tide and investigate the curious configurations of tidal pools and rock crests.

Seclusion While you will see the occasional house nearby, you are likely to have this spot and this section of shore more or less to yourself.

70 WA-WA-KIE ROAD— KAY DUBOIS TRAIL

A 1.5 km forest trail running parallel to the shore, with several easy points of access near its northern end

Location, signs and parking As you disembark at Quathiaski Cove, follow the ferry traffic straight ahead, turning left onto Harper Road for a little under half a kilometre, and right onto Heriot Bay Road. About 700 m along, the road makes a sharp left turn. Just before the sharp left, you can also cut across this corner by turning onto School Cove Road and rejoining Heriot Bay Road 300 m later. About 2.5 km from the beginning of Heriot Bay Road, turn right down Smiths Road. Toward its end, about 3 km along, this road hairpins down a bank to an open gravel area. Turn right onto Wa-Wa-Kie Road and drive about 600 m to its end beside a house in a paved turnaround. Straight ahead you will see a little slot in the vegetation and a sign reading TRAIL PARKING. Although you are likely to be the only car here, if the spot happens to be taken, you will find fairly easy parking along the edge of the approach road.

Path Kay Dubois Trail runs parallel to the shore, but it is close to the shore only at its northern end, since it gradually rises up the forested bank toward its southern end at Sutil Road. In the absence of a single, well-beaten path onto the shore, you can find your way fairly easily to the beach once you have walked a few dozen metres along the level, well-graded trail.

Beach Like most of the other access spots on this section of coast, this one begins with a stunning wealth of beach logs and driftwood. About 100 m wide at low tide, the shore is composed primarily of rounded, barnacle-covered rocks and dotted with a few particularly large boulders near the low-tide line. Picnicking or even just nestling down for an afternoon's contemplation is more attractively done here than at some of the other access points to this stretch of shore. Depending on what the previous winter's storms have decided to do in their gigantic game of pick-up sticks, you may or may not find some open areas of polished gravel among the logs.

Suitability for children If releasing energy, collecting crabs and starfish and hurling rocks are what your children do naturally, then they can find plenty of distractions here while you find a little deep inner peace. The picnic spots among the logs can also add to their contentment and distraction. Still, this shore is probably a lot rockier and a lot rougher than most children find ideal. Provide them with tough water shoes, and life will be easier for the entire family.

Suitability for groups A walking group could make this the beginning of a tip-top hour or two's outing, using the shore as a picnicking or resting area. Other sorts of groups, though, are likely to be much happier elsewhere.

View Because the southern part of the generally straight coastline curves out gradually toward Francisco Point, your eyes will naturally be drawn down this coast and its tapering treeline. The fact that the horizon is wide open directly south gives you some idea of the size of the waves that can build up in the Strait of Georgia and drive so many logs ashore here. Most likely, though, you will be busiest drinking in the magnificent view across Sutil Channel, roughly 7 or 8 km wide at this point. Across this open stretch are the steep-sided bumps of Cortes Island and the more gentle curves of the smaller islands around it. Most eye-catching, though, especially in early spring when the snow still lies deep at higher altitudes, are the crags and peaks of the Coast Range.

Winds, sun and shade If the wind is up to its usual tricks, you will be fully aware that this is not a particularly well-sheltered shore, though you won't feel the wind directly. The trees crowd forward to the shoreline and, because of the orientation of the coastline, cast deep shade across the upper beach from about noon onward.

Beachcombing Although you can walk for several kilometres in either direction, you will probably most enjoy turning to your right. First you will come across some huge tidal pools and, if you persevere, will eventually round the tip of Francisco Point and discover an entirely new panorama open before you. Be warned, though. Walking on the rough surface of the beach is most enjoyable if you have tough shoes and aren't prone to twisted ankles.

Seclusion Once you start along the trail and make your way to the beach, you will be leaving the world of niggling worries and aggressive sounds far behind you. Celebrate the fact that this is one of the most untouched sections of easily walked, accessible coast in the Salish Sea.

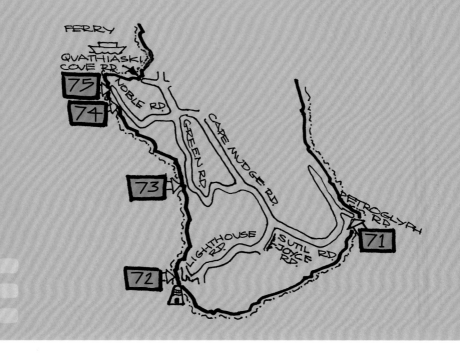

71
PETROGLYPH ROAD
Remarkable for its petro-
glyphs, the closest access to
Francisco Point via a sweep
of rocky shore

Location, signs and parking Make your way up Quathiaski Cove Road, and turn left onto Harper Road for a little under half a kilometre. After a right turn onto Heriot Bay Road, about 700 m along, turn right onto Cape Mudge Road at a T-junction and follow it for roughly 4 km. Swing left at a fork in the road onto Sutil Road. A little over 2 km along, turn right down Petroglyph Road and follow it more or less to its end. Where the pavement ends and the road dives down the steep treed bank to the right, you will see a parking spot straight ahead, or, if it is full, lots of room along the nearby shoulder of the road. En route to the shore, posted high on a tree, you will see a sign prohibiting overnight parking and camping.

Path The roadbed, about 50 m long, is steep and rough by vehicle standards and by the standards of those with walking difficulties. Others might puff a little on the way back to the vehicle but will otherwise find it easy and obvious.

Beach Located near the southeastern tip of Quadra Island and subject to the strong forces of wind and wave, the shore here is one of the most interesting parts of the long, gently shelving coastline around the south-ern end of the island. Widening to about 200 m of intertidal flats, the beach at low tide also has some huge, shallow tidal pools. Like much of the rest of the shoreline along the southeastern tip of the island, the beach here collects lots of logs, but they are not nearly as congested here as at most points and thus provide strategic spots in which to position yourself and your picnic ingredients for an afternoon's quiet pleasures.

Suitability for children Although the path to the shore isn't a joy, the shore is varied and interesting enough that most children who aren't wedded to the idea of a sandy beach can find lots to do. In addition, the shore is sufficiently free from significant hazards that parents can keep their vigilance level fairly low. Even the most robust children will be freest to explore and ramble if you make sure you have equally robust water shoes—and, perhaps, a good supply of snacks. Hunting for petro-glyphs will clearly appeal to the Indiana Jones in most children.

Suitability for groups Though you will find nothing in the way of facili-ties here, you will also find nothing in the way of congestion. With comparatively easy roadside parking and a beach that dishes up space and quiet in spades, this is a good spot to bring a few cars of beach explorers who are interested in trying to find the elusive petroglyphs. While your explorers are here, they will find plenty of attractive spots for picnicking and intriguing distances to set out for. Still, this is not even remotely like a developed and gentle bit of park, so select your group carefully.

View The most obvious eye candy is arranged in splendid fashion directly across the open waters in the form of immoderately picturesque snow-clad peaks. The forested ridges and crests of several islands decorate the middle ground of the view, Marina, Cortes and Hernando most prom-inently. Almost as striking, though, is the shoreline of Quadra itself, sweeping far to the north.

Winds, sun and shade Whether a southeast wind is gently fanning the Strait of Georgia or whipping it into breakers, you will be fully aware of its effects. Northwest winds likewise flow along the beach, but less directly. The mornings are by far the sunniest part of the day, though the lower beach is in sun throughout the course of a sunny day.

Beachcombing Beachcombing is probably the chief attraction for most visitors to this fascinating chunk of shore. Hunting for petroglyphs, in particular the "sea wolf," which faces toward the sea on a large boulder, will be high on most visitors' list. Also beckoning is the walk along the shore, perhaps via some of the huge tidal pools, to Francisco Point, remarkable for its petroglyphs and lofty banks. Rounding this point, just a few hundred metres to the right, beachcombers will suddenly find themselves with the whole wide vista of the southern straits and Vancouver Island mountains opening before them. The hardiest souls will carry on an additional 5 or so 6 km to Cape Mudge and the lighthouse, possibly arranging a car pickup there.

Seclusion You might have the opportunity to exchange comments on the weather and view with one or two other beach visitors. Otherwise, though, expect to experience wonderful isolation. Because the few local houses are well tucked away in the trees and high above the shore, you will probably be alone with the "sea wolf" and whatever other lucky guests you have brought to share the spot with you.

Quadra: Strathcona Park from Lighthouse Road

72
LIGHTHOUSE ROAD
Shoreside parking beside Cape Mudge lighthouse and easy access to a long beach with a loose, sandy upper shore and a lower shore of rounded rock

Location, signs and parking With your copy of *To the Lighthouse* firmly in hand as you depart the ferry, take the first right turn onto Green Road and follow it for a little over half a kilometre. Turn left onto Noble Road for almost 1 km and right again onto Cape Mudge Road. Between 3 and 4 km along, turn right onto Joyce Road for about 1.5 km and right yet again onto your destination road, Lighthouse Road. As you approach the end of the road, some 2 km along, you will see a large commercial sign helping you with the slightly confusing choice of direction. The sign, welcoming you to "Tsa-Kwa-Luten," directs you to turn left if you are after accommodation, RV check-in and the seafood restaurant—all of potential interest. For now, however, note the fork on the road straight ahead, the one to the left being to Cape Mudge lighthouse, your destination. Once you reach the bottom of the slope, you can turn right toward the RV park drive—and also right to the edge of the shore. Strictly speaking, this is reserve land, so you should probably use this access only if you are a guest of the RV park. It is unlikely, however, that you will be creating a problem if, in foul weather, you position your vehicle there for as long as it takes to scoff your shrimp pitas while enjoying the view. Otherwise, take the left fork and find yourself a spot in the large gravel parking lot in clear sight of the lighthouse.

Path From the edge of the parking lot, you need take only a few steps to reach the upper shore. Under some conditions you can easily launch a kayak here, but you will have to be careful with your timing. If you arrive when the tide is low, you can face an awkward trudge to the waterline. More important, though, you should avoid paddling if a strong southeast wind is blowing, and especially if that wind is combined with a strong south-flowing current out of Discovery Passage. This combination of forces, meeting over the extensive shallows at the south end of the island, are a recipe for treacherous waters. Oops.

Beach The entire southern end of Quadra is covered by a stretch of similar shoreline. Those with picnicking on their mind or with little wiggling children in their arms will be most pleased with the highest part of the beach. Here, tucked behind a phalanx of weathered beach logs, the soft, sugary sand makes an inviting spot for lunching and lounging. Low tide reveals some 100 m of wave-rounded rock, increasingly large toward the low-tide line. Be aware that, except at high tide and near the water's edge, the water is generally more than a little nippy because of the strong currents flowing through Discovery Passage.

Suitability for children Little children, of course, will be happiest in the giant sandbox of the upper beach. Older and more stable children may be eager to hunt for dried kelp bulbs or climb some of the giant boulders that dot the lower shore. The beach is not well suited to swimming, but, of course, when the tide is high, almost any child will show no hesitation in getting thoroughly wet, in spite of cautious words from sensible parents.

Suitability for groups This is one of the better spots on the island to bring a cavalcade of guests. The ample parking and the even more ample expanse of shore mean that congestion and overcrowding are the least of your concerns. Do ensure, however, that your crowd realizes they will find no facilities here and shouldn't expect the acres of flat sand that most crowds seem to seek out when on the prowl for their annual shareholders' picnic.

View The view is one of the glories of this spot, both along the sweeping shoreline of this end of the island and also across Discovery Passage to the south end of Campbell River and the mountains of Strathcona Park beyond. Those with a good eye can also spot distant Mount Arrowsmith and the tiny but distinctive hump of Hornby Island. Come at the right time, too, and you may find yourself with a close-up view of freighters, fishing boats and even Alaska cruise ships, all making their way through the only deepwater channel between Vancouver Island and the mainland.

Winds, sun and shade Both northwest and southeast winds run largely parallel to the coast here, but you will find some protection behind the logs, especially during a northwest wind and especially if you walk to your left down the curving shoreline.

Beachcombing This is the perfect spot to exercise your wanderlust—and your ankles. Though walking over the rocks can be a little awkward, once you get into the rhythm you can stride great distances in either direction. For the longest walks, though, and for dramatic changes in view, head to your left and the southern tip of the island. Low tide reveals weirdly configured bars extending several hundred metres into the straits. The high, sandy cliffs of Cape Mudge itself add to the unusual geography of this whole strip of shoreline. With nearly 20 km of shore walking available, this part of Quadra Island probably has the most extensive beachcombing of any of the islands in the Salish Sea.

Seclusion You are likely to see a few people here, especially if you walk to your left and below the shorefront resort. The beach is so vast, however, that these few people—and you—seem mere grains of sand.

73 NUYUMBALEES
CULTURAL CENTRE
A gradually sloping, pebbly shore, facing across Discovery Passage, is part of a visit to the cultural centre

Location, signs and parking Many of the routes around Quadra Island are scenic, but this one is unusually so. In fact, for about 1 km, you will be driving next to the shore, with magnificent views across Discovery Passage. Not only scenic but as easy as falling off a log, the route begins with a right turn onto Green Road as you drive away from the ferry. Approximately 3 km later, you will come to "Cape Mudge Village," as it has been called, a First Nation settlement on a gorgeous area of flat land next to the water. Simply turn toward the village and follow the signs to the Nuyumbalees Cultural Centre. It would be criminal not to include a visit to this jaw-droppingly beautiful museum as part of your tour of Quadra Island. You will find plenty of parking by the cultural centre.

Path While it would be inappropriate to come into this First Nation community unless you are visiting the cultural centre, once here, you need only cross the road from the centre and walk through a grassy field to appreciate both the carved totems there and the shoreline behind. While you won't find an obvious path from the grassy area onto the shore, you will find it easy to take the few steps down the slope.

Beach One of the most welcoming beaches on the east side of Quadra Island, the shore here deserves at least a brief visit. Although a few jagged boulders dot the upper beach, the gradually sloping shore is composed mostly of fine gravel, stretching far away into the distance in either direction. In fact, if you have planned a long-distance shore walk around the whole southern end of the island, you will inevitably pass this section.

Suitability for children If children have accompanied you in your visit to the cultural centre, they can comfortably and safely also visit this adjoining bit of shore.

Suitability for groups As part of their visit to the cultural centre, your entourage will naturally want to appreciate the totems near the shore. Here they will find lots of space and a good viewpoint.

View It is really the view that will draw you to the shore here, both of Quadra Island itself and of Vancouver Island, across Discovery Passage. Because your viewpoint is positioned in the middle of a long, curving chunk of shoreline, you can see about 5 km of Quadra's west coast from this one spot. If you have brought your binoculars, you will be in an especially good position to enjoy the banquet spread of "big island" features spread before you. The first part of a sunny day in early spring is the very best time to enjoy the view. The Vancouver Island Ranges, lit from the east and startlingly white with snow, are worth every pixel your digital camera assigns to them.

Winds, sun and shade As long as you are not facing rain—or worse—the elements are not of much concern to you during a short visit. You will notice, though, that prevailing winds tend to run parallel to the shore in either direction.

Beachcombing If you have parked outside reserve land and are in the middle of a long trek, you will find this section of shore makes for easy strolling.

Seclusion This beach is in the middle of a village, but the shore is likely to be quiet and beautifully peaceful.

74
NOBLE ROAD—SOUTH
A little beach of jagged boulders, good for car picnicking, with magnificent views across Discovery Passage to Campbell River and the Island mountains

Location, signs and parking Head up the hill from the ferry terminal and take the first road on your right, Green Road. Follow it for about half a kilometre until the intersection with Noble Road. Turn right, and just over half a kilometre later, you will find a small, looping gravel strip off the side of the road in full view of the water. You will see no signs to guide or restrict you, but you will hardly need them. This is a spot to seek out when the sun has turned tail on you and you find yourself with a sumptuous picnic and nowhere attractive to eat it. Come here, and you can enjoy a beautiful view of mountains and boat traffic while putting paid to those crab croissant sandwiches and steaming cups of coffee.

Path While only two or three metres of wild grass separate you from the shore, you won't find a well-prepared route down the little drop onto the jagged boulders.

Beach You will be hard-pressed to apply the term "beach" to this steep shore of large, angular boulders. While few would choose this spot who want to visit the shore rather than to enjoy the view, the more curious and adventurous will find some rewards in making their way over the rocks. The icy currents that sweep by this part of the coast are rich with nutrients—much to the delight of the critters that lurk under the boulders.

Suitability for children While the smallest children might be a little dismayed with this shore, older, more adventurous ones will not. Parents may be content to sit and drink in the view—but children worth their salt will find this rocky tangle, however restricted, a good place for hurling rocks into the deep water or hunting down seashells and bizarre little animals.

Suitability for groups If you have come to Quadra Island with a minor entourage, you can lead them here with the knowledge that you will find room for two or three other cars at this waterfront car-picnicking spot.

View The view is the main attraction of this spot. Whether you are interested in the busy boat traffic navigating the treacherous waters of Discovery Passage or the peaks of Strathcona Park towering above Campbell River, come with binoculars and a camera, and you will find it hard to tear yourself away. If you spend the day touring Quadra Island, consider swinging by here in the evening for a ringside seat on the sun setting over the Island peaks. On the other hand, if you want to photograph the peaks when they are posing most decoratively, choose a sunny day in the early spring and arrive in the morning.

Winds, sun and shade While winds rarely blow directly onto the shore, both prevailing winds do whistle up and down Discovery Passage, sometimes whipping it into a minor frenzy.

Beachcombing This is a spot for staying more or less put while letting your eyes roam. Even so, if you're up for a little exploration, wandering around the low-tide line and poking under rocks might yield some fascinating discoveries in the form of leather stars, chitons and, if you're lucky, leafy hornmouths.

Seclusion This spot happens to be located at a break in a largely continuous sequence of shorefront houses. Even so, little local traffic uses this dead-end road and only the few visitors, like yourself, who know of the spot's existence are likely to come here. Enjoy the sense of being at a secret window onto a splendid little chunk of scenery.

Quadra: Discovery Passage from Noble Road—North

75

NOBLE ROAD—NORTH
A virtually "secret" spot with
a steep rocky shore and a
splendid view up Discovery
Passage

Location, signs and parking Trundle off the ferry and take the first turn right onto Green Road. About half a kilometre later, at a crossroad, turn right onto Noble Road and follow it to its northern end as it swings around to run parallel to the shore. You will see a steep driveway running uphill straight ahead, a road-width track angling downward toward the shore, and a small parking area with a sign forbidding overnight parking and camping.

Path Although it is theoretically possible for skookum vehicles to drive down the track toward the shore, you are best off parking on Noble Road and walking the few dozen metres to a small level area immediately above the shore. Most visitors will be happy using this small area to find a grassy or mossy hillock and drinking in the view, but it is possible to climb over the steep, ragged rocks onto the shore for a better view into Quathiaski Cove, immediately to the north.

Beach It is hard to find many beaches on Quadra more rugged and steep. The area of rough boulders immediately below the access can be traversed, but on either side, solid-rock outcroppings are slippery with fucus at low tide. Don't write off the spot, though, if you are looking for an utterly isolated viewpoint with pleasant, grassy spots for meditating on nature or the pleasures of picnicking. Those looking for an access for shore fishing will immediately notice that the bull kelp growing up against the low-tide rocks is a sure sign of a steep drop-off. Be aware that the water is generally icy along this part of the island, since the strong currents that sweep past create powerful upwellings.

Suitability for children Small children could hardly find a spot less conducive to survival. Older children with an overdose of gumption and curiosity can happily clamber over the jungle gym of boulders while their more circumspect elders savour the view or the sandwiches.

Suitability for groups The spot is much too small and the parking much too limited for more than a few visitors at a time.

View The view is the real glory of this access. Similar to the view from the nearby shorefront parking area half a kilometre south along Noble Road, that here allows you an even more spectacular vista of Discovery Passage, past craggy little Grouse Island along the coast of Quadra Island toward April Point. Quathiaski Cove is tucked largely out of sight around the bluff to the right. If you have brought binoculars and maps, you will soon discover that this is a superb spot to view many of the highest peaks of Strathcona Park. From Mount Albert Edward, Mount Washington and Alexandra Peak to the south, your view sweeps across the range toward Big Den Mountain and Crown Mountain, among many others. This also happens to be one of the best spots on Quadra for magnificent views of sunsets over the highest mountains on Vancouver Island.

Winds, sun and shade If you perch above the shore, you will have a little protection from the wind, but the shore itself is subject to both northwest and southeast winds funnelling up and down Discovery Passage. The afternoon is by far the sunniest part of the day.

Beachcombing Wandering along the shore should be the last thing on your mind if you seek out this hidden little spot. Pick your way over the rocks, by all means. But go for a seaside stroll? No.

Seclusion Although several lucky house owners cluster along this rocky section of the coast, from this little nook, you will feel wonderfully tucked out of sight. Since this is the end of an out-of-the-way dead-end road, you need share the spot only with whichever soulmate you have told your secret.

While you're here . . . Also near to the ferry terminal, but on its northern side, is the public access at the end of Ferry Road accessible from Pidcock Road. Here you will find a lovely little view spot over Quathiaski Cove and Grouse Island, as well as a slightly overgrown path down a few steps to a small gravel shore.

PART 5 Cortes Island

FOR THOSE VANCOUVER ISLANDERS more or less familiar with the islands of the Gulf of Georgia, Cortes Island is a little mysterious and remote. The reasons aren't hard to find. It *is* remote, and, up to a point, it is also mysterious. Actually lying much closer to the mainland than to Vancouver Island, Cortes Island is reached only by a small, infrequent ferry from Quadra Island. In addition, almost all of the island's residents are clustered around the southern end. With the most convoluted and deeply indented shoreline of any of the settled islands, Cortes Island, and most of its northern section, is a barely penetrated landscape of high, forested ridges and long inlets and bays. Add to these the fact that the island is composed mostly of black rock with some areas of granite, and you may decide to put Cortes into the file "To Be Visited . . . Later." If you did so, however, you would miss out on some of the most memorable and beautiful experiences to be found in all of the islands. First, consider the 40-minute ferry trip from Quadra Island. Take this trip on a clear day in spring, when the tooth-sharp crags of the Coast Mountains are thick with snow, and you will be convinced you have found the most spectacular mini-cruise in British Columbia. Relish the fact. That is exactly what you've done. Once you arrive on Cortes Island, you won't find a huge number of beaches, but those you do find, some of them public parks, rival any of the most popular beaches in the Salish Sea for their acres of fine sand and warm swimming water. In addition, some of the hidden spots are as hidden as any you can find anywhere. These are not just somewhat "secret," they are truly isolated—and deeply beautiful.

The map shows roads and numbered beach locations: 77, 78, 79, 76. Road labels include COULTER BAY RD, SAWMILL RD, JARDING TON BAY RD, SEAVISTA RD, HARBOUR RD, FERRY.

76

SEAVISTA ROAD

An isolated beach of mixed gravel and rock within walking distance of the ferry

Location, signs and parking If you happened to have come to Cortes as a foot passenger or simply want a beach almost certain to be empty, go up Harbour Road for about half a kilometre and turn left onto Seavista Road. Less than a kilometre along Seavista Road will bring you to a fork in the road and, straight ahead, a road-width gravel track. You won't see an obvious parking spot but will have no difficulty pulling onto the shoulder near this gravel track.

Path An easy stroll about 100 m down this roadbed through a thick second-growth stand of firs and cedar will bring you to the shore. A flat area next to huge signs alerts boaters to the existence of an underwater cable and signals them not to anchor.

Beach Immediately in front of the grassy area, logs sometimes collect, often loosely scattered rather than tidily backed up against the bank. The most appealing part of the upper beach for picnickers or sunbathers is to the left of the access point, past a patch of boulders. While this area of coarse sand and pebbles is immediately in front of private property, as yet no one has built here. Since the entire shore to the low-tide line is covered with boulders beyond this part of the beach, most visitors will find strolling down the beach toward the water's edge most attractive close to the access.

Suitability for children Don't select this spot if your primary purpose is to give your little ones an afternoon at the beach. On the other hand, you may well choose this isolated and attractive bay to savour its more subtle adult pleasures, confident that most children will find lots of opportunities for beach play. Since the shore slopes gradually, you needn't worry overmuch about setting your children free to create watery mayhem or molest the critters under the rocks. Water shoes are crucial for everyone's peace of mind.

Suitability for groups Bring a small group to this beautiful, quiet spot for a peaceful bit of communing with each other or with nature. Be aware that your group will have to be up for a tromp from their car to the shore and, of course, will find no facilities.

View This is the only beach access spot on Cortes Island that allows an unrestricted view across Sutil Channel toward Quadra Island. While the western end of Marina Island is visible beyond the headland to the left end of the beach, this expansive view otherwise is most distinctive for the long curve of boulder shore sweeping to the north and west.

Winds, sun and shade Largely protected from northwest winds, this spot is fairly exposed to winds from the southeast. Storm lovers, too, may appreciate the fact that not just winds but also the large waves sweeping up Sutil Channel can wash ashore in this bay, particularly along the shore to the right of the access spot. While the beach can be a little dark with shade during the early part of the day, it becomes increasingly sunny in the course of the afternoon. If you're here toward the evening, in fact, you may want to position yourself for a great front seat on a full-blown sunset.

Beachcombing While beach walking isn't particularly easy, it can be immensely rewarding on this isolated piece of wave-swept coast. If you are not prone to twisted ankles and wear sturdy shoes, head to the right of the access. You will be able to walk for well over 1 km around the headland and along the shore of Plunger Pass, which separates this headland from the picturesque Subtle Islands just offshore.

Seclusion Although one very large house stands firm along the shore to the right of this bit of curving coast, this house is the only encroachment on what is otherwise a wild and open piece of shoreline. Even on a hot day, you are likely to be inspected only by eagles and seals.

While you're here . . . Even closer to the ferry terminal is the small beach a few dozen metres along the shore to the west of the ferry dock. This gravel beach can be reached by a public path leading down from the roadside or by a shorter path from the ferry parking lot below the road. This is a good beach to visit while waiting for the ferry. It is also a good place to launch a kayak if you want to avoid ferry congestion and bring your kayak across without a car—though you will have to carry your kayak more than 150 m in total.

77
SAWMILL ROAD
A broad track through cedars and swordferns to a deeply inset little bay with a gravel and rock shore

Location, signs and parking For those who have come to the island on bicycles, this is one of the most accessible shore spots to visit. Simply head away from the ferry along Harbour Road for about 1.5 km and, at the T-junction, turn left onto Carrington Bay Road for 200 or 300 m. Sawmill Road, on your left, ends about 1 km later in a functional but small turnaround area.

Path If you have come by car, park here and walk the 100 m to the shore down the sloping dirt road, past cedars and swordferns. This roadbed can be a little muddy and rutted but is smooth enough that it is occasionally used to launch boats.

Beach You will find a small area of fine pebbles at the uppermost part of the beach. Since it is largely overhung with cedar boughs and lacks handy perching logs, you are unlikely to want to pause here for a picnic. At low tide, the small bay reveals about 100 m of gravel. To the left, the gravel shoreline ends abruptly at a steep wall of forests and high cliffs. To the right, the gravel merges into uneven rock and, after a small headland, stretches for a few hundred metres.

Suitability for children Given the alternatives on the distant south end of Cortes Island, you will find little reason to single this spot out for your little eager beavers. If, however, you want to explore the spot yourself, you can be comfortable letting your children wander over the tidal flats looking among the rocks for hermit crabs, ochre starfish, frilled dog whelks and limpets without much fear that any child will come a cropper amongst steep slippery rocks.

Suitability for groups Few groups would find this a welcoming or even interesting spot unless they are naturalists, photographers or painters. In this case, a small group will be well contented with the picturesque view, especially if they walk along the shore a little.

View Indeed, it is the view, in many ways a classic combination of fjord-land ingredients that makes the spot well worth visiting. A tiny, heavily treed islet in the middle of the bay is framed by the dramatically steep shoreline to the west. Looking out of the bay beyond Sutil Channel, you will see the high, forested ridges and crests of Read Island around Burdwood Bay. Some toters of sketchbooks and cameras will be intrigued by the hulk of an abandoned fishing boat to the left of the bay. Others might just find it ugly.

Winds, sun and shade You will have few worries about a wind knocking over an easel. Although you can expect some northwesterlies to create a bit of a stir here, you can equally expect barely a riffle or waft if the wind is from the southeast. Late afternoon is the sunniest part of the day. During the first part of the day, heavy shadows cover most of the upper shore.

Beachcombing At low tide, you can explore your way along the shore for a few hundred metres to the right. Come with sturdy shoes, however, and a curiosity tuned to appreciating the close-up world of intertidal critters.

Seclusion Apart from a private residence well hidden among the trees to the left of the access road, you are unlikely even to be aware of the existence of fellow humans. Almost all visitors to the island head to the south end of Cortes and its large sandy beaches. Don't be surprised if you have this little hidden cove entirely to yourself.

78
COULTER BAY
The best kayak-launching spot during a strong southeasterly, providing access to the sheltered waters north of Cortes Island

Location, signs and parking The directions to this remote location are as simple as the distance is short. Head your vehicle and kayak away from the ferry along Harbour Road until the T-junction about 1.5 km later, and turn left onto Carrington Bay Road. Keep left, and the road will eventually turn into Coulter Bay Road. This road ends a little under 3 km away at the head of a well-protected bay. You will see a huge gravel parking area where you can leave your Lamborghini to explore this hidden spot, to take some photos or sketch the picturesque view. If you've brought your kayak, drive directly to the shore, being careful not to go too far onto the soft surface of gravel and mud. In fact, you will be happiest if you come at or near high tide, but you can get your kayak to the water at just about any tide if you don't mind slightly squelchy footing. The only relevant sign, posted by Fisheries, bears the ghoulish image of a skull and crossbones superimposed on a giant clam. In fact, rather than prohibiting you from collecting shellfish, the sign merely warns you to check that there has been no paralytic poisoning before you begin your collecting.

Path It is the absence of a path that makes this a good spot for launching—as the tire tracks usually criss-crossing the surface of the beach suggest. Don't expect anything fancy by way of a launching ramp. Though the slope to the shore is gradual, it is just pebbles and gravel.

Beach This is not the kind of beach you would seek out if you are planning the conventional kind of beaching activities. Because it is so well protected from the wind and waves, it is rather murky and overhung with trees. Even for those not intending to launch kayaks, however, it is well worth visiting as a picturesque view spot, especially at high tide.

Suitability for children Don't bring your children here for a day's outing. If, however, you want to explore the spot yourself, you can expect them to wander and prod safely around the shore without worrying about them tripping over hazardous boulders or falling down steep rocky drop-offs.

Suitability for groups Very few groups would thank you for bringing them here. Because the bay is sheltered, it can be a good bird-spotting area, though, and sketchers will find some intriguing subjects.

View Apart from its value as a launching spot, this small, deeply inset bay makes for attractive views because it is nearly blocked from the open waters of Coulter Channel by Coulter Island. Though this island and two other tiny islets are connected at low tide, at high tide, when the flats are covered, they make for a picturesque combination of miniature seascape features, especially if you make your way along the shore beyond the launching area.

Winds, sun and shade Are winds howling elsewhere around the island? You are unlikely to feel much more than a faint stirring here. In fact, if you are about to begin a kayaking venture, you may be lulled a little into false confidence unless you check the conditions. Though late afternoon is the sunniest part of the day, it is unlikely that the presence of sun or shade will matter much to most visitors.

Beachcombing Don't come here with the expectation of walking along the shore. Beyond the launching area and the head of the bay, most of the shoreline is far too steep and slippery for comfortable walking.

Seclusion Though occasional houses peer from the trees around the bay, and though the spot is well used for launching even large boats, the spot is hidden from most visitors.

79 CARRINGTON BAY REGIONAL PARK

A long forested walk to a remarkable spot between two grassy knolls where tides wash in and out of Carrington Lagoon

Location, signs and parking From the ferry, head up Harbour Road until the junction with Carrington Bay Road, about 1 km along. Turn left. Roughly 2 km later, look for a distinctive pull-off where the road turns sharply left. Currently, no sign is posted at this trailhead, but one is planned, so it may be there when you arrive. It is also possible to approach via so-called Jimmy Smith Way off Whaletown Road, but this is a rough gravel track and therefore less desirable.

Path Probably the most isolated regional park in the Northern Gulf Islands, this spot can be reached only by means of considerable, though attractive, walking. The well-maintained trails are mostly roadbeds used occasionally by forest service vehicles and "quads." The two- to three-kilometre walk, mostly through old moss-covered firs and sword-ferns, also passes some waterfalls. By the shore itself, you will see an interesting, airy outhouse-with-a-view, particularly useful to those who camp here.

Beach The path brings you to the mouth of one of the tidal lagoons for which Cortes Island is remarkable among the islands of the Salish Sea. Like the lagoons at Von Donop Inlet and Manson's Landing, this one fills on an incoming tide and, on a dropping tide, becomes a cascade of rushing water flowing out of the lagoon. In this case, a small wooden bridge spans the narrow gap between two rocky ridges through which the water splashes. The upper beach facing outward into Carrington Bay is mostly slab-like igneous rock merging into a rocky lower beach about 40 m wide. While the smooth rocky area or the adjacent sun-bleached patch of grass are good picnic spots, the gravelly uppermost shore on the east side of the small bay is probably the most welcoming for picnics.

Suitability for children The length of the trail here will discourage your bringing wee folk who are too large to be comfortable in a backpack and too small to undertake a mini-hike. Add to that the fact that the beach isn't wonderful for the littlest children, and you may want to postpone a visit here for a few years. This is a great spot for the adventurous crowd, though; it has been a favourite campout for many of the island's elementary schoolchildren.

Suitability for groups If you make sure any group you shepherd here is properly prepared for the walk and the isolation, you can come confident that you won't feel the slightest twinge about invading a residential neighbourhood. The area is the spectacular opposite of residential.

View You won't find many other island views in the Salish Sea where you will feel so much as if you are looking at a lake rather than the ocean. Because Carrington Bay is so long and curved, you can see only out a narrow gap into Sutil Channel. Needless to say, though, the heavily forested crests around the bay and around the lagoon off the bay make for some quintessential West Coast scenery.

Winds, sun and shade The first part of the day is shadowy on much of the beach, but the treeless rocky area by the lagoon's entrance is in sun throughout the day. This almost landlocked spot is largely protected from southeast winds and somewhat protected from northwest winds.

Beachcombing If you have not already had enough walking by the time you get to this spot, you can explore farther along the shore of Carrington Bay. Choose low tide, though, and go to your right. After about a kilometre, the fairly steep shore becomes probably too steep for the comfort of all but the most intrepid.

Seclusion While this can be a popular spot with islanders, rarely will you see more than the odd person from whom to learn a little island lore. The chances are high that you will have the spot to yourself. Even more to the point, you won't see a trace of civilization's incursions onto this splendid wilderness spot.

80

SQUIRREL COVE

Waterfront parking for easy launching of kayaks in a protected cove with adjacent shops

Location, signs and parking Having completed probably the most scenic minor sea cruise on the British Columbia coast, hunker down for one of the most convoluted island explorations on the British Columbia coast. From the ferry terminal in Whaletown Bay, follow Harbour Road about 1.5 km to a T-junction. Turn right onto Carrington Bay Road for just over 1 km and, at another T-junction, left onto Whaletown Road. Now settle back for a winding road, delivering you about 11 km later to signposted Squirrel Cove. Here you will find not just a little restaurant and shop but lots of shorefront parking. Before making a beeline for the shore, pause to look at the large sign at the back of the parking area, full of information about the history of shellfish on Cortes Island. The only other significant sign is beside a concrete launching ramp, with information about charges (currently eight dollars).

Path This is a perfect spot for those with walking difficulties or those who find themselves more interested in paddling kayaks than in lugging them long distances. Except for the minor barricades of shore-stabilizing boulders and a few logs, nothing much lies between you and the shore. If the weather has become treacherously unwelcoming during your visit to the island, this is a good spot to enjoy your picnic while enjoying a picturesque waterfront view.

Beach You will find yourself on a long stretch of gradually sloping gravel shore. Because this is, as the cove in its name suggests, well protected from the lashes of waves, the gravel is somewhat jagged and becomes increasingly so toward the low-tide line. Though the tide usually retreats only a few dozen metres, the shore is gradual and even enough to offer few impediments. Although it's perhaps not the most enticing picnic area on Cortes Island, if you have arrived around lunchtime or picked up a few delectables from the nearby shop, you can find a pleasant spot to perch along the pebbly upper shore, best to the left of the launching ramp.

Suitability for children Given the splendid alternatives on the island, don't seek this spot out as a place to bring your children for an afternoon of beach fun. After all, the pleasures of gravel and rock for most children play a very distant second fiddle to the pleasures of sand and tidal pools found elsewhere. Still, children being children, in the absence of alternatives they can be let loose with few worries that they will come a cropper or find nothing to amuse them. A beach is, after all, a beach. And water? Everyone can hope that you brought a change of shoes.

Suitability for groups If parking, washrooms and shore access are your chief concerns, this is an easy and welcoming spot for a minor slew of cars and explorers. Most groups, however, intent on lolling and frolicking, will be much happier at one of the island's gorgeous parks.

View The view is one of the huge pleasures of this spot. Intriguing, picturesque and varied, it cries out to be captured on film or sketchpad. Look to your left along the shore, and you will see a minor shipwreck and, in the distance, the First Nation settlement, Klahoose, the site of the Oyster Festival on the May holiday weekend. What you don't see is that Squirrel Cove disappears behind a headland far into the interior of Cortes Island, separated by only a narrow strip of land from Von Donop Inlet cutting into the island from the northwest. Most visitors, however, will find that their eyes are drawn immediately to look across Desolation Sound to West Redonda Island and, beyond it, the jagged crags of the Coast Range. Come on a clear spring day, when the mountains are still deep in snow, and you will be hard-pressed to restrict your "oohs" and "aws."

Winds, sun and shade This spot comes by its name "cove" honestly—but not completely so. Somewhat exposed to the north, it can become more than a little windy. During stormy weather, however, when the wind is almost always from the southeast, the cove is snugged well out of the blasts. In fact, on a hot day, without wind and without a trace of shade, the shore can become a minor oven.

Beachcombing Come with sturdy shoes and a little wanderlust, and head to your right out of Squirrel Cove for a solid shore trek. You will soon pass the Gnat Road shore access and see, stretching before you, more than 2 km of expansive, rocky shore dotted at points with large boulders.

Seclusion By Cortes Island standards, this spot can be considered busy. Most visitors come because of the government wharf, the private launching pad or the shop, however. Even then, the spot is never crowded. Walk a short distance along the shore and you will realize how much of the island is still unsettled.

81
GNAT ROAD
A zigzagging wooded trail to a secluded rocky shore with a magnificent mountain view

Location, signs and parking From the ferry terminal in Whaletown Bay, head out along Harbour Road about 1.5 km to a T-junction. Note the signs to Smelt Bay and Manson's Landing parks. Turn right onto Carrington Bay Road for just over 1 km and, at another T-junction, left onto Whaletown Road. This long, twisting road, after 11 km or so, will take you past Squirrel Cove and its various shops and facilities. A few hundred metres later, after the road turns sharply right (Squirrel Cove Road at this point), look for tiny Gnat Road on your left. A few dozen metres down this dead-end road, you will see plenty of room to park and a blue-and-white sign announcing the beginning of Gnat Road Trail.

View of Cortes Island from Cortes ferry

Path This carefully cleared but sometimes rugged trail leads, for about 200 m, first through a stand of small alders and then down a steep cedar-covered bank. At points the trail is bordered with rocks and is well graded, but is not well suited to those with walking difficulties because of the steep bank.

Beach The trail to the beach emerges from under a large cedar into a clutter of logs and an upper shore of fine gravel. This is a welcoming spot to spread out your beach feast or to take up temporary residence with your journal or ukulele. Farther down, the gradually sloping beach is covered with increasingly large, rounded granite boulders.

Suitability for children Children who have been primed for a venture into the wilds should enjoy the sense of exploring the forest trail and the iso-lated shore. Choose low tide if their interests include peering under rocks for limpets and chitons. Choose high tide, however, if getting thoroughly doused is a priority. In either case, forget to bring water shoes at your peril. As for the stubbiest and most vulnerable little ones, take them elsewhere.

Suitability for groups While you can anticipate parking for several cars and need not worry about having a noisy impact on neighbours—there aren't any—don't bring a group here that has an interest in easy access to a sandy shore and lots of facilities. A group keen on exploring a section of shore with a magnificent view, however, will be impressed with your choice.

View For mountain lovers, this spot will vie for a top position among the most beautiful view spots on any of the islands in the Salish Sea. First off, you will be impressed by the steep shores of West Redonda Island across Desolation Sound. Then, farther to your right, let your eyes drink in the crags and crests of the mountains behind and to the south of Toba Inlet.

Winds, sun and shade Because this coast of Cortes Island faces almost due east, the prevailing winds run largely parallel to the shore, funnelling up and down Desolation Sound. Morning is the sunniest part of the day on the upper beach, since the high wooded banks create deep shade in the afternoon.

Beachcombing While some will choose to explore this largely secluded chunk of coastline from nearby Squirrel Cove, others will find this starting point more beautiful. Head to your right for more than 2 km of discovery over gradually sloping, rocky shore. For a different kind of walk, turn left and follow the shore to Squirrel Cove, its government wharf and, if you're peckish, a tasty pick-me-up from a local business.

Seclusion While not complete wilderness, this whole section of coast is largely unpeopled. Except for occasional houses peering from the high, forested bank, you will see few traces of fellow humans. For companionship, you just might have to make do with gulls and seals.

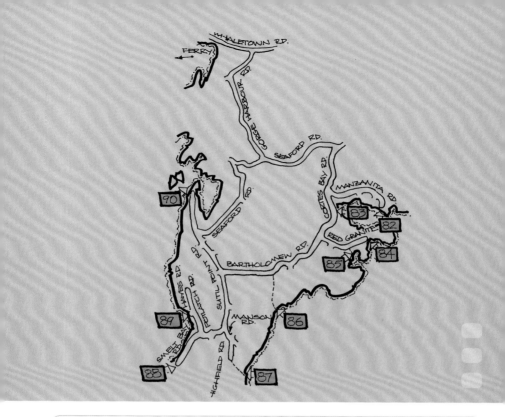

82

MANZANITA ROAD

A short, forested trail to one end of a quiet, rocky bay thick with spectacular amounts of driftwood logs

Location, signs and parking Bracing yourself for a bit of an adventure in navigation, head off the ferry along Harbour Road for about 1.5 km and turn right onto Carrington Bay Road for just over 1 km to the next T-junction. A left onto Whaletown Road will bring you, approximately 6 km later, to a fork in the road. Turn right onto Gorge Harbour Road until the next T-junction, almost 4 km later. Turn left onto Seaford Road for almost 2 km, then right onto Cortes Bay Road for roughly 2 km, forking left onto Manzanita Road and following it for well over 1 km to a capacious gravel turnaround. You won't see any signs, helpful or otherwise, but you will see a path near the end of the parking area. You have a clear sight of your destination through the trunks of the firs.

Path A short path, only a dozen or so metres, brings you easily down a slight slope to the beach. Generally clear, it is bordered by knee-high salal that can crowd enthusiastically onto the path during the summer. Those with walking difficulties should find the path manageable, but may find getting onto the beach itself a bit of an ordeal. Read on.

Beach Your first impression of the beach will be of wood—a lot of wood. This gently sloping and deeply inset little bay is clearly a kind of black hole for every passing log and chunk of driftwood. Below the swath of logs, this little bay, roughly 100 m long, is almost entirely covered with fist-sized rocks. Depending on which pickup-sticks configuration of logs the last winter storm has created, you should be able to find convenient ready-made benches and picnic tables.

Suitability for children This is not a spot for those wee ones who need a playpen of soft sand. It is, however, a great place to explore for galumphing older children eager to clamber over the mountains of logs, hurl rocks or practise a little entry-level rock climbing on the granite outcroppings at either end of the beach.

Suitability for groups If you are looking for easy parking and a quiet picnic spot where you and your beach buddies can be your collective selves, this is one good option. Be aware, however, that you don't have the beach completely to yourselves and that, of course, you will find no facilities—beyond the all-purpose logs.

View This is the kind of picturesque view, complex and convoluted, that you might expect of an island's shoreline. A series of overlapping rocky points to your right largely conceals Cortes Bay, with its clearly visible navigation light and barely visible government wharf. Heavily forested Red Granite Point, directly opposite, will appeal to those interested in combining beach visits with walking trails. To the south, you can pick out the tiny Cod Rocks (aka Three Islets), and, in sequence, Twin, Hernando and Savary Islands.

Winds, sun and shade It isn't just the geography of the bay that makes it a magnet for drifting logs. It is also the wind. The southeast winds funnelling up the straits and past the islands blow directly into this little bay. Northwest winds, however, almost entirely skirt it. Midday is the sunniest time of day. Looking for shade from the blistering rays? Come later in the afternoon.

Beachcombing While walking the length of the bay is enticing, walking beyond the bay in either direction is not. Take the time to pry up some of the rocks on the lower beach and investigate the slimy world of chitons, limpets and frilled dog whelks.

Seclusion When you see the glint of sunlight on the large windows peering out from the trees at the right end of the beach, you will realize that you are not quite free from inspection. On the whole, though, the spot creates a sense of untouched shore and barely touched forest.

83 BLIND CREEK BOAT RAMP
The best kayaking launching spot for access to the southeast coast of Cortes Island and Desolation Sound

Location, signs and parking If you are toting your beloved kayaks, head expectantly off the ferry along Harbour Road for about 1.5 km and turn right onto Carrington Bay Road for just over 1 km to a T-junction. Turn left onto Whaletown Road and, approximately 6 km later, turn right onto Gorge Harbour Road until the next T-junction almost 4 km later. Turn left onto Seaford Road for almost 2 km, then right onto Cortes Bay Road for roughly 2 km. Where the road runs directly along the shoreline of Cortes Bay, slow down and decide whether you wish to park on the wide gravel shoulder closer to the ramp or to the little beach at the end of the bay. A spanking new natural cedar sign identifies BLIND CREEK BOAT RAMP and, among other things, notes that the ramp becomes slippery with algae at low tide. At the beach end of the parking area, you will see another sign with dire and graphic warnings about shellfish poisoning.

Path If you are heading for the little beach, you have a short, slightly scrambly descent past large, irregular boulders. If, however, you have come to this spot to get your brightly coloured pleasure craft into the water, a skookum, newly constructed concrete ramp paves your way to the waterline.

Beach Because the beach at the end of the bay is protected from the swirling waters of wind-driven waves, it tends to be a little muddy. Composed of small gravel, however, it is easily explored and, at low tide, can yield some interesting specimens cowering away from the full force of the open coast. Some 75 m long, the upper, log-lined shore makes for a pleasant bit of tromping.

Suitability for children Children can, of course, find any shore a source of imaginative (and wet) play. You might be assured that the younger set can keep themselves entertained while you fuss around with your kayaks before launching, but don't go out of your way to bring your children here for an afternoon's play.

Suitability for groups If you happen to have a minor flotilla of adventure-bound kayakers, you can launch at any tide, under any wind conditions, and find lots of parking space. Other groups? Shepherd them elsewhere.

View If you are on a photography or sketching venture, you will want to come here on your tour of local beauty spots. The combination of forested bumps, near and distant, and the window you get onto the peaks of the Coast Mountains make for some memorable compositions.

Winds, sun and shade One of the reasons this makes a great launching spot is its protection from waves, and, for the most part, wind. While shade is not an issue for kayakers, you might note that a few shady alders adjoin the parking area.

Beachcombing The little beach is easy enough to traverse for exploring, but otherwise you could hardly choose a spot less conducive to extensive shore walking.

Seclusion The bay is quiet and largely isolated. You might trip over only a few other lovers of the coast and its watery pleasures.

84

RED GRANITE ROAD

A small, rocky bay, thick with logs, great for car picnicking during a southeasterly storm

Location, signs and parking Head along Harbour Road for about 1.5 km and spot the right turn for Smelt Bay Park on Carrington Bay Road. Just over 1 km to the next T-junction take a left onto Whaletown Road. About 6 km later turn right onto Gorge Harbour Road until the next T-junction, almost 4 km later. Swing left onto Seaford Road for almost 2 km, then right onto Cortes Bay Road for roughly 3 km. Take Red Granite Road on your left and follow it for about 1 km until nearly its end, where you find the road in clear sight of a small bay opposite a collection of cabins belonging to the Seattle Yacht Club. Planning a beach fire and a yodel-along? Note the sign atop a shorefront stump telling you in no uncertain terms that fires of any sort are not welcome here.

Path While you can park just a few metres from the shore on an exposed bit of flat, bare ground, getting across the crowd of logs on the shore can be a bit of a stumble. Be particularly wary if the logs are wet. You can manage a kayak the short, level distance to the shore, but you will be most pleased with yourself about your choice of launching spots if you come at or near high tide.

Beach About 100 m wide, this small rocky bay is directly exposed to the southeast and a generous chunk of the Strait of Georgia. Facing directly south, like two or three other similar bays on this coast, it is a virtual magnet for logs and driftwood. Although the shore surface is mostly rough gravel and small rocks, it is separated into two sides by a large tidal pool or shallow inlet. You won't find any silky-soft sand or even comfortable pebbles for perching long, but you will find log after log after log of improvisable benches and picnic tables.

Suitability for children This is not a beach for tender little feet toddling in and out of wavelets. It is, however, a great spot for older, adventurous children whose notion of exploring intriguing shore goes beyond building sandcastles. The wild, exposed shore, with its wave-worn rocks and logs, is a playground of imagination-stirring possibilities.

Suitability for groups You can bring a few carefully chosen cohorts here, secure in the knowledge that you will find easy parking, easy shore access and plenty of room well away from neighbouring houses. These cohorts do need careful choosing, however, because here they will find no facilities and no sand. What they will find is a gorgeous morsel of near wilderness.

View Ragged rock promontories, ornamented with weathered firs, frame a distant perspective on a sequence of overlapping islands extending many kilometres to the south. You will need good binoculars and a detailed map to identify the dozens of little islands on the east side of the passage but should easily pick out nearby Three Islets, and possibly, Powell Islets. On the west side, the low skylines of Twin, Hernando and Savary Islands extend far into the distance.

Winds, sun and shade If the strait is dishing up even a minor waft of southeast wind, you will feel it here. Warm-weather northwesterlies, however, leave you largely untouched—and, if the day is hot, possibly baking. You won't find shade. Be warned.

Beachcombing You will want to walk the 100 m of this enclosed little bay's shoreline. You will not want to walk much beyond it. If you do have restless limbs, however, and would like to explore a little varied terrain, your legs will find some possibilities of being stretched along a trail that starts from the end of Red Granite Road, virtually beside this beach, and runs along the crest of Red Granite Point.

Seclusion If you swivel your head behind you, you will be aware of a few buildings dotting the area across the road and beside the bay. Keep your view-seeking eyes trained toward the sea, however, and you'll feel you are in an untouched bit of wilderness.

85
WINDY BAY
An isolated rocky bay exposed to southeast winds but protected from northwest winds

Location, signs and parking The directions for this spot are largely the same as those for nearly adjacent Red Granite Road beach. Head along Harbour Road for about 1.5 km and spot the right turn for Smelt Bay Park onto Carrington Bay Road. Just over 1 km to the next T-junction, take a left onto Whaletown Road. About 6 km later, turn right onto Gorge Harbour Road until the next T-junction, almost 4 km later. Swing left onto Seaford Road for almost 2 km, then right onto Cortes Bay Road for roughly 3 km. Take Red Granite Road on your left. About half a kilometre later, after a sharp turn in the road, look for an unsignposted track heading toward the shore on your right.

Path Although you may have the impression that you are invading private property, you are okay if you keep to your right as you descend the track. After about 150 m, you will find yourself passing some old fruit trees and then reaching the upper shore.

Beach If you are after a comfortable nestling spot to consume your munch-ables, keep to the centre part of the curving shoreline. Here, depending on what the winter storms have decided to do with the logs and small rocks, you should be able to find several pleasant areas of pebbles and ready-made backrests. The beach is at its prettiest at high tide. It is at its most biologically interesting at low tide, when the denizens of the deliciously gooey sub-boulder worlds can be inspected. At very low tides, beds of eelgrass and gravelly sand reveal even more interesting creatures.

Suitability for children This is the kind of beach most adults will savour and children will tolerate. At or near high tide, it could provide enough ingredients in the form of magic pebbles, driftwood boats and splash-able water to keep most children engaged, though water shoes are an absolute necessity. Parents can relax and turn their attention to a little self-indulgent basking.

Suitability for groups A few carloads of lovers of isolated and wild beauty spots could come to this spot confident that they will find lots of space, beauty and quiet without intruding on nearby neighbours. What they won't find, of course, is even a trace of anything in the form of a facility

View In fact, this spot is more within a cove than a bay, in spite of its name. As a result, the view is almost entirely of the nearly enclosing fore-shore, extending farther on the west of the bay than on the east. Because the entire shore is richly forested, however, the visual effect is not of entrapment but of escape.

Winds, sun and shade This is, unsurprisingly, called Windy Bay for a good reason. Not just southeasterly storms but even southeasterly breezes, usually on the chilly side, funnel directly into this narrowing bay. When the wind is from the northwest, however, as it often is when the weather is good, the name of the bay could hardly seem less appropriate. In fact, if you are looking to cool off on a hot day, you will be hard-pressed to do so unless you take to the water or manage to find a few spots under overhanging branches to the left of the bay.

Beachcombing Though the bay is not very large, the shore of broken rock to the right of the access spot is likely to beckon to just about any beach explorer eager to enjoy the shifting views and a sense of immersion in apparently untouched nature. Outside Windy Bay, though, the shore becomes steep and difficult.

Seclusion Seclusion is not quite complete, though the only signs of humanity you are likely to see are in the form of a few houses peering through the trees from the distant end of the bay. On the beach itself, the chances of your meeting a single solitary soul are few.

86
HANK'S BEACH
A long track down a forested
bank to a level grassy area
and a loose gravel beach
with lots of low-tide sand

Location, signs and parking Navigating to the south end of the island is no mean feat, but since this whole area has the most spectacular beaches on the island, you will want to hone your navigational skills. Head along Harbour Road for about 1.5 km and turn right on Carrington Bay Road, toward Smelt Bay Park. Go just over 1 km to the next T-junction and take a left onto Whaletown Road. About 6 km later, turn right onto Gorge Harbour Road until the next T-junction, almost 4 km later. Turn right onto Seaford Road and follow it until another T-junction, about 3 km along. A left onto Sutil Point Road for about 1.5 km and a left onto Bartholomew Road will bring you, about 1.5 km later, to a grassy pull-off area outside a yellow metal gate. Apart from a small sign forbidding camping and fires, you will have scant evidence that you are at Hank's Beach Forest Conservation Park, opened in 2011.

Path About a kilometre of forest track, mostly old roadbed, leads toward the shore. Though more than one of the tracks will take you to the shore, to get to the beach, turn left when you come to a kind of intersection of tracks. As you descend toward the shore, you will see an open grassy area above a mass of beach logs separating you from the loose gravel beach.

Beach Your impression of the beach will vary enormously, depending on whether you arrive at high or low tide. Striking at all tide levels, the beach is probably best enjoyed at low tide, when the retreating water reveals a whole section of sandy shore extending far along the shoreline, well past the gravel beach and rocky headland at the south end of the beach. The upper beach, thick with tangled logs, is probably best for picnicking or lounging, though you will obviously be most comfortable if you bring a beach towel or blanket.

Suitability for children You will have to be organized in remembering each and every item to cope with childhood emergencies as you begin your long trek to the shore. Once you've set up your camp of towels and treats on the beach, you can sit back with every expectation that the low-tide sand will provide more entertainment than you possibly can. Do be aware, though, that the sandy bottom drops off fairly quickly into deep water just below the low-tide line.

Suitability for groups As with children, so with groups. This beach has everything a group will need or love—except easy access to the parking area. In the case of groups, too, the lack of facilities can be an issue, so make sure your Brownie pack's 50th reunion knows what to expect.

View The most striking element of your view is the more northerly Twin Island, with its southerly sibling tucked behind it. The entire sweep of view is, however, coloured with a plethora of overlapping mountain peaks, crests, ridges and islands. Most distinctive, perhaps, is the cliffy shore of Cortes Island itself to the north, and, far to the south, the northern tip of Texada Island.

Winds, sun and shade All air movement from the southeast squalls makes its way unimpeded onto the shore. If you are feeling just a little chilly, though, you can find a little protection by snuggling up to the rocky headland to the south. If winds were to behave themselves, you should get a little protection from northwesterlies, but, particularly around these

Cortes: Hank's Beach

islands, winds stray a good deal from the compass directions assigned to them. On a high-UV day, make sure sun protection is included in your beach bag—it will be the only sun protection you'll find here.

Beachcombing Beachcombers of all stripes and hues will want to make a special note of this spot. Low tide is crucial to beachcombing pleasure, but midday low tides are very much the norm during summer months. Turn north, and you will find pleasant, isolated wandering for a few hundred metres. Turn south, however, and you will find the world is your oyster—or at least this corner of it is. Carrying a little backpack of supplies, you can begin a major shorefront trek around the entire southern tip of the island, arriving more than 12 km later at Manson's Landing.

Seclusion To add to the perfection of this spot, you will likely enjoy it without seeing a single solitary soul—other than the lucky ones accompanying you.

87
MOON ROAD
A well-prepared trail and board-walk to a magnificent stretch of exposed beach composed of alternating bars of rock and hard, white sand

Location, signs and parking Like the other spots near the south end of the island, the Moon Road access requires a graduate degree in navigation to reach from the ferry, but it is more than worth the effort. First, note that you will not find Moon Road on your road map. Take Harbour Road for about 1.5 km and turn right on Carrington Bay Road. Toodle along, just over 1 km, to the next T-junction, and veer left onto Whaletown Road. About 6 km later, turn right onto Gorge Harbour Road until the next T-junction, almost 4 km later. Turn right onto Seaford Road and follow it until another T-junction, about 3 km along, then go left onto Sutil Point Road for about 3 km. Turn left onto Highfield Road. As you near the end of the road, and in sight of the open coast, slow down to a crawl so that you don't miss the small, freshly painted green-and-white sign saying

MOON ROAD ACCESS TRAIL. You won't see much of a parking area but should have no problem finding room along the shoulder of the road.

Path An impressively crafted path, about 100 m long, leads past a variety of flora, including a fine thicket of skunk cabbage and some beautiful cedars. Boardwalks with curvilinear borders, driftwood handrails and a few board-and-gravel steps make getting to the shore part of the pleasure. The only trick in reaching the shore itself is making your way over the dense mass of storm-tossed logs at the upper edge of the beach.

Beach You won't find any other beach bordering on the Salish Sea that so closely approximates the kind of wild beach you can otherwise find only on the west coast of Vancouver Island. Largely exposed to the entire fetch of the Strait of Georgia, this gradually sloping shore, piled high with wave-battered logs, feels wide open to the ocean. More than 100 m of low-tide beach is composed of bands of rock and boulders along with large stretches of fine, hard silvery sand. On the upper beach, though, how much dry sand is available for spreading out your über-picnic depends on the whim of the previous winter's storms.

Suitability for children Along with a few other spots on the south end of Cortes Island, this is one of the most child-friendly beaches in all of the islands of the Salish Sea. The comparatively easy approach to the shore, the long, level stretches of sand and usually warm water all invite any beachy bit of romping the typical child can concoct. Depending on the age and interests of your children, consider bringing Frisbees, kites, skimboards, buckets and spades—all can be thoroughly enjoyed. A word of caution, though: at some tides, sections of barnacled rock can be hidden by the turquoise waters. Water shoes and a little care should keep the number of yelps of distress to a minimum.

Suitability for groups The only parking for this spot is along the shoulder of the road, and facilities are nonexistent. Otherwise, this beach is large enough and remote enough from private houses that even the most fertile extended family could frolic and feast here. It is no accident that the builders of Hollyhock Retreat Centre chose the adjacent bit of shore for their many visitors.

View The view from this beach is almost as spectacular as the beach itself. The graceful curve of the shore sweeps to the southern tip of the

Cortes: View from Moon Road

island, some 2 km distant. To the west, the double mounds of nearby Twin Islands lead across Baker Passage to Hernando Island and, beyond, the open waters of the Strait of Georgia. The backdrop to all of this are the ragged peaks of the Coast Range behind Malaspina Peninsula.

Winds, sun and shade While the sun beats on the shore most directly during the first part of the day, the low shoreline and distance from beach to trees mean that UV rays will find you throughout the day. If the breeze is from the northwest, it will run largely parallel to and slightly offshore, so you may feel little of it. Come when a southeasterly is blowing, however, and you will know exactly how so much wave-driven driftwood came to be mounded up against the shorefront vegetation.

Beachcombing This beach an excellent choice for not only those who wish to stay put but also those who want to stride off those picnic doughnuts. You can walk for a considerable distance in either direction on the generally level shore. Turn to the right and time your walk for low tide if you want a major trek. Not only can you make your way around the southern tip of the island, but you can also undertake an ambitious hike to Manson's Landing, some 10 km distant.

Seclusion While this relatively new access trail is not yet well known, it does bring you to a section of shore near a popular retreat centre. In good weather you can expect to see others enjoying the beach. After walking just a short distance, however, you should see almost no one. Time to cast aside the bobby pins and undo the braids.

88 SMELT BAY PROVINCIAL PARK

A full-facility park, including waterfront parking for easy access to a spectacular stretch of firm, silver sand

Location, signs and parking While this park is about as far from the ferry terminal as you can get by road, many beach-lovers and first-time visitors to Cortes Island will make a beeline to this amazingly beautiful beach. You need only follow blue-and-white provincial park signs to make your way here, but keep track of distances and roads so you can visit some other beaches while you are here. Thus, note that your route begins with your taking Harbour Road for about 1.5 km and turning right onto Carrington Bay Road. Just over 1 km to the next T-junction, you will turn left onto Whaletown Road. About 6 km later, you will have to turn onto Gorge Harbour Road until the next T-junction, almost 4 km later. Turn right onto Seaford Road and follow it until another T-junction, about 3 km along. A left onto Sutil Point Road for about 3.5 km will bring you to Smelt Bay Road on your left, and soon the park and the end of your quest. As a day visitor, you can park in the shade of some waterfront firs or carry on to the parking lot, closer to the washrooms and large grassy field. The important signs to note here are those prohibiting camping or overnight parking and instructing Bessie the basset hound to stay on her leash.

Path Visitors with mammoth feasts, trunkloads of paraphernalia and seats full of wobbly family members will be delighted that they can park virtually on the beach without even thinking about paths. Kayakers will be equally happy only if they come at mid to high tide, when the waterline is within easy reach.

Beach This is very much like one of the classic sandy beaches for which Vancouver Island is famous. Stretching for kilometres, the upper beach of sugary white sand and weathered logs invites more feasting and flopping than you can imagine. At low tide, a band of mid-beach pebbles gives way to almost 100 m of firm, silver sand and warm, toe-friendly tidal pools. To the left of the parking area, the tidal flats become increasingly expansive, at their most extreme extending more than a kilometre into the strait.

Suitability for children Suitable for children? It is difficult to be moderate about a beach that is quite so immoderate in what it offers the beach-loving child. In practical terms, the shorefront parking and washrooms can keep crises to a minimum. The huge, sandy beach and usually warm water provide all the traditional pleasures of a sandy beach. At low tide, unload the kites, Frisbees, skimboards, buckets and spades. At mid or high tide, whip out the towels and inflatable orcas. To keep everyone happy, though, do bring water shoes or crocs for negotiating the area of mid-beach pebbles.

Suitability for groups Along with nearby Manson's Landing, Smelt Bay is one of the two best spots on Cortes Island for your annual onslaught of visiting cousins, step-uncles and half-sisters. The ample parking and facilities, large grassy field and endless expanses of empty beach are the blank slate for an afternoon of beachy bliss. A practical note, however: for the aging aunts and their ilk, consider bringing beach chairs, and for spreading out your feast, consider bringing a folding table. Picnic tables are one ingredient you will find missing from this otherwise perfect group spot.

View The closest landforms are the nearly circular Marina Island and, to the north, the heavily indented shoreline of Cortes Island near Gorge Harbour. Across Sutil Channel lies Francisco Point at the southern end of Quadra Island and, behind it, the graceful skyline of the Vancouver Island mountains. If you have been unable to tear yourself away from this beach and the evening is approaching, you will find this to be one of the best sunset-viewing spots on the island.

Winds, sun and shade Although this is a fairly exposed piece of low shoreline, it is surprisingly shielded from southeast winds. Northwest breezes, however, are common visitors to the beach. For protection from burning rays, shorefront firs dot the approach road along the beach and provide shelter well into the afternoon.

Beachcombing Only the most indolent and sun-sated will not yield to the temptation to wander far from base camp out along the low-tide stretches of sand. In fact, you can walk for kilometres in either direction, as far as Manson's Landing to the north, or many more kilometres all around Sutil Point, the southernmost tip of the island, and up its eastern shore as far as Hank's Beach. Most distinctive, though, is the kilometre-long stretch of rocky tidal flats extending far to the south.

Seclusion On a hot summer's day, you will find many fellow beach-lovers here (though the most popular swimming hole for islanders is Hague Lake, which you will have passed on your way here). Even at its busiest, though, this spot allows you to feel that any city-bound stresses are far, far distant.

89
HAYES ROAD
Steep stairs down a wooded bank to a sandy beach with tidal pools and clusters of boulders

Location, signs and parking In quest of one of the distant but delectable sandy beaches of southern Cortes? Take Harbour Road for about 1.5 km and turn right on Carrington Bay Road. Amble just over 1 km to the next T-junction and swing left onto Whaletown Road. About 6 km later, turn right onto Gorge Harbour Road until the next T-junction, approximately 4 km later. Turning right onto Seaford Road, carry on until another T-junction, about 3 km. Turn right onto Sutil Point Road for almost 4 km, then right onto Potlatch Road. About half a kilometre along Potlatch, you will see on your left an approach to private drives.

You can find spots for a few cars in the turnaround area but will have to be careful not to block the driveways. You should be able to see a green-and-white sign, nearly at ground level, saying HAYES ROAD BEACH ACCESS TRAIL beside a broad clear track. Another sign, high on a fir, bears the warning STEEP TRAIL.

Path In spite of the warning, you need not worry overmuch about cata-pulting to your doom. The trail is not especially steep and, in any case, is carefully prepared with a series of board-and-soil steps. A potentially slip-pery plank bridge is covered with asphalt shingles. Clearly, however, you are not likely to single out this spot if you have a carful of centenarians.

Beach The trail deposits you in a patch of loose gravel beneath overhang-ing alders. Not the prettiest part of the beach for a picnic, it leads to a much more appealing long section of upper shore composed of sugary white sand. If you are toting toddlers or edibles, head a short distance in either direction and find a spot with a few logs to set up camp in a nest of sand or pebbles. This comparatively steep section of upper beach leads to long tidal flats with fascinating arrangements of sandbars, tidal pools and rocks.

Suitability for children While most families would prefer nearby Smelt Bay, those who want a quiet, sheltered sandy beach might well select this spot—but only if they are prepared to cope with the steep descent and—be warned—the equally steep ascent. Small children will find plenty of sand for building more sandcastles than they can cope with. Older children can be equally rambunctious charging around on the sand or, equipped with water shoes, heading out along the tidal flats to the low-tide line, some 300 m away.

Suitability for groups Parking isn't easy, and the steep descent will not appeal to some groups, but if you have two or three cars' worth of soul-mates intent on dissecting each other's personal lives over croissants and brie, you may prize the quiet of this intriguing piece of shore.

View Since the coastline curves significantly here, most striking is your view of the shore sweeping to Smelt Bay Park, about 1 km away. The low profile of Marina Island, about 3 km away, is framed by Quadra Island, across Sutil Channel.

Winds, sun and shade Because of the curve of the shore, this end of Smelt Bay is more protected from northwesterlies than the public park at the other end, but, conversely, more exposed to southeasterlies. The morning can be a little heavy with shade. Even during the afternoon, however, you can cower in the shade of overhanging alders, well away from the burning rays of the blistering sun.

Beachcombing This spot is a beachcomber's paradise. If covering long distance is one of your druthers, head south and, especially when the tide is out, you can march purposefully for many kilometres around the entire south end of the island and for a few kilometres up the eastern side. If, however, exploring long tidal flats and pools is your idea of shorefront-wandering bliss, you need only select a low tide and head straight out toward the waterline.

Seclusion As you will have noticed as you began your descent down the bank, this access is far from houses. Once on the beach, however, well out of sight, you will most likely not just feel secluded but actually be secluded. Don't be surprised if you begin purring audibly.

While you're here . . . From the opposite end of Hayes Road, about half a kilometre east, you can enter the Siskin Forest Trail system for an idyllic saunter through a few kilometres of trails.

90 MANSON'S LANDING PROVINCIAL PARK
One of the most unusual configurations of shoreline and beach in the Salish Sea, good for launching kayaks and riding inner tubes through a narrow channel

Location, signs and parking Take Harbour Road for about 1.5 km and turn right on Carrington Bay Road. Amble just over 1 km to the next T-junction and swing left onto Whaletown Road. About 6 km later, turn right onto Gorge Harbour Road until the next T-junction, approximately 4 km later. Turning right onto Seaford Road, carry on until another T-junction, about 3 km. While you are actually within park boundaries at this point, you will want to turn right onto Sutil Point Road and follow it more or less to its end, about 1 km later. You will find yourself in a large parking area. You can choose to stop here or to carry on along a narrow gravel road. This road has no parking down it but does take you to a handy spot, 100 m along, where you can easily unload your kayaks and beach goods. Note the location of the washrooms off the entrance road to the parking area. At different points in the park, you will see signs warning you of the dangers of contaminated shellfish and, a little inconsistently, telling you that you are allowed only recreational limits (as opposed to commercial limits) to your daily take.

Path Since the parking lot is located about 100 m from the tip of a narrowing spit, you can choose to get quick access to the beach by walking the few metres across a small strip of grass. Alternatively, you may choose to walk past a picnic table along a little treed path running the length of the spit and taking you toward its tip. As you approach the end of this section, note the eroded bank revealing a section of midden, a remnant of an ancient First Nation habitation.

Beach This fascinating spot consists of several different kinds of shore. A long, narrowing spit of coarse sand and pebbles encloses a lagoon that largely empties at low tide and is dotted with two picturesquely rocky islets. Outside the spit, an upper shore of loose dry sand and convenient beach logs stretches for a considerable distance along the treed shoreline. Sloping fairly steeply toward the low-tide line, this sun-baked area is best for afternoon swimming when the tide is in, since the lower shore is mostly pebbles and gravel. Kayakers arriving at low tide will probably find their easiest route to water is not the launching area but the beach next to the parking lot.

Suitability for children Children of most stripes will love this spot. The littlest ones can heap mounds of sugary sand over their feet before toddling toward the generally warm water. Those with adventure glinting in their eyes will thank their parents for bringing them here with flotation toys or PFDs and arriving when a high tide is just beginning its descent. Warmed in the shallow lagoon, the outflowing water can provide lots of swirling fun—though parents will want to monitor closely the safety of children whose swimming skills are sketchy. While it is possible to ride the current into the lagoon on an incoming tide, the water is, of course, considerably cooler when flowing from the deeper outer bay. Whatever the size of your children, you will be happiest if they are happiest—and that translates as "Don't forget water shoes."

Suitability for groups Along with Smelt Bay Provincial Park, Manson's Landing Provincial Park is the best spot on the island for a minor invasion of breeders of hairless chihuahuas—or plain old picnickers and sun worshippers. While you will find only a few picnic tables, you will find the washrooms and extensive, easily accessible beach conducive to an afternoon's indolence and sunburn.

View You will regret not bringing a camera to this unusual and beautiful spot. Wander around the entire spit for varying views across the heavily forested lagoon, past the boat wharf, along the coast of Cortes or out to Marina Island, just over 2 km across the protected waters.

Winds, sun and shade One of the advantages of this convoluted shoreline is the fact that, on a windy day, you can either escape the gusts or seek out the cooling breezes by positioning yourself outside or inside the spit. A little protected from northwest winds, the outer shore is largely exposed to southeast winds. Shade, like wind exposure, is readily available. While the afternoon is the sunniest part of the day, you can find sun or shade throughout the day by selecting your spot.

Beachcombing Most beach wanderers will be content to explore the edges of the spit and its borders with the lagoon. Those who have planned properly and want a major expedition should come with sturdy shoes, a day pack, and enough energy to walk more than 10 km around the entire southern end of the island. Long-distance explorers who want only a one-way challenge can arrange car pickups at the Moon Road access or Hank's Beach access. Choose mid to low tide to maximize your route along the shore.

Seclusion This is a gorgeous public park. It is, however, rarely a crowded park. Islanders generally prefer to go to nearby bathtub-warm Hague Lake. In fact, you may well want to visit this curious lake, at one point in its geographical history an extension of Manson's Lagoon, and still lined at some points with beach sand.

While you're here . . . Note that one trail leads from this part of the park along the edge of the lagoon to Hague Lake, and another runs through the forest to the museum and tourist information office, about 1 km south.

Best Bets

All beachgoers will find favourite spots and for the most personal of reasons. Perhaps one beach will become a favourite because of the configuration of tidal pools. Another one might have a particularly cozy little nest among beach logs. Yet another might provide easy access for those with walking difficulties. As a starting point, however, many will find the following recommendations handy.

(G)	Gabriola
(D)	Denman
(H)	Hornby
(Q)	Quadra
(C)	Cortes
(T)	Thetis

81 (C)	Gnat Road
85 (C)	Windy Bay
86 (C)	Hank's Beach
87 (C)	Moon Road
89 (C)	Hayes Road
90 (C)	Manson's Landing Provincial Park

1. Varied Shore

1 (G)	Descanso Bay Regional Park
6 (G)	Taylor Bay Road
7 (G)	Gabriola Sands Provincial Park
8 (G)	Decourcy Drive
10 (G)	Tinson Road
11 (G)	Berry Point Road
17 (G)	Joyce Lockwood Community Park
19 (G)	Drumbeg Provincial Park
22 (G)	Spring Beach Drive
23 (G)	El Verano Drive
28 (D)	Chrisman Road—North
33 (D)	Bill Mee Regional Park
36 (H)	Phipps Point
39 (H)	Ostby Road
40 (H)	Oyster Place
44 (H)	Isabelle Place
45 (H)	Shaen Place—Whaling Station Bay
46 (H)	Maude Road—Whaling Station Bay
51 (H)	Shields Road—Tribune Bay
52 (H)	Little Tribune Bay
53 (H)	Sandpiper Beach
54 (H)	Ford Cove
55 (H)	Mount Geoffrey Escarpment shoreline
58 (Q)	Shellalligan Pass Trail
61 (Q)	Redonda Drive
62 (Q)	Marina Drive
72 (Q)	Lighthouse Road

2. Car picnicking

6 (G)	Taylor Bay Road
13 (G)	Orlebar Point
21 (G)	Gray Road
24 (G)	Ferne Road
25 (G)	Descanso Bay Road
32 (D)	East Road
35 (D)	Hinton Road
36 (H)	Phipps Point
42 (H)	Clam Shell Place
43 (H)	Myrl Place
44 (H)	Isabelle Place
45 (H)	Shaen Place—Whaling Station Bay
47 (H)	Moya Road—Whaling Station Bay
48 (H)	Carling Road—Whaling Station Bay
52 (H)	Little Tribune Bay
55 (H)	Mount Geoffrey Escarpment shoreline
56 (Q)	Whalebone Cove Road
59 (Q)	Valdes Drive
64 (Q)	Heriot Bay Road
66 (Q)	Rebecca Spit Provincial Park
68 (Q)	Edgeware Road
69 (Q)	Smiths Road
74 (Q)	Noble Road—South
80 (C)	Squirrel Cove
83 (C)	Blind Creek Boat Ramp
84 (C)	Red Granite Road
88 (C)	Smelt Bay Provincial Park

7. Long beach walks

8. Those with walking difficulties

9. Walking on trails

10. Seclusion

11. Afternoon sun

52 (H)   Little Tribune Bay
54 (H)   Ford Cove
55 (H)   Mount Geoffrey Escarpment
         shoreline
56 (Q)   Whalebone Cove Road
66 (Q)   Rebecca Spit Provincial Park
72 (Q)   Lighthouse Road
73 (Q)   Nuyumbalees Cultural Centre
74 (Q)   Noble Road—South
75 (Q)   Noble Road—North
77 (C)   Sawmill Road
79 (C)   Carrington Bay Regional Park
84 (C)   Red Granite Road
85 (C)   Windy Bay
86 (C)   Hank's Beach
87 (C)   Moon Road
88 (C)   Smelt Bay Provincial Park
89 (C)   Hayes Road
90 (C)   Manson's Landing Provincial Park

12. Medium or large groups

1 (G)   Descanso Bay Regional Park
7 (G)   Gabriola Sands Provincial Park
10 (G)   Tinson Road
17 (G)   Joyce Lockwood Community Park
19 (G)   Drumbeg Provincial Park
24 (G)   Ferne Road
29 (D)   Gladstone Way (medium)
30 (D)   Fillongley Provincial Park
31 (D)   Mabel Road (medium)
32 (D)   East Road (medium)
34 (D)   Boyle Point Provincial Park
37 (H)   Grassy Point (medium)
38 (H)   Hidden Community Park (medium)
47 (H)   Moya Road—Whaling Station Bay
         (medium)
50 (H)   Tribune Bay Provincial Park
51 (H)   Shields Road—Tribune Bay
52 (H)   Little Tribune Bay
53 (H)   Sandpiper Beach
58 (Q)   Shellalligan Pass Trail
66 (Q)   Rebecca Spit Provincial Park
67 (Q)   Milford Road (medium)
72 (Q)   Lighthouse Road
79 (C)   Carrington Bay Regional Park
81 (C)   Gnat Road
87 (C)   Moon Road
86 (C)   Hank's Beach
88 (C)   Smelt Bay Provincial Park

90 (C)   Manson's Landing Provincial Park

13. Flying kites, throwing Frisbees

1 (G)   Descanso Bay Regional Park
6 (G)   Taylor Bay Road
7 (G)   Gabriola Sands Provincial Park
9 (G)   Decourcy Drive—Northwest
11 (G)   Berry Point Road
15 (G)   Sandwell Provincial Park
17 (G)   Joyce Lockwood Community Park
21 (G)   Gray Road
30 (D)   Fillongley Provincial Park
31 (D)   Mabel Road
32 (D)   East Road
35 (D)   Hinton Road
37 (H)   Grassy Point
38 (H)   Hidden Community Park
40 (H)   Oyster Place
42 (H)   Clam Shell Place
45 (H)   Shaen Place—Whaling Station Bay
46 (H)   Maude Road—Whaling Station Bay
47 (H)   Moya Road—Whaling Station Bay
48 (H)   Carling Road—Whaling Station Bay
50 (H)   Tribune Bay Provincial Park
51 (H)   Shields Road—Tribune Bay
52 (H)   Little Tribune Bay
62 (Q)   Marina Drive
64 (Q)   Heriot Bay Road
65 (Q)   Heriot Bay Road staircase
66 (Q)   Rebecca Spit Provincial Park
72 (Q)   Lighthouse Road
86 (C)   Hank's Beach
87 (C)   Moon Road
88 (C)   Smelt Bay Provincial Park
89 (C)   Hayes Road
90 (C)   Manson's Landing Provincial Park

14. Bird or sea mammal viewing

8 (G)   Decourcy Drive
9 (G)   Decourcy Drive—Northwest
10 (G)   Tinson Road
12 (G)   Sea Girt Road
14 (G)   Bells Landing
16 (G)   Killerwhale Lookout
19 (G)   Drumbeg Provincial Park
30 (D)   Fillongley Provincial Park
33 (D)   Bill Mee Regional Park
34 (D)   Boyle Point Provincial Park
36 (H)   Phipps Point
37 (H)   Grassy Point

49 (H)	Texada Drive
54 (H)	Ford Cove
55 (H)	Mount Geoffrey Escarpment shoreline
56 (Q)	Whalebone Cove Road
57 (Q)	Hoskyn Channel Landing Community Park
58 (Q)	Shellalligan Pass Trail
65 (Q)	Heriot Bay Road staircase
66 (Q)	Rebecca Spit Provincial Park
68 (Q)	Edgeware Road
74 (Q)	Noble Road—South
78 (C)	Coulter Bay (high tide)
79 (C)	Carrington Bay Regional Park
81 (C)	Gnat Road
83 (C)	Blind Creek Boat Ramp
88 (C)	Smelt Bay Provincial Park
90 (C)	Manson's Landing Provincial Park

15. Protection from a southeast wind

1 (G)	Descanso Bay Regional Park
2 (G)	McConvey Road
4 (G)	Malaspina Drive
6 (G)	Taylor Bay Road
7 (G)	Gabriola Sands Provincial Park
9 (G)	Decourcy Drive—Northwest
11 (G)	Berry Point Road
23 (G)	El Verano Drive
24 (G)	Ferne Road
25 (G)	Descanso Bay Road
27 (D)	Chrisman Road—South
28 (D)	Chrisman Road—North
29 (D)	Gladstone Way
36 (H)	Phipps Point
37 (H)	Grassy Point
38 (H)	Hidden Community Park
39 (H)	Ostby Road
44 (H)	Isabelle Place
47 (H)	Moya Road—Whaling Station Bay
48 (H)	Carling Road—Whaling Station Bay
54 (H)	Ford Cove
56 (Q)	Whalebone Cove Road
65 (Q)	Heriot Bay Road staircase
66 (Q)	Rebecca Spit Provincial Park
77 (C)	Sawmill Road
78 (C)	Coulter Bay
80 (C)	Squirrel Cove

90 (C)	Manson's Landing Provincial Park

16. Protection from a northwest wind

7 (G)	Gabriola Sands Provincial Park
10 (G)	Tinson Road
18 (G)	Dragon's Lane
19 (G)	Drumbeg Provincial Park
20 (G)	Stalker Road
21 (G)	Gray Road
22 (G)	Spring Beach Drive
23 (G)	El Verano Drive
34 (D)	Boyle Point Provincial Park
35 (D)	Hinton Road
50 (H)	Tribune Bay Provincial Park
51 (H)	Shields Road—Tribune Bay
52 (H)	Little Tribune Bay
53 (H)	Sandpiper Beach
57 (Q)	Hoskyn Channel Landing Community Park
58 (Q)	Shellalligan Pass Trail
59 (Q)	Valdes Drive
60 (Q)	Breton Road
61 (Q)	Redonda Drive
62 (Q)	Marina Drive
76 (C)	Seavista Road
79 (C)	Carrington Bay Regional Park
82 (C)	Manzanita Road
83 (C)	Blind Creek Boat Ramp
84 (C)	Red Granite Road
85 (C)	Windy Bay
87 (C)	Moon Road

Index to Entries

Acknowledgements

Thanks to Bill Thompson for great help in hunting down beaches on Gabriola, Denman and Hornby Islands—all by bicycle; to Lucy Sawyer for local knowledge of Quadra Island; to Conrad Dombrowski for local knowledge and photographs of Cortes Island; and to Wanda Dombrowski and Bruce Whittington for local promotion.

Cortes: Manson's Landing Provincial Park

THEO DOMBROWSKI is a retired teacher who was involved for many years in international education, primarily at Lester B. Pearson College of the Pacific outside Victoria, BC. A writer, photographer and artist, he has a Ph.D. in English and spent many years teaching literature and writing. He studied drawing and painting at the Banff School of Fine Arts and the University of Victoria Fine Arts Department and has worked as a professional artist. He lives in Nanoose Bay, BC. Theo is donating his proceeds from sales of this book to the local environmental group Georgia Strait Alliance and to the international humanitarian support group Médecins Sans Frontières/Doctors Without Borders (MSF). Originals and copies of the illustrations in this book can be purchased by contacting the author at booksandart@shaw.ca. Proceeds will go to MSF.

OTHER BOOKS IN THE
SECRET BEACHES SERIES

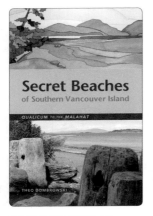

**SECRET BEACHES OF
SOUTHERN VANCOUVER ISLAND**

Qualicum to the Malahat

ISBN 978-1-894974-97-4

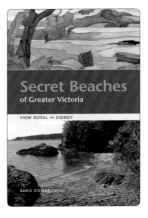

**SECRET BEACHES OF
GREATER VICTORIA**

View Royal to Sidney

ISBN 978-1-894974-98-1

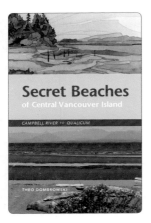

**SECRET BEACHES OF
CENTRAL VANCOUVER ISLAND**

Campbell River to Qualicum

ISBN 978-1-926936-03-1

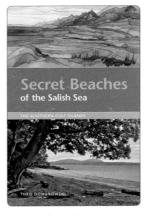

**SECRET BEACHES OF
THE SALISH SEA**

The Southern Gulf Islands

ISBN 978-1-927051-30-6